George Orwell

1984

Focus Study Guide
by
Edward Morneau

Teacher Edition

Published by
©rαπiⱯIHƎΔρ
™ Pending
Salem, MA

Copyright © 2016
by Edward Morneau

All Rights Reserved
CranialHeap
www.cranialheap.com
emorneau@gmail.com

George Orwell, *1984*. Study guide. Literature, film, writing, politics, patriotism, nationalism, fascism, language, genres, archetypes, Christopher Hitchens, and assessments.

Cover Design: E. Morneau
Cover Solutions: Bruce Jones
CranialHeap Design: Mischa Archer

Excerpts form NINETEEN EIGHTY-FOUR by George Orwell. Copyright © 1949 by Houghton Mifflin Harcourt Publishing Company, renewed 1977 by Sonia Brownell Orwell. Printed by permission of Houghton Mifflin Harcourt Publishing Company. All rights reserved.

Politics and the English Language by George Orwell (Copyright © George Orwell, 1946); *Notes on Nationalism* by George Orwell (Copyright © George Orwell, 1945). Reprinted by permission of Bill Hamilton as the Literary Executor of the Estate of the Late Sonia Browne Orwell.

ISBN-13: 978-1508813040
ISBN-10: 1508813043

From *Orwell Matters* by Christopher Hitchens:

*Frederic Warburg, Orwell's publisher, could barely recover from shock after reading it: "Here is a study in pessimism unrelieved, except by the thought that if a man can conceive of **1984**, he can also will to avoid it."*

[...]

Orwell's views have been vindicated by time. What he illustrates by his commitment to language as the partner of truth is that 'views' do not really count; that it matters not what you think, but how you think; and that politics are relatively unimportant, while principles have a way of enduring, as do the few irreducible individuals who maintain allegiance to them.

From Julie Treloar, English & Dystopian Literature Teacher:

*Ed Morneau's Study Focus Guide on **1984** is incredibly comprehensive. It is clearly written by a veteran teacher who knows how to scaffold ideas and concepts effectively. This guide begins with essential questions and suggestions in how to apply these questions. He gives the instructor leeway to interpret the text in a dizzying variety of perspectives, rather than insisting on one analysis. Of course, there are the basic (and very helpful) questions for each chapter and essay options, but what truly separates this guide from others, and where it really sings, is that it contains an almost overwhelming amount of specific connection from the text to events to events from recent history. Both new educators and Orwell die-hards will learn something new from Morneau's guide.*

DEDICATION

Dedicated to the teachers and students who take heed and inspire others to take heed of Mr. Orwell's 'savage roar.'

Introduction

1984 George Orwell Focus Study Guide is one in a series of educational units designed to help students with an understanding and appreciation of great and still relevant literature. Teachers new to the profession and seasoned teachers will find practical tools for reading Orwell's text as well as related materials that amplify his ideas.

This guide is different from others in its approach to *1984* as a work that needs to be read and understood on a number of levels. As a reading experience it is the touchstone of most dystopian literature and uses the 'anti-utopian' codes in maximally efficient ways. As a satire, its extremes are imaginative, but critical in understanding the nearly unbelievable abuses of power of which people are capable and for which history has its political progenitors and practitioners. *1984* is also about the power of language as it is related to the way we think and express ourselves. And because language is at the root of dystopia's deception, the extremes of propaganda and their effects are revealed through Orwell's text and characters in ways that deserve closer scrutiny.

This guide also moves the student from a familiar acquaintance with Orwell's powerful story to a series of ways students can assess the value of *1984* in contemporary, scholarly, and critical ways. When Edward Snowden leaked the NSA memos regarding the abuse of privacy, sales of *1984* spiked, reminding us that, while Orwell claimed his book was not a prophecy, it is, as he asserted, 'a warning.'

As one of *1984's* more powerful motifs, the idea of revisionism informs the narrative throughout. From the redacting of war heroes from historical record, performed by Winston in the Ministry of Truth, to making words meaningless, obscure and eliminating language itself, Orwell instructs us to look deeply into the well of human experience and language that invigorate self-delusion and political deception.

Included in this unit are high stakes testing questions geared to retention (Not included in Teacher Edition). While critics of high stakes testing decry rote learning as an inauthentic measurement of achievement, I provide some common sense assessments that test a basic knowledge of *1984*. It is expected through contemplative and research-based writing, students will more deeply explore the profound themes and consequences of Orwell's novel. The writing assessments and suggested assignments are modeled throughout. As most schools have district-based rubrics, I choose the modeling paradigm as it has more universal applications for composition and critical thinking.

Writing and research are significant pursuits of scholarship, and any achievement in scholarship should lead to an exploration of knowledge beyond this text. Hopefully the resources included in this *focus guide* will encourage students to consider the greater context of literature.

The "idea" of Orwell as a literary and political abstraction is permanent in our social and political culture, as the term ==Orwellian== has taken prominence in all manner of conversation, for better or worse. "…[We] commonly use the term 'Orwellian' in one of two ways. To describe a state of affair as 'Orwellian' is to imply crushing tyranny and fear and conformism. To describe a piece of writing as 'Orwellian' is to recognize that human resistance to these terrors is unquenchable" (Hitchens 5). It is my hope that this guide helps to clarify these distinctions.

Beyond the text, Orwell's thoughts on ==language, fascism, *realpolitik*==, and his satirical theories regarding the ==structures of human behavior== reveal a mind that is critically engaged. This unit is an attempt to pass on this engagement to the student.

NOTE

For those who are familiar with *1984*, Section 39 of this guide may be a good starting point to become reacquainted with Orwell. This section is built almost entirely around the late Christopher Hitchens' appreciation (and defense) of Orwell—*Why Orwell Matters*. It is here where we discover many of the origins of concepts, events, contexts, and experiences that inform his work. I have annotated the book with a focus on *1984*, specifically.

For those readers who want to enjoy the suspense and the profound ideas of *1984*, it is best you skip this section and return to it after you have completed the novel.

All references are to the Signet Classic Edition of *1984*:

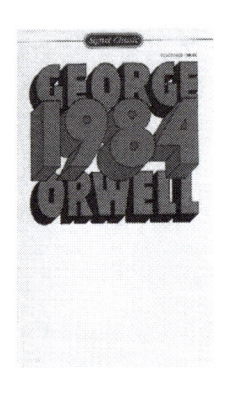

Penguin / Houghton Mifflin Harcourt Publishing Company. New York & London, 1949

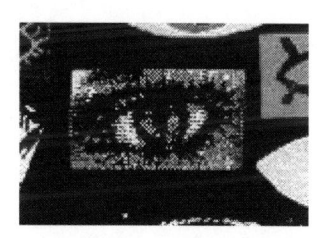

CONTENTS

Literary Theory   Student Edition Location

1. What Is Literature?—12 13
2. What Is a Genre?—13 15
3. Essential Questions to Apply to All Readings—15 18
4. Applying These Questions—16 19

Archetypes and Myth

5. Mythology and the Essence of Literature—21 26
6. Archetypes—22 27
7. Archetypal Rhythms to Literature—23 29
8. Dystopia / Anti-utopia Codes—26 33
9. *1984* as Satire—28 36

Political Theory

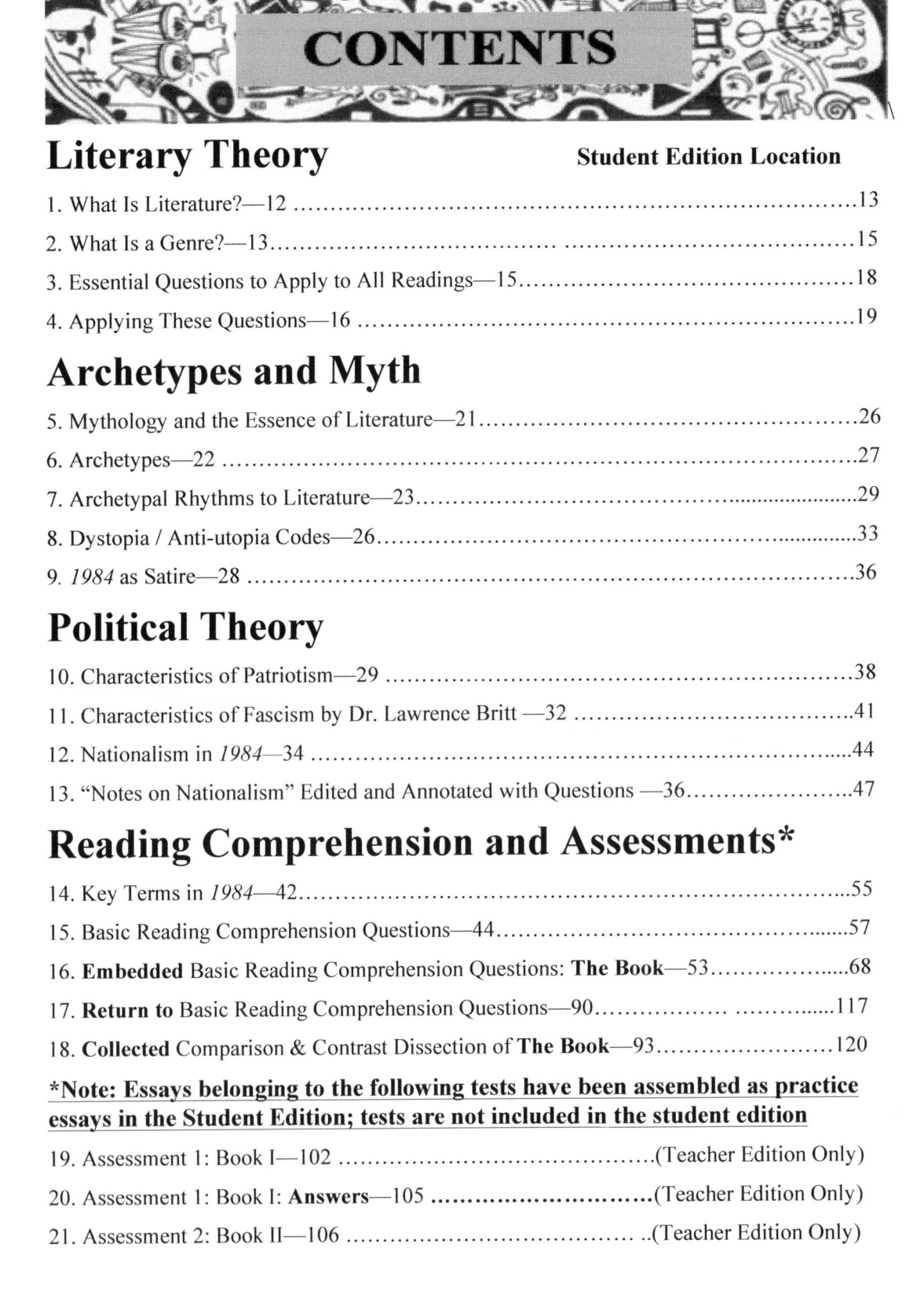

10. Characteristics of Patriotism—29 38
11. Characteristics of Fascism by Dr. Lawrence Britt —32 41
12. Nationalism in *1984*—34 44
13. "Notes on Nationalism" Edited and Annotated with Questions —36 47

Reading Comprehension and Assessments*

14. Key Terms in *1984*—42 55
15. Basic Reading Comprehension Questions—44 57
16. **Embedded** Basic Reading Comprehension Questions: **The Book**—53 68
17. **Return to** Basic Reading Comprehension Questions—90 117
18. **Collected** Comparison & Contrast Dissection of **The Book**—93 120

Note: Essays belonging to the following tests have been assembled as practice essays in the Student Edition; tests are not included in the student edition

19. Assessment 1: Book I—102 ....(Teacher Edition Only)
20. Assessment 1: Book I: **Answers**—105 ....(Teacher Edition Only)
21. Assessment 2: Book II—106 ....(Teacher Edition Only)

22. Assessment 2: Book II: **Answers**—110 ....(Teacher Edition Only)
23. Assessment 3: Whole Book—111 ....(Teacher Edition Only)
24. Assessment 3: Whole Book: **Answers**—114 ....(Teacher Edition Only)
25. Assessment 4: Codes, Nationalism, M. Radford's *1984*—115 .... (Teacher Edition Only)
26. Assessment 4: Codes, Nationalism, M. Radford's *1984*: **Answers** ....116 .... (Teacher Edition Only)

Composition and Sample Writings

27. *1984* by George Orwell: Formal Essay Assignments / Options—119......................136
28. General Five-Paragraph Rubric—121 139
29. Samples of the Motivator & the Conclusion—122.. 140
30. *1984* Sample Essay: Introduction and Body—124 143
31. Sample 'Free Write' for George Orwell's *1984*. Concept: *Doublethink*—125 145

Rubrics, Research and Film

32. First Draft Rubric Corrections FORM—128... 149
33. First Draft Rubric Corrections **Sample**—129 150
34. Formal and Collaborative Approach to Research—130......................................152
35. Introduction to Dystopian Film—135 158
36. Sample Essays: Free Write: 'Paradise Lost'—137... 161
37. Sample: Structured Research Essay on Dystopian Film: Model—139.................. 163

Projects

38. *1984*: Projects—145 171

Special Sections

39. *Why Orwell Matters* by Christopher Hitchens: Annotated—147 174
40. Annotated questions on "Politics and the English Language" (1946)—169...............202
41. George Orwell: "Notes on Nationalism" (Full Text)—183 221
42. Thoughts on *Newspeak*—197 239

Bibliographies

43. Dystopian Literature—199 242
44. Dystopian Film—206 251
45. Familiar Dystopian Comics—208...252
* Appendix **Practice Essay Test Questions** (Student Edition, **Section 19**)—210............132

Other Resources

Hanna Arendt on "Adolph Eichmann": **http://remember.org/eichmann/ownwords.htm**

Aristotle. *The Poetics.* **http://classics.mit.edu/Aristotle/poetics.html**

Bibliography of Dystopian Literature
http://en.wikipedia.org/wiki/List_of_dystopian_literature

Bibliography of Dystopian Film:
https://www.mtholyoke.edu/acad/intrel/orwell46.htmhttp://en.wikipedia.org/wiki/

Bibliography of Dystopian Comics
http://www.utopiaanddystopia.com/dystopian-fiction/list-of-dystopian-comics/

Dr. Lawrence Britt. "Fourteen Defining Characteristics Of Fascism."
Source: Free Inquiry.co/ 5-28-2003 Liberty Forum Courtesy of Jeff Rense. **(Rense.com) www.ratical.org/ratville/CAH/fasci14chars.htm**

James Burnham. **http://www.k-1.com/Orwell/site/work/essays/burnham.html**

Joseph Campbell. *The Hero Has a Thousand Faces*; *The Power of Myth.* California: New World Library. **http://www.amazon.com/Thousand-Faces-Collected-Joseph-Campbell/dp/1577315936**

Northrup Frye on "archetypes and myths":
http://edweb.tusd.k12.az.us/dherring/ap/consider/frye/indexfryeov.htm'

Christopher Hitchens. *Why Orwell Matters.* Basic Books: New York. 2002

Stuart Jeffries. "What would George Orwell have made of the world in 2013?" *The Guardian.* **http://www.theguardian.com/books/2013/jan/24/george-orwell-britain-in-2013**

George Orwell on "Nationalism": **http://www.resort.com/~pri/Orwell/nationalism.html**

**George Orwell's "Politics and the English Language":
https://www.mtholyoke.edu/acad/intrel/orwell46.htm**

U.S. Patriots United. "Characteristics of Patriotism."
http://uspatriotsunited.blogspot.com/2005/07/ten-characteristics-of-true-us-patriot.html

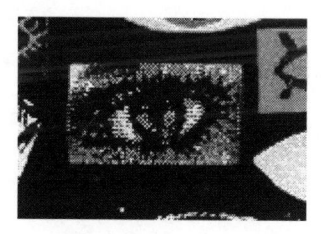

1. What Is Literature?

Literature expresses itself as a substitution for human experience. When we encounter a great story or poem, we are at a safe distance from the conflicts, crises, and environments of powerful stories. Often we would like to immerse ourselves in these stories and join with, or be, the characters that experience the effects and events of the story. Often we are glad that we are at a distance. As there is no substitute for experience, literature is the closest thing we have to gaining wisdom from inexperience. Literature is central to every culture and allows people to frame the remembrance of experience as something historical or something imagined. Literature, therefore, becomes a personal and social experience. We learn from inferences about literary experience and caution ourselves and others through the lessons learned from history and imagination. Literature raises compelling questions about experience and follows a pattern of inquiry regarding human nature. Genre study forms the blueprint of this inquiry.

Something to Consider

There is concern from some child experts that today's children are living a life outside of personal experiences—living a 'vicarious life'—living through secondary experiences. Television, video, cinema, video games, and personal media all play a role of replacing actual flesh and blood experiences in life, making children passive witnesses to life instead of active participants. The over-scheduling of a child's life robs her of the excitement of inventing her own time and the thrill of exercising spontaneity and invention. And because media activities usually consign children to the inside, the experience of the outer world is denied to them, exchanged for the safety and ease of the inner asylum or sanctuary of structured activity. Often without realizing it, good parents referee their child's engagement in life, urging them to participate or watch. Too much of one inhibits the other: too much structure and participation denies a child the free time he needs to invent his own "time"; too much spectator time denies the child the opportunity to actualize his life.

Literature should not escape this scrutiny. Is reading a passive experience? Is it an experience that conjures, that activates? Is there a point when literature denies a child more profound personal experiences by providing her with already conjured imaginary ones? When reading George Orwell's *1984*, we discover a hideous world where language has been obliterated, reading and writing is forbidden, and any stray thought is a crime. The central character, Winston Smith, discovers through reading the rudimentary political structures that created this dystopia. Much to his misfortune, the act of discovery condemns him to torture and possible death. His discovery is a passive one, and considering the resulting catastrophe, would he have better off if he did not read?

2. What Is a Genre?

The following notes and questions were gleaned from my reading of the works of Aristotle, Northrup Frye, and Joseph Campbell.

A genre often establishes itself through quantity and familiarity. If writers, artists, and filmmakers create a volume of work based on some universal aspect of human experience, the work usually reveals universal codes, motifs, themes, characterizations, symbols, archetypes, and artifacts that remind readers and spectators that they've entered a familiar realm. It is the job of writers/artists/filmmakers to make this familiarity fresh and embellish it with distinction as well as their own humanity. **If enough creators do this then a genre is established or refined.**

Genre has a generic pedigree easily replaced by words like 'kind,' 'form,' and 'type.' The effort of categorizing is to represent a consistent set of conventions that define a genre. In literature there are the established genres (kinds or types) of Fiction, Non-Fiction, Poetry, Short Story, Drama, Biography, and Autobiography. Within each of these broad categorizations, you may discover more categories. Within Fiction you will discover Myth, Fable, and Folklore. In Non-Fiction there are the Essay, Editorial, Report, Paper, Monograph, Profile and a whole range of other journalistic kinds of non-fiction writing. In the Short Story form there are stories built around types of writing: Diary narration, Letter narration, Point of View narration, Monologues, and anything of a short nature that makes an attempt to tell a story, no matter how abstract the ingredients are used.

In film and literature, genres are categorized by narrative themes or settings: Romance, Drama, Comedy, Detective, Film Noir, Gangster, Western, Horror, Science Fiction, Fantasy, Animation, and even Pixar and Disney are considered stylistic genres based on forms of animation that are consistent with their films. Within Dramatic Film, there are subgenres: the Buddy Movie, the Boxing Movie, the Musical, the Prison Film, and so on. In other words each of the genres can be broken down into sub-categories, and if the conventions defining these sub-categories are repeated enough and the changes within these conventions remain fresh, some emerge as major genres, such as Dystopian Film and Dystopian Literature, which are both derived, in part, from Science Fiction, which sits under the umbrella of Fiction.

The important thing to know is that the genre functions mostly as a psychological tool—something familiar to the reader to wedge him or her further and further into the matrix of the story, the characters, and all the other aspects of storytelling, including style, voice, and audience. The last three elements attract readers who love language, inflection, and the idea of belonging to a community of readers, respectively. The genre gives comfort to those who need to believe that they belong to this world and share a familiarity with it, no matter how much the work challenges the familiar codes and assumptions in order to reshape the genre. The genre functions as a way to delineate changes within its own codes and as a way to arouse conscience and consequence within the reader. I can think of no better example of this than in John Steinbeck's *Of Mice and Men*. In this classic work, we see the genre setting of the "modern" West transitioning into redefining the conscience, or lack thereof, of men. As codes of male isolation and misogyny become central to the narrative, one character is presented with an impossible choice regarding the fate of his friend. As a result, the codes of what comprise drama, point of view, time, setting, and the shifting nature of characters confronting each other, collapse into the reader's own psychological makeup.

Finally, genre study allows intellect to organize itself around a set of values. Recognizing the value of literary perceptions often means shattering stereotypes and pursuing a deeper read of an author's imagination, fueling our imaginations to reorder our lives according to the depth and variety of our perceptions. One cannot forget a great book or a great film, or any great work of art, for that matter, if one brings to the effort an understanding the deeper intentions of the artist. The genre helps organize this effort and appreciation.

Something to Consider

Genre is so appealing because it represents universality and certainty. It corresponds to what is predictable for the sake of challenging what is predicted. The norms of any society are cast upon its children, and these children are expected to conform to these norms so traditions persist, but the greatest stories from any culture are those made dynamic by how individuals subvert these expectations. Every good story has a turning point, and in this juncture, what has been predicted by convention is liberated by change. This change is discovered through character and conflict, making it necessary for the certainties and universalities to be questioned. What results from difficult questions and equally difficult choices are expressions of imagination, acts of heroism, and the birth of new codes resulting in more complex genres with greater features. If a student begins her understanding of literature by asking how she is a 'genre' unto herself, she will then discover what she shares with and what sets her apart from her culture. In her 'story,' she will attempt to discover and reconcile both and either jettison the rituals and conventions she rejects to cultivate an individual, dynamic humanity, or she will remain static and unchanging, each for better or worse.

3. Essential Questions

Note: For clarity and to avoid misogyny, I use personal plural pronouns as the collective pronoun for men and women.

- How do we perceive our world?
- What forces go into shaping the way we behave or perceive our world?
- What forces distort or clarify our perceptions?
- What role do we have or play in shaping our own experiences?
- What natural and real factors distort or clarify our experiences?
- How accurate is our concept of self and world?
- How accurate are our value judgments?
- As part of human definition, what values do we find valid and meaningful?
- How does the author limit our concept of self and our ability to make judgments?
- How much power or control can we achieve, if any?
- What are the obstacles before us that prevent us from achievement?
- Why does contemporary literature focus on our common humanity? What has happened to the concept of the Hero in literature?
- In whatever role we choose, what are the nature of success and the consequence of failure?
- How much choice, in fact, does exist for us?
- Are our destinies and the decisions we make to achieve this destinies pre-determined?
- What forces outside of us do we invoke to find relevance, happiness and permanence?

Dear Teacher: Please feel free to add to this list:

- _____
- _____
- _____
- _____
- _____
- _____
- _____
- _____
- _____

4. Applying These Questions

In applying these questions we will turn to specific references regarding *1984*. To help and challenge the student, we will provide some possible sample answers with **detail** and some answers with **direction** in order to explore detail. **Note:** Spoiler alert: Some of this information reveals plot movement and character development.

• How do we perceive our world?

Detail: There are several characters who see the world through different lenses: Winston through remembrance and curiosity; Julia through personal rebellion and love; O'Brien through the consolidation and application of power; Charrington through an intermediary relationship between memory and ruthlessness; Goldstein through myth, history, and revolution; the Proles through living memory, indifference, and ignorance; and minor characters, like Parsons and Symes, through obedience and self-deception. **The student would go on to explain these perceptions using further detail from the text.**

• What forces go into shaping the way we behave or perceive our world?

Direction: The forces of dystopia shape how each character behaves and sees his or her world. Each character is subject to the influence of one or more dystopian codes. **The student must identify these forces and render their effect on each character.**

• What forces distort or clarify our perceptions?

Detail. Winston's perceptions are distorted through tormented memories of how the world was before Big Brother. He is also riddled with an unrelenting curiosity as to why the world has become so brutal and unforgiving. His is a journey through the very understanding of Orwell's ideas, however limited his understanding is by factors beyond his control and by the forces of the State. Conversely, Julia and O'Brien show certainty in their perceptions. For Julia, she is not perplexed by Big Brother, but she is also not given to anything but a personal rebellion against the State. Her distortions are complex and may contribute to the idea that cynicism and indifference fuel Big Brother's hold on power. O'Brien is thoroughly bleached of the requisite humanity that tempers power; he exists for the sake of power and nothing else. His character is the very force of distortion. **The student would be wise to add details to they key points and choose minor characters to amplify these distortions (e.g., Parsons and Symes).**

- **What role do we have or play in shaping our own experience?**

Direction: Winston is the dupe for O'Brien. He is oblivious in following O'Brien's carefully constructed path for Winston's self-destruction. With every discovery Winston makes regarding the machinations of Big Brother, he plays the unwitting tool of O'Brien's *realpolitik*. **Students would explore other characters in greater detail and ask questions like, "Is O'Brien's experience his own or is it shaped by delusion?"**

- **What natural and real factors distort or clarify our experiences?**

Detail and Direction: Julia is naturally belligerent, having to cope with the disappearance of what is essential to practicing womanhood. Her rebellion is reduced to a sexual rebellion until she meets Winston, who understands both the rigid exterior of Julia's defense mechanisms, but cultivates the tender loyalty she shows to loving Winston. In refusing to betray Winston, she gives into the natural impulse for human love. However, in reality, her love is doomed by the conditions of *Oceania* that subvert her humanity. **Students should not ignore the fine details Orwell uses to embellish Julia's character.**

- **How accurate is our concept of self and our world?**

Detail and Direction: O'Brien presents a specific vision of human dystopia. His accuracy as expressed in his interrogation of Winston is debatable, expressing the failure of human beings to confront fascism after they have allowed it to settle into their lives in exchange for the preservation of a small, elite part of the species who functions as institutional saviors and protectors—even if their institutional protection is accomplished through brute force and deception. His concept is the darker side of Orwell's. **It is the business of the reader to challenge this concept.**

- **How accurate are our value judgments?**

Detail and Direction: When Symes celebrates the destruction of words, he is placing a value on their disappearance. What is this value? O'Brien would claim words cloud reality and that only words useful to the attainment of power have real value. As a linguist, Symes goes along, which is contrary to the logic of his intellect. Yet, how do we, as students, value words, especially if we do not embrace their shades of meaning through study and the habits of reading? **Amplify this by virtue of how Symes contributes to the distortion of his own logic. Also, what other characters (e.g., Parsons) suffer from false values they embrace?**

- **As part of human definition, what values do we find valid and meaningful?**

Direction: Orwell is criticized by some as being too cynical, with no room in his narrative for hope. Yet, with a deeper read **students should be able to abstract hope from his story, especially through characters like Winston, Julia and the figure of Emmanuel Goldstein.**

- **How does the author limit our concept of self and our ability to make judgments?**

Direction: Writer James Burnham's work on the 'Managerial Revolution' had an enormous impact on Orwell and contributed much to the superstructures of *1984's* bureaucratic ministries which all inhibit humanity, social growth and future hope for the citizens of Oceania. **Students should have a basic understanding of his ideas.**

http://www.k-1.com/Orwell/site/work/essays/burnham.html

The concept of 'The Johari Window' is equally useful in bringing this inhibition down to a personal level and is therefore essential in understanding Orwell's characters and their limitations.

https://www.usc.edu/hsc/ebnet/Cc/awareness/Johari%20windowexplain.pdf

Detail: Orwell makes Parsons stupid, surrounds him with 'Hitler Youth-like' children who rat him out, and equips him with an unquestioning enthusiasm that sabotages his own life. Consequently, he is the perfect effect of the totalitarian stooge. **How does Orwell limit other characters in order for them to perform his literary ends?**

- **How much power or control can we achieve, if any?**

Direction and Detail: This is a good way to explore O'Brien's concept of power and Winston's opposition to it during the interrogation. This can be rooted through Winston's reading of Goldstein's 'book' and the subsequent discovery he makes after being tortured. [**Again, a deeper reading of Julia's character may serve as a respite from O'Brien's matter-of-fact conceits and Winston's growing terror and befuddlement.**]

Specifically, the trajectory of O'Brien's character is the very process of how power gathers itself through deception (luring and tricking Winston and Julia into believing in Goldstein and The Brotherhood, for example); how the constituents of power rationalize the goals of absolute power (O'Brien's brutal interrogation of Winston); and how the results of implacable power (the virtual collapse of society and total denial of human rights), all demonstrate the process and consequence of acquiring power.

- **What are the obstacles before us that prevent us from achievement?**

Direction: What are the actual obstacles in Oceania that prevent the natural inclinations of human behavior and subvert the basic rights of humanity? **Students should explore aspects of setting, routine, objects, and language, propaganda, busy work, and other details to bring context to what obstructs these characters.**

- **Why does contemporary literature focus on our common humanity? What has happened to the concept of the Hero in literature?**

Direction and Detail: The Proles represent a common humanity that fascinates Winston, but is ignored by Julia. Is this Orwell's way of trying to locate nobility in character; or because of Julia's indifference, is it Orwell's way of dispensing with the idea that heroes are possible in such a world? **It is important for the student to arrive at some definition of what a classic hero is, and by reasoning, explore why heroes in contemporary society are either rare or contrived.**

One detail regarding common humanity may be abstracted from Winston's uncommon suspicion of Big Brother. Another regarding Julia's potential for heroic stature is her refusal to betray Winston in the presence of O'Brien.

- **In whatever role we choose, what are the nature of success and the consequence of failure?**

Direction: It seems that only the forces of Big Brother succeed in *1984*. The nature of this success is born from the concentration and application of absolute power over humanity. Winston attempts to challenge this success, and **it is up to the student to understand and bring context to his challenges on the student's own terms.** Failure is the prescription for all rebellions against Big Brother. Yet, Orwell gives us characters that illustrate the Party's failure. **Again a deeper read will reveal Big Brother's failure over the individual.**

- **How much choice, in fact, does exist for humanity?**

Direction: Orwell seems to subtract choice from his characters and leave them to suffer by the forces *1984's* totalitarian exercise of absolute power. This power forces terrible choices upon these characters, most of them counter to the human side of their enterprise and happiness. **It is up to the student to locate moments of choice where the character does not lose sight of his or her humanity. It is also up to the reader to glean from the experience of Orwell's story what constraints we need to put on power that robs us of our humanity.**

- **Are our destinies and the decisions we make to achieve this destiny pre-determined? What forces outside of humanity do we invoke to find relevance, happiness and permanence?**

Direction and Detail: O'Brien leaves us with a most brutal image of human destiny. Winston's conjures an alternative destiny. How do both support or refute the idea of choice and pre-determination? **It is important that students think beyond the text and question the nature of what is fated for them based on what prior experiences they have had, and those forces that create a destiny not of their choosing.**

When O'Brien reveals the nature of Goldstein's 'book,' does this revelation suggest that knowledge and truth do not matter to the rigors of power? Or does knowledge create the possibility of altering fate? Why is Julia so resigned to being defeated? Is she plugged into some universal truth regarding power or human nature? Is *1984* itself an essay in the form of a story a plea for people to pay closer attention to each other so that our differences, ambitions, and dreams be understood before they become corrupted?

Something to Consider

It is important for students to remember that dystopian literature like *1984* grew out of the genre of science fiction. Serious science fiction often employs codes that factor out the survival of human beings. In the short history of humanity it is apparent to writers, philosophers, scientists, and historians that humankind has the capacity to destroy itself and often participates in this self-destruction willingly or without thought. We are a puzzling species, in conflict with our own intellect and at war with nature. Science fiction writers accept our oblivion, but write tales that attempt to get to the root of humanity's galactic hubris that has or may bring about our demise. That said, consider O'Brien's sermon to Winston regarding human value not as something eventual and profound, but as something forgettable and irrelevant. Whereas in most science fiction, and even in some dystopian narratives, there is an often-elegant reflection of the inevitable grace and relevance of humanity as a 'remembered species' at best—one from which other cosmic intellects may learn. O'Brien's vision of humanity is nihilistic, void of elegance, and belonging to a totality shaped within a party devoid of unreliable memory, fashioning instead a realization of God itself defined as power, where remembrance is irrelevant, the future impossible, and all time is present **now**, eradicating hope.

5. Mythology & the Essence of Literature

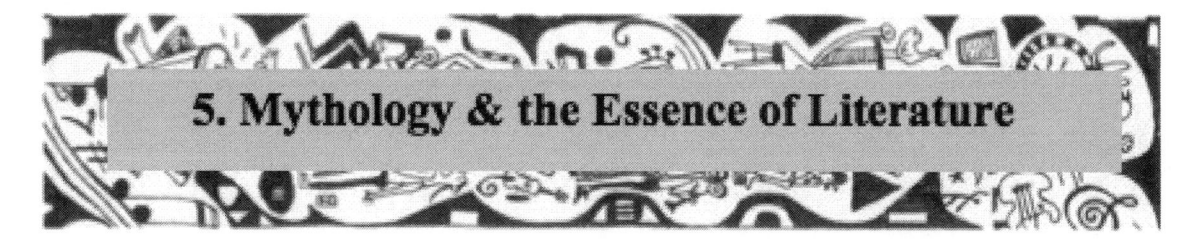

Literature and Human imagination attempt to do the following:

- present a social vision
- reveal the human situation as it is, as it should be, and as it could be
- give shape to human experience
- reveal the imaginative possibilities within each of us and within society itself
- nourish our ability to handle fears, embrace hope, and live a truly human life
- engage imagination, for without a person's capacity to create and re-create, there could be no change, no reform, and no vision of a world we would want to live in.

Something to Consider

Mythology and literature are the answers to "I don't know." A child's first brush with triumph or tragedy is through the earliest tales she reads or is taught. Intellects as profound as Einstein, Dickinson, e.e. cummings, and Shakespeare exercise triumph and tragedy in remarkably different ways, but the records of these triumphs and tragedies are understood through the written word, through the specific literature of each individual's effort. In Emily Dickinson and cummings' case, respectively, the compression of language and emotion through poetry, or a slice of life through a short story, allow for understanding and imagination to expand on the brevity of each form of literature. Without literature humanity cannot remember or reflect on what it knows and remembers, nor can it imagine what is and what lies beyond experience.

6. Archetypes

The unifying principles of literature are **archetypes**, which are the building blocks of **genres**.

- Archetypes are recurring images, character types, symbols, motifs, and narrative patterns.
- Archetypes are manifested in myths, legends, the *Bible* and other holy books, classics, contemporary literature, films, comics, video games, songs and advertisements.
- When connected, archetypes make one aware of the imaginative experience of literature, and also bring shape to order and structure to human experience.
- Conventions determine the ways in which stories may be told. Literature grows out of recognizable conventions and imaginative applications of these conventions. Every form in literature has a pedigree, and we can trace its descent back to ancient times.
- Literature begins in myth, which is our imaginative effort to explain the natural world in human terms. Its conceit has always been identity, with seeing the unity in things rather than the distinctions that sabotage unity and reveal doubt and calamity.
- Literature is Humanity's search for harmony with a universe from which it seems distinctly cut off. It is a metaphorical quest for identity and unity with the universe, as it once was in the beginning, in the *Golden Age,* before the fall from innocence.

Something to Consider

What are the new clusters of information and artifact that may create a new archetype? If you are an avid fan of cinema, a recent development in the artifacts of many genres of films is the presence of cell phones. This personal media has a ubiquitous presence in films about espionage, crime, forensic detective work, legal dramas, situation comedies, and almost every modern incarnation of plot-driven storytelling rooted in today's world. Breaking down the relevance of cell phones to plot movement in modern story telling creates an order of space and time relevant to film's dependence on 'suspension of disbelief.' While we worry about cell phone battery life in our daily lives, this concern is dispensed with in cell phone-driven cinema, making the cell phone equal to the gun in resolving stories. Entire conflicts and crises are dependent on cell phone constructs. It is nearly impossible to imagine some film forms without the constant presence of something **that is a constant presence** in our own lives, and shapes how we communicate and connect with each other, making the cell phone an artifact in an archetypal structure.

7. Archetypal Rhythms to Literature

There are two fundamental **rhythms** to literature: **Cyclical** and **Dialectal**

A. The **Cyclical Rhythm** springs from

    1. the cycles of nature

    2. the passing of seasons

    3. the rituals of life, death, and rebirth

        a. The **rising cycle movement** (Comedy) consists of birth, marriage, and resurrection;

        b. The **falling cycle movement** (Tragedy) consists of death, metamorphosis, and sacrifice.

B. The **Dialectical Rhythm** expresses a desire to be liberated from the cycles that often limit us, to create a free human society that will transcend time and last forever.

C. The two rhythms create opposing worlds:

    1. The **Dialectical** movement projects a paradise above our world, free from the cycles that inhibit change;

    2. The **Cyclical** movement binds us to an indifferent world.

D. From these two opposing worlds, emerge the four types of imaginative experience—**Romance, Tragedy, Satire-Irony,** and **Comedy**—which are expressed in four types of imaginative plots.

Tragedy is opposed to **Comedy**; **Romance** is opposed to **Satire-Irony**. None are mutually exclusive, meaning a story can contain elements of more than one imaginative experience.

    1. **Romance**

        a. engages the archetypal themes of conflict, adventure and triumph;

        b. is characterized by a world of innocence and remembrance; and

        c. usually consists of a **hero's quest**

            1) involving a perilous journey,

            2) engaging in a crucial struggle that tests the hero,

            3) resulting in triumph and exaltation when the test is completed,

4) even if the hero dies. [A rebirth of the hero's stature is established in remembrance.]

d. Two central characters of a quest story are

1) the **hero** (protagonist), who is associated with spring, dawn, order, fertility, and youth;

2) and the **adversary** (antagonist), who is associated with winter, darkness, confusion, sterility, and old age.

e. The **settings** usually fulfill our desire for order and meaning and offer possibilities of magic, mystery, and miracles.

f. **Visions** and **revelations** unify quests of a 'heavenly' world with the 'lower' world (Earth).

g. Romance almost always deals with some kind of progress towards fulfillment.

2. **Tragedy**

a. **Catastrophes are** driven by the archetypal themes of tragedy, where humanity tries to understand a world that can crush human greatness. **Catastrophe** is

b. characterized by a **loss of innocence,**

c. features a person (**hero**) who suffers or dies for some cause, usually a nation (state);

d. the **motif** of victory through defeat sometimes emerges;

e. characters are immersed in a **world of experience;**

f. some are victims of **fate and time;**

g. heroes become **isolated** from society, which is slow to fathom impending catastrophe; and

h. some heroes live in a world of **pity (elos)** for their experience, far below what is normal.

i. Extreme tragedy expresses its ironic tone in settings of madness and prison—literal and figurative—and promotes **fear (phobos)** in the reader.

3. **Satire-Irony**

a. ridicules mythical (**cyclical**) patterns of experience;

b. gives form to an ambiguous world without heroes;

c. demands an implicit moral standard, not an inferred one;

d. needs an object to attack;

e. grants that the world is full of folly, crime and injustice;

f. however, sees the world as worth reforming (unlike **Parody**, which laughs it off as unsalvageable and only worthy of ridicule).

g. Conventions are objects of attack;

h. exaggerate for effect;

i. its settings are crowded; action, frenzied; and

j. questions our capacity to reason and perceive.

k. Extreme use of satire presents invective and torrential abuse of other archetypes, reveals bitterness and resignation, and function within extreme plot constructions.

4. **Comedy** is

a. the rise and recognition of a new, free society;

b. its plots stretch from romantic to ironic;

c. features the presence of a **blocking figure;**

d. deals with themes of **illusion** and **reality**.

e. Resolutions in comedy usually dissolve disguises, hypocrisies, obsessions, and things unknown;

f. central movement of comedy is that the hero outwits the blocking figure; and

g. love conquers all.

Summary: Literature historically reflects the possibility of civilization evolving. Contemporary literature concerns itself more and more with purely human problems and conflicts (**Realism**) and how we make congress with the outer world (**Naturalism**). This is our quest. Once we lose our quest we seek ways to unify the outer world with the human one. Literature offers us a panoramic view of the human condition. Our responsibility as learners is to discover the possibilities literature provides by freeing the imagination to create a vision that will make a free human society a reality.

8. Dystopia—Anti-Utopia Codes

Dystopian literature is a subgenre of science fiction and satire and is the opposite of utopian literature. Plato's *Republic* is the original source of Western utopian political thought, which was systematized and further explored by Sir Thomas More in his book *Utopia,* written during the bloody reign of Henry the Eighth. Both Plato and More present a political and social vision of how society could organize itself for the benefit of all its citizens and allow them to thrive and grow as individuals, as citizens, and as collective members of society. War, poverty, ignorance and corruption are eradicated by diplomacy, shared wealth, education and mutual trust. The most imaginative conceptions of the utopian state are *Atlantis* and *The Garden of Eden*, where humankind is one and righteous with the temporal, metaphysical, and the divine.

Subsequent writers, leery of human nature, scoffed at the idea that human beings could attain such perfection and would ridicule this vision. Early dystopian works like *Gulliver's Travels* by Jonathan Swift and *Erehwon* ("nowhere" spelled backwards) by Samuel Butler, ridiculed humankind and revealed that human virtues are too complex to align themselves with perfection.

During the colonialization of indigenous peoples by European powers, and after the Industrial Revolution, realpolitik, totalitarianism, and genocide gripped the imaginations of writers who churned out works satirizing any hope for civilizing humankind. Books like Yevgeny Zamyatin's *We,* Aldous Huxley's *Brave New World,* and George Orwell's *1984*, present chilling visions of a social state in which society has lost its ability to bring people together in any hopeful way. These dystopian societies dehumanize its members, marginalize the majority for the benefit of the few, almost always enslave or "disappear" fringe groups, and brutally punish and discourage those brave souls who attempt to bring order, justice, and hope back to society.

Dystopian literature is critical; therefore, it is an argument. Almost all dystopian literature and film embrace all or some of the following codes in order to pursue their respective arguments:

Codes:

- The masses are oppressed because…
- Authority is corrupt.
- There must be blind obedience to authority
- A faceless, well-equipped police state enforces laws
- Minorities are persecuted
- The use of terror and torture are instruments of order
- There are no governmental checks and balances
- Civil and human rights are eliminated

- Free movement is suspended
- Books are banned or burned, or both
- Language is corrupted, convoluted, misused, reduced
- Propaganda and brainwashing techniques are used
- The consumption of alcohol, drugs and pornography is encouraged or tolerated
- The presence of an enemy is necessary, whether real or fictional
- The concentration of power is in the hands of a few
- Society is divided into a caste system
- There is a calculated dissemination of money
- Religion is either eliminated or amplified to extremes
- The establishment of authority borders on the semi-divine
- There is a constant conflict between the inner world and outer world
- People never had so good, though things have never been worse

Like the terms Orwell uses to define the political and social thought of the *1984* society, it is equally important for the reader to bring modern context to these dystopian codes. For example, the concept of **a faceless, well-equipped police state enforcing laws** is currently under scrutiny in many Western democratic countries, such as England, France, and the United States. In these countries we see heavily armed and aggressive police forces engaging in para-military actions in civil affairs. In the USA, the *Homeland Security Act* of 2004 gives municipalities across America access to military equipment to combat urban and rural unrest. In addition, with the end of the Iraq and Afghanistan Wars, surplus military equipment, including high powered explosives, firearms, and heavily armed Humvees and the like, are available to local cities and towns to supplement their law enforcement abilities. Critics fear that the 'militarization' of ordinary police in American towns will lead to a permanent and implacable martial state.

Something to Consider

It's not enough to know what a dystopian society looks like. What does a utopian society look like? What are the contrary codes to dystopia? Taking each of the codes above, develop a list of utopian codes. For instance, if in a dystopia "the masses are oppressed because...," in a utopia,

- The masses are free to live as they wish because...
- Authority is fair and law and order reflect justice...
- Authority can be challenged and changed...
- Enforcers of the law care for the community and consider the rights of citizenry.

Students should finish the utopian list, articulating each opposite of the dystopian codes, and then come to some consensus as a group. This is the first step in establishing utopia.

9. *1984* as Satire

Orwell intended *1984* as a warning and not a prophecy. However, many of the observations he made when he finished writing his novel in 1948 seem prophetic. Orwell considered his novel to be a work of satire, and therefore its exaggerations are for effect. Satire has specific requirements. Generally satire is an archetype that uses irony for effect to ridicule the romance archetype by revealing defeat, confusion and anarchy, and the loss of heroic archetypal themes.

Satire

- ridicules mythical (cyclical) patterns of experience
- gives form to ambiguous world without heroes
- demands an implicit moral standard, not an inferred one*
- needs object to attack
- grants that the world is full of folly, crime and injustice
- however, sees the world as worth reforming (unlike Parody, which laughs it off as unsalvageable and only worthy of ridicule)
- conventions are objects of attack
- exaggerates for effect
- its settings are crowded; its action is frenzied
- questions our capacity to reason and perceive
- extreme use of satire (as in Orwell's *1984*) presents invective and torrential abuse of other archetypes, reveals bitterness and resignation, and functions within extreme plot constructions.

*Example: Oceania has no laws, which **implies** that people are free to do anything they want. However, *thoughtcrime, facecrime, and sexcrime* **infer** that there are no freedoms of any kind. Are there modern examples that show the collision of what is implicit and what is inferred?

Something to Consider

Using the above codes of satire, consider each as it applies to *1984*. For example, in terms of satire's need to ridicule, what is ridiculed in *1984*? Some of this is obvious: language is degraded, as is sex, family, love, and free speech. O'Brien ridicules all of human nature as unworthy of any beneficial consideration except as it serves the implacable power of what O'Brien calls "The New Inheritors."

How are the other codes of satire represented by *1984*?

10. Characteristics of Patriotism

Note: It is expected that students challenge these characteristics.

This list of ten characteristics of 'A True US Patriot' was compiled by a group of US Citizens both here and abroad and published in 2005 on the Web Site, US Patriots Unite:

(http://uspatriotsunited.blogspot.com/2005/07/ten-characteristics-of-true-us-patriot.html)

The impetus behind this is as follows, as stated by the Web writers:

Let this list serve to help remind those who serve us that these terms were not meant to be bandied about like a club, bludgeoning opponents into submission.

We, the People of the United States of America, finding ourselves repeatedly misled by those charged with the care and governance of our nation, know that partisan politics have resulted in a serious breach of the public trust:

- *We have suffered attacks against our Constitutional rights and the founding tenets of this Democratic Republic*
- *We have suffered the infringement of our freedoms.*
- *We have suffered insult to our honor and integrity as proud citizens.*
- *We do hereby now and forever reject the bastardization of this nation's core principles through this proclamation, and define this reminder to our wayward leaders just what it takes to be a True US Patriot:*

1. ***A True US Patriot* realizes if the rights of one are violated, the rights of all are at risk, and objects to any attempt to alter the Constitution in order to specifically undermine the rights and freedoms of others, ensuring that the Constitution will never be amended to endorse discrimination of any kind.**

2. ***A True US Patriot* holds the founding principles of the Declaration of Independence to be self-evident, and defends the Constitutional rights of others even when those rights conflict with personal and religious beliefs; believing that all men are created equal, even in times of war, the basic principles of**

humanity apply not only to one group of people or nation, but to all.

3. *A True US Patriot* supports the checks and balances within the three branches of government and rejects any attempts to circumvent or undermine them.

4. *A True US Patriot* exercises the right to openly challenge and hold accountable at all times, even and most particularly in times of war, those who do not honor their oaths of office, who purposely mislead the nation, who abdicate responsibility when those in their employ are caught engaging in criminal and unethical activities, and who fail to serve the nation with integrity.

5. *A True US Patriot* recognizes the contributions of the older generation and values the potential of the next, and that in order to promote the general Welfare, and secure the Blessings of Liberty to ourselves, our elders, and our Posterity, we must ensure that the basic rights of those we hold dear to access quality healthcare and education is steadfastly supported, uncompromisingly and without discrimination based on race, color, creed, gender, or orientation.

6. *A True US Patriot* believes that human rights are inherent to the human condition and should not be given to non-living entities; the rights of corporations should not equal or exceed the rights of any individual, and the right to fair and equal trade as well as fair and equal pay are a vital part of those expectations.

7. *A True US Patriot* recalls that our citizens consist of the tired and the poor, huddled masses yearning to breathe free, the 'wretched refuse', and homeless, tempest-tossed people, and welcomes fair and balanced immigration with managed borders to ensure an open policy while maintaining and increasing security for both those who would call this land their home as well as those who already dwell within.

8. *A True US Patriot* respects the personal religious choices of others, refrains from imposing his or her own beliefs upon others, refuses to support war in the name of religion, and offers foreign humanitarian aid unconditionally without tying it to religious dogma.

9. *A True US Patriot* knows that due process of law and the protections against illegal search and seizure are core principles upon which our nation is founded, and the respect of an individual's right to privacy and security within his or her home is critical to the preservation of our freedom.

10. *A True US Patriot* **respects the diversity and culture of all nations, recognizing that our continued success lay not in spite of other nations but in alliance with them in a uniform approach toward promoting the global general welfare.**

These ten basic tenets characterizing a True US Patriot can perhaps best be summed up in the words of Eric Zorn of the Chicago Tribune, paraphrased below:

A True US Patriot **loves what his country stands for, not necessarily what his or her country does, and will not shrink from holding America to her ideals.**

Something to Consider

After challenging these definitions, do a WEB search on 'nationalism.' Compare patriotism to nationalism. What are the differences and similarities, if any? Later in this guide, we encounter Orwell's "Notes on Nationalism." Are they different than what you researched? How so? What do they share with Orwell's definitions? Do tenets of patriotism collide with tenets of nationalism? Most importantly, what tenets of either do we as Americans practice? Be specific.

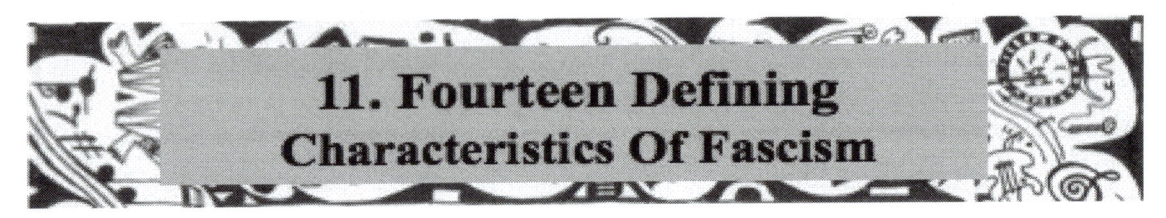

11. Fourteen Defining Characteristics Of Fascism

By Dr. Lawrence Britt

Note: It is expected that students challenge these characteristics.

Dr. Lawrence Britt has examined the fascist regimes of Hitler (Germany), Mussolini (Italy), Franco (Spain), Suharto (Indonesia) and several Latin American regimes. Britt found 14 defining characteristics common to each:

1. Powerful and Continuing Nationalism – Fascist regimes tend to make constant use of patriotic mottos, slogans, symbols, songs, and other paraphernalia. Flags are seen everywhere, as are flag symbols on clothing and in public displays.

2. Disdain for the Recognition of Human Rights – Because of fear of enemies and the need for security, the people in fascist regimes are persuaded that human rights can be ignored in certain cases because of "need." The people tend to look the other way or even approve of torture, summary executions, assassinations, long incarcerations of prisoners, etc.

3. Identification of Enemies/Scapegoats as a Unifying Cause – The people are rallied into a unifying patriotic frenzy over the need to eliminate a perceived common threat or foe: racial, ethnic or religious minorities; liberals; communists; socialists; terrorists, etc.

4. Supremacy of the Military – Even when there are widespread domestic problems, the military is given a disproportionate amount of government funding, and the domestic agenda is neglected. Soldiers and military service are glamorized.

5. Rampant Sexism – The governments of fascist nations tend to be almost exclusively male-dominated. Under fascist regimes, traditional gender roles are made more rigid. Divorce, abortion and homosexuality are suppressed and the state is represented as the ultimate guardian of the family institution.

6. Controlled Mass Media – Sometimes the media is directly controlled by the government, but in other cases, the media is indirectly controlled by government regulation, or sympathetic media spokespeople and executives. Censorship, especially in wartime, is very common.

7. Obsession with National Security – Fear is used as a motivational tool by the government over the masses.

8. Religion and Government are Intertwined – Governments in fascist nations tend to use the most common religion in the nation as a tool to manipulate public opinion. Religious rhetoric and terminology is common from government leaders, even when the major tenets of the religion are diametrically opposed to the government's policies or actions.

9. Corporate Power is Protected – The industrial and business aristocracies of a fascist nation are often the ones who put the government leaders into power, creating a mutually beneficial business/government relationship and power elite.

10. Labor Power is Suppressed – Because the organizing power of labor is the only real threat to a fascist government, labor unions are either eliminated entirely, or are severely suppressed.

11. Disdain for Intellectuals and the Arts – Fascist nations tend to promote and tolerate open hostility to higher education, and academia. It is not uncommon for professors and other academics to be censored or even arrested. Free expression in the arts and letters is openly attacked.

12. Obsession with Crime and Punishment – Under fascist regimes, the police are given almost limitless power to enforce laws. The people are often willing to overlook police abuses and even forego civil liberties in the name of patriotism. There is often a national police force with virtually unlimited power in fascist nations.

13. Rampant Cronyism and Corruption – Fascist regimes are almost always governed by groups of friends and associates who appoint each other to government positions and use governmental power and authority to protect their friends from accountability. It is not uncommon in fascist regimes for national resources and even treasures to be appropriated or even outright stolen by government leaders.

14. Fraudulent Elections – Sometimes elections in fascist nations are a complete sham. Other times elections are manipulated by smear campaigns against or even assassination of opposition candidates, use of legislation to control voting numbers or political district boundaries, and manipulation of the media. Fascist nations also typically use their judiciaries to manipulate or control elections.

Source: Free Inquiry.co/ 5-28-2003, Liberty Forum, Courtesy of Jeff Rense (Rense.com)

Something to Consider

In his interrogation of Winston, O'Brien refers to the Proles as "animals," inferring a kind of random, subhuman brainlessness about them, making them easily malleable and easy to control. Appealing to their base instincts and tranquilizing them with pornography, alcohol, impoverishment, the constant threat of war, and powerlessness, Big Brother is able to keep the masses under total control. Is this how existing oligarchies keep their masses under control?

Winston, however, sees the Proles as the essential connection to the past, the last memory of better times, and possessing noble virtues all their own, even believing they are the key to overthrowing Big Brother. O'Brien scoffs at this idea as ridiculous. Is the larger inference that the mass of humanity, when left to its own resolve, fails to defend the very rights it relies on to be free and content? How many of us know and defend the very rights we are denied? And if we do not know and defend them, why should they be employed on our behalf?

12. Nationalism in *1984*

A review of *nationalism* is necessary to understand *1984*. Orwell's experience as an imperial policeman in Burma, a corporal in The Spanish Civil War, a prisoner of war, a sergeant in the Home Guard during World War II, a journalist, essayist, radio broadcaster, and writing correspondent, all informed his theories regarding political and military oppression and refined his intellectual and critical view of the corrupting influences of mass media and the power elite. His insight into the hysteria of political loyalty and the functions of an 'invisible' bureaucratic, faceless managerial society are keys to understanding the darkest allusions present in his political writing.

A combined understanding of *1984* and Nationalism will also lead to an understanding of *totalitarianism*, which best reflects the monolithic form of rule that persists in the world of *1984*. The philosopher and Holocaust scholar, Hannah Arendt, attributed the emergence of *totalitarianism* to what she referred to as 'the banality of evil'—a conclusion on the 'disease' that infects the ordinary, the mediocre, and the unthinking. To Arendt this is a 'new' kind of human being who places his complete trust for all endeavors in the hands of one governing entity. As an observer of the 'Trial of Adolf Eichmann,' Arendt wrote in a series of controversial articles for *The New Yorker* that the 'Final Solution'—the eradication of European Jews— was conceived in all its brutality, but more so in its planning, by the 'unthinking' conditions that grew from blind obedience to authority. In his testimony in Jerusalem, Eichmann deflects all responsibility to Nazi law and Nazi intimidation. When Chief Prosecutor Attorney Gideon Hausner asks Eichmann to reflect on the moral consequences of his participation in The Final Solution, Eichmann buries his moral culpability under the defense that he was "just following orders," and went on to say that his was the expedient and efficient thing to do as a servant of the state. In his final statement before sentencing, he pleaded for leniency of sentence, saying,

> *I did try to leave my position, to leave for the front, for honest battle. But I was held fast in those dark duties. Once again I would stress that I am guilty of having been obedient, having subordinated myself to my official duties and the obligations of war service and my oath of allegiance and my oath of office, and in addition, once the war started, there was also martial law.*

(http://remember.org/eichmann/ownwords.htm)

Arendt is therefore appalled that the nightmare of genocide was born not entirely out of monstrousness but out of the moral vacuum of the unthinking and the obedient. Orwell takes the 'nobility of obedience' one step further and fabricates the identity of the authority as the idea of a mythical, all-powerful, brutal, but 'loving' nature that demands spiritual allegiance. Whereas *totalitarian* and *fascist* regimes were identified with 'real' personalities— Franco, Hitler, Mussolini, Stalin, Pol Pot, Idi Amin, and Pinochet to name a few—in Orwell's world, 'Big Brother' is the abstraction of power for power's sake (as represented by O'Brien—the only character other than Charrington, the head of the Thought Police, who comes closest to an actual flesh and blood authoritarian figure). By the end of Orwell's novel, the suffering, fate, and resulting delusional fealty to his torturer and his 'love' of Big Brother, Winston's predicament is beyond ordinary human understanding.

In his greatest use of irony, Orwell's last maxim—'God is Power'—exercises the concept of *doublethink* to define God not as something kind, but something brutal; not as something holy, but unholy. Like all of Big Brother's maxims, God disappears under the idea of Power itself. O'Brien admits that he himself will wither away, the only thing remaining will be the Power to which Winston becomes loyal, making Winston's loyalty even more of a delusion.

Something to Consider

How does one define and practice his or her patriotism? Are paying taxes, obeying the laws, flying a flag, wearing a ribbon, and going to a parade or rally or protest enough? Is protesting patriotic, or is it civic mistrust? How much civic mistrust can a citizenry tolerate before it degrades into a form of, or a force of, outright anarchy? If the freedom of a society leads to civil unrest, is an enforced kind of nationalism more desired, owing to the unpredictability of human nature when people cannot self-regulate?

Considering human nature, does the variety of human psychologies shaped by natural forces or by social forces shed a dim light on how realistic it is to expect people to behave when given freedom? Is patriotism an idealized view of nationalism?

In countries where an imposed, extreme version of nationalism persists, such as North Korea, what is the end game? Is it to immobilize, enslave, and imprison an entire nation of people, guaranteeing privileges only to the elite and subordinates who work the machinery of nationalism into a highly structured form of totalitarianism? If it is a virtual incarceration of a nation's people, in a republic such as the United States, how can we explain our own enormous prison rate and not consider the same nationalistic implications?

13. Edited Notes and Annotated Questions on George Orwell's 'Notes on Nationalism' (1945)

> Note: The full text of Orwell's 'Notes on Nationalism' (1945) is included near the end of this guide.
>
> [...]—My edits/omissions; ***boldface italics***—mine; boxed text—annotated questions.

[...]

By *"nationalism"* I mean first of all the habit of assuming that human beings can be classified like insects and that whole blocks of millions or tens of millions of people can be confidently labeled "good" or "bad." But secondly—and this is much more important—***I mean the habit of identifying oneself with a single nation or other unit, placing it beyond good and evil** and recognizing no other duty than that of advancing its interests.*

> **Questions:**
>
> 1. If human beings are considered social animals, is it possible to exist outside of a collective unit, generally speaking?
>
> 2. Born into families, would we not do just about anything to protect our families? Is loyalty to a nation just another extension of other particular loyalties?
>
> 3. Are not good and evil relative terms?
>
> 4. Does loyalty provide a grey area for good and evil?
>
> 5. Is it possible for a governing body to reveal its interests without compromising the common good?
>
> 6. If power corrupts, and if it takes varied types power and advantages to rise to leadership roles in government, how can the advancing interests of those in power be different from those who are subject to power?

Nationalism is not to be confused with patriotism. Both words are normally used in so vague a way that any definition is liable to be challenged, but one must draw a distinction between them, since two different and even opposing ideas are involved. ***By "patriotism" I mean devotion to a particular place and a particular way of life**, which one believes to be the best in the world but has no wish to force on other people. Patriotism is of its nature defensive, both militarily and culturally. Nationalism, on the other hand, is **inseparable from the desire for power**. The abiding purpose of every nationalist is to* *secure more power and more prestige, not for himself but for the nation or other unit in which he has chosen to sink his own individuality.*

> 7. Is it possible to separate altruism from the desire to influence others to be altruistic?
>
> 8. If a nation believes its ideals are best for other nations, but other nations reject these ideals, should a nation isolate itself from those nations that do not share its ideals?
>
> 9. If, as Orwell says, **Patriotism is of its nature defensive, both militarily and culturally**, is it not inevitable that military defense naturally becomes offensive?
>
> 10. Who or what defines *cultural patriotism*?
>
> 11. How can **prestige** distort a person's individuality?
>
> 12. Can an individual be truly patriotic?

So long as it is applied merely to the more notorious and identifiable nationalist movements in Germany, Japan, and other countries, all this is obvious enough. Confronted with a phenomenon like Nazism, which we can observe from the outside, nearly all of us would say much the same things about it. But here I must repeat what I said above, that I am only using the word "nationalism" for lack of a better. Nationalism, in the extended sense in which I am using the word, includes such movements and tendencies as Communism, political Catholicism, Zionism, Anti-Semitism, Trotskyism and Pacifism. *It does not necessarily mean loyalty to a government or a country, still less to one's own country, and it is not even strictly necessary that the units in which it deals should actually exist.* To name a few obvious examples, Jewry, Islam, Christendom, the Proletariat and the White Race are all of them objects of passionate nationalistic feeling: but their existence can be seriously questioned, and there is no definition of any one of them that would be universally accepted.

> 13. What is the nature of individual-to-individual **loyalty**?
>
> 14. When **loyalty** radiates out to larger groups, like teams and clubs, does it naturally "thin," bowing to the strength of the weakest member?
>
> 15. If Orwell's *examples—Jewry, Islam, Christendom, the Proletariat and the White Race*—lack enough definition to be the object of **nationalistic passion**, what definition justifies *patriotic fervor*?
>
> 16. Are there universal passions to warrant either **nationalism** or **patriotism**?
>
> 17. Can these passions actually define each impulse more clearly?

[…]

OBSESSION. *As nearly as possible, no nationalist ever thinks, talks, or writes about anything except the superiority of his own power unit. It is difficult if not impossible for any nationalist to conceal his allegiance.* The smallest slur upon his own unit, or any implied praise of a rival organization, fills him with uneasiness, which he can relieve only by making some sharp retort. If the chosen unit is an actual country, such as

Ireland or India, he will generally claim superiority for it not only in military power and political virtue, but in art, literature, sport, structure of the language, the physical beauty of the inhabitants, and perhaps even in climate, scenery and cooking. He will show great sensitiveness about such things as the correct display of flags, relative size of headlines and the order in which different countries are named.

> 18. As obsessions tend to distort reality, what realities does an individual distort if he or she is **nationalistic**?
>
> 19. What realities are neglected if a nation practices a collective **nationalism**?
>
> 20. How does a **culture** suffer from these distortions?
>
> 21. In psychological terms, an obsession with **superiority** indicates an ignorance of **inferiority**. How does this apply to a person and a nation?
>
> 22. In obsessing over the **artifacts** of passionate **nationalism**, how does an individual distort the meaning of those **artifacts**?
>
> 23. If competition is considered healthy, how does **nationalism** sabotage competition?

[…]

    INSTABILITY: The intensity with which they are held does not prevent *nationalist loyalties from being transferable*. To begin with, as I have pointed out already, they can be and often are fastened upon some foreign country. One quite commonly finds that great national leaders, or the founders of nationalist movements, do not even belong to the country they have glorified. Sometimes they are outright foreigners, or more often they come from peripheral areas where nationality is doubtful. Examples are Stalin, Hitler, Napoleon, de Valera, Disraeli, Poincare, Beaverbrook. The Pan-German movement was in part the creation of an Englishman, Houston Chamberlain.

> 24. Why would a foreign power *fasten upon some other foreign country* nationalistic loyalties?
>
> 25. How is this type of 'foreign born nationalism' a way to define and possibly mythologize and propagandize another nation's identity and sovereignty?
>
> 26. To what purpose?
>
> 27. The examples to which Orwell alludes are from the last century. Are their contemporary examples of this *transference*?

[…]

INDIFFERENCE TO REALITY. *All nationalists have the power of not seeing resemblances between similar sets of facts.* A British Tory will defend self-determination in Europe and oppose it in India with no feeling of inconsistency. Actions are held to be good or bad, not on their own merits, but according to who does them, and there is almost no kind of outrage -- torture, the use of hostages, forced labor, mass deportations, imprisonment without trial, forgery, assassination, the bombing of civilians

-- which **does not change its moral color when it is committed by "our" side. The Liberal News Chronicle published, as an example of shocking barbarity, photographs of Russians hanged by the Germans, and then a year or two later published with warm approval almost exactly similar photographs of Germans hanged by the Russians.** It is the same with historical events. ***History is thought of largely in nationalist terms***, and such things as the Inquisition, the tortures of the Star Chamber, the exploits of the English buccaneers (Sir Francis Drake, for instance, who was given to sinking Spanish prisoners alive), the Reign of Terror, the heroes of the Mutiny blowing hundreds of Indians from the guns, or Cromwell's soldiers slashing Irishwomen's faces with razors, become morally neutral or even meritorious when it is felt that they were done in the "right" cause. If one looks back over the past quarter of a century, one finds that there was hardly a single year when atrocity stories were not being reported from some part of the world; and yet in not one single case were these atrocities -- in Spain, Russia, China, Hungary, Mexico, Amritsar, Smyrna -- believed in and disapproved of by the English intelligentsia as a whole. **Whether such deeds were reprehensible, or even whether they happened, was always decided according to political predilection.**

---

28. We often choose to be indifferent in our own lives, selecting occasions to act and ignoring other occasions when we should act, but don't. What do the occasions of acting on our conscience look like?

29. Why do we choose to ignore other opportunities to act?

30. How is intelligence compromised when one acts with **indifference**?

31. How does this **indifference** help define Orwell's concept of *doublethink*?

32. Is there such a thing as a **right cause?** Are rights universal? Which ones? Why?

33. If you understand the simplest notion of **political predilection**, why do politics fail humanity?

34. It is largely believed that during the Iraq War, the United States tortured "enemy combatants" and defended this behavior on the grounds that valuable intelligence could be obtained through this behavior. How is this irrational?

The nationalist not only does not disapprove of atrocities committed by his own side, but he has a remarkable capacity for not even hearing about them. For quite six years the English admirers of Hitler contrived not to learn of the existence of Dachau and Buchenwald. And those who are loudest in denouncing the German concentration camps are often quite unaware, or only very dimly aware, that there are also concentration camps in Russia. Huge events like the Ukraine famine of 1933, involving the deaths of millions of people, have actually escaped the attention of the majority of English Russophiles. Many English people have heard almost nothing about the extermination of German and Polish Jews during the present war. Their own anti-Semitism has caused this vast crime to **bounce off their consciousness**. In nationalist thought there are facts which are both true and untrue, known and unknown. **A known fact may be so unbearable that it is habitually pushed aside and not allowed to enter into logical processes, or**

on the other hand it may enter into every calculation and yet never be admitted as a fact, even in one's own mind.

> 35. Why do people and nations have selective historical memories?
>
> 36. What events in American history do people try to conveniently forget, and for what reasons do they want to forget them?
>
> 37. Why do things **bounce off our consciences?** Is this part of Orwell's process of 'disappearing' the truth?
>
> 38. How does this process erode one's grasp of reality? Explain, using a familiar example.
>
> 39. If reality is evaded through this process, what happens to 'truth'?

Every nationalist is haunted by the belief that the past can be altered. He spends part of his time in a fantasy world in which things happen as they should -- in which, for example, the Spanish Armada was a success or the Russian Revolution was crushed in 1918 -- and he will transfer fragments of this world to the history books whenever possible. Much of the propagandist writing of our time amounts to plain forgery. Material facts are suppressed, dates altered, quotations removed from their context and doctored so as to change their meaning. Events which it is felt ought not to have happened are left unmentioned and ultimately denied. In 1927 Chiang Kai Chek boiled hundreds of Communists alive, and yet within ten years he had become one of the heroes of the Left. The re-alignment of world politics had brought him into the anti-Fascist camp, and so it was felt that the boiling of the Communists "didn't count", or perhaps had not happened. The primary aim of propaganda is, of course, to influence contemporary opinion, but those who rewrite history do probably believe with part of their minds that they are actually thrusting facts into the past. When one considers the elaborate forgeries that have been committed in order to show that Trotsky did not play a valuable part in the Russian civil war, it is difficult to feel that the people responsible are merely lying. **More probably they feel that their own version was what happened in the sight of God, and that one is justified in rearranging the records accordingly**.

> 40. In rearranging reality, how is the nationalist haunted by time.
>
> 41. What is the personal process by which we all alter the past to conform to the present?
>
> 42. What happens when a nation acquires the habit of revising its past?
>
> 43. What impact does altering the past have on the future?
>
> 44. What are contemporary examples of historical revisionism?

Indifference to objective truth *is encouraged by the sealing-off of one part of the world from another, which makes it harder and harder to discover what is actually happening.* There can often be a genuine doubt about the most enormous events. For example, it is impossible to calculate within millions, perhaps even tens of millions, the number of deaths caused by the present war. The calamities that are constantly being reported -- battles, massacres, famines, revolutions -- tend to inspire in the average person a feeling of unreality. One has no way of verifying the facts, one is not even fully certain that they have happened, and one is always presented with totally different interpretations from different sources. What were the rights and wrongs of the Warsaw rising of August 1944? Is it true about the German gas ovens in Poland? Who was really to blame for the Bengal famine? Probably the truth is discoverable, but the facts will be so dishonestly set forth in almost any newspaper that the ordinary reader can be forgiven either for swallowing lies or failing to form an opinion. The general uncertainty as to what is really happening makes it easier to cling to lunatic beliefs. Since nothing is ever quite proved or disproved, the most unmistakable fact can be impudently denied. Moreover, although endlessly brooding on power, victory, defeat, revenge, the nationalist is often somewhat uninterested in what happens in the real world. What he wants is to feel that his own unit is getting the better of some other unit, and he can more easily do this by scoring off an adversary than by examining the facts to see whether they support him. All nationalist controversy is at the debating-society level. It is always entirely inconclusive, since each contestant invariably believes himself to have won the victory. Some nationalists are not far from schizophrenia, living quite happily amid dreams of power and conquest which have no connection with the physical world.

---

45. What are the benefits of **isolationism**?

46. What are the perils of **isolationism**?

47. Why is it important for historians to tell the truth?

48. Why do some historians lie?

49. Winston Churchill's maxim, "History is written by the victors," suggests the peril of subjectivity. How do we pursue an objective history of an event?

50. In *1984*, why does Winston Smith spend so much effort trying to remember the past through those who lived it? What does this suggest about memory and authentic history?

Something to Consider

In thinking about your own patriotic temperament, are there any tenets in your love of country that are unavoidably nationalistic? Are there actions you would take that reflect a customized, personalized nationalism?

14. Key Terms: Define

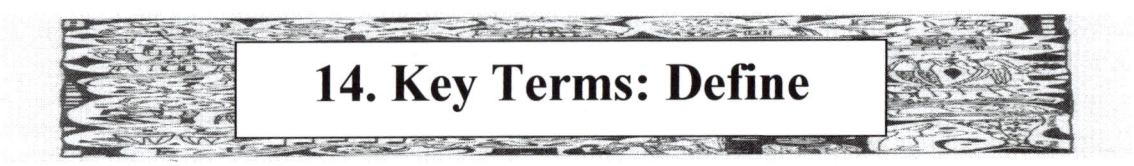

1984 is a dynamic narrative, full of the force of ideas and characters. Many of the ideas are compressed into specific terminology, which has to be understood in order to follow the narrative. As these concepts are embedded in the narrative, it is important to keep tract of where they occur, what they mean, and how you understand them. One way of decoding Orwell's language is to apply it to the contemporary world. This will come in handy when you get to "The Book"—"Emmanuel Goldstein's *Theory and Practice of Oligarchical Collectivism*"—the 'illegal' text embedded within *1984,* which explains the origins and theories of Orwell's brutal and dehumanizing dystopia.

For example, when we encounter the term *Victory*, as in *Victory Gin* or *Victory Cigarettes*, we associate Orwell's use of victory with failure, which is one of our first exposures to the broad concept of *Doublethink*:

#	Term	Page	Definition & Relevance
1.	*Victory*		Anything *Victory* is an example of *doublethink,* which is cruelly ironic. There is no 'victory' of any kind in *1984*, as war is never ending, commerce is crumbling, the decline of human progress is everywhere, and personal dignity and acts of individuality are defeated at every turn. Using smaller examples, tobacco falls out of *Victory Cigarettes* and *Victory Gin* tastes like rotten vinegar. Today, products are advertised to be the "best," "the most effective," " the most watched," etc. Pharmaceuticals claim to cure ailments, but warn against dire consequences, like "feelings of suicide." In the larger scheme, the idea of *victory* distorts public service when someone 'wins' an election, but nothing is legislatively accomplished.

Victory	Freedom Is Slavery	Oldspeak
Hate Week	Ignorance Is Strength	Overfullfilment
Thoughtcrime	Speakwrite Machines	Versificator
Big Brother	Doublethink	Pornosec
Telescreen	Novel Writing Machines	Facecrime
INGSOC	Anti Sex League	Blackwhite
Ninth 3-Year Plan	Brotherhood	Duckspeak
Ministry of Truth	"the book"	Facecrime
Ministry of Love	Inner Party	Doubleplusungood
Ministry of Plenty	Outer Party	Newspeak
Ministry of Peace	Proles	Crimestop
Airstrip One	Emmanuel Goldstein	Artsem
Oceania	Sports Committee	God Is Power
Newspeak	The Spies	*Under the spreading chestnut tree…*
War Is Peace	Golden Country	*Oranges and lemons…*

THIS CHART CAN BE COPIED FOR EDUCATIONAL PURPOSES

#	Term	Page	Definition & Relevance

15. Reading Comprehension Questions

1984 is a novel and must be read as a story whose plotlines hinge on the movement of principal characters through a maze of impossible conditions. These conditions are an invention of an extreme, but fully realized dystopian view of the future. Though we are far past the year '1984', the novel presents permanent implications for a future where dignity and humanity have no place in the power structure of social order. Moving from page to page, the reader can gather Winston's journey through this dystopian world and assemble, bit-by-bit, Orwell's intensely detailed puzzle of political and cultural atrophy. With an accumulation of knowledge and growing insight into Orwell's totalitarian world, we can also experience Winston's memory, which is the motif Orwell uses to hold onto whatever humanity remains of Winston while he is losing his sanity and soul.

When reading the text, notice Orwell's exaggerations according to the **satirical** and **dystopian** criteria previously mentioned, then determine if these exaggerations reveal fundamental truths that exist in our present day reality.

Note: There are many questions below, some basic to plot reading, some for inferential reading, and others for larger discussions. The teacher should gauge student reading comprehension level and make the effort to assign questions accordingly. There is much discussion by educational theorists about 'busy work' and the drag that 'homework' sometimes has on a student's sustained effort to enjoy and challenge what she reads. I suggest teachers should find creative and efficient ways to use these questions without imposing a burden on the student.

CHRONOLOGY OF ENCOUNTERING TERMS / MOTIFS

13 O'Clock	Memory Holes	"Under the spreading chestnut tree…"
Victory Mansions	Overfullfillment	Ownlife
Hate Week	Versificator	Lottery
Big Brother Is Watching You	Pornosec	Golden Country
Telescreen	Duckspeak	Pornosec
INGSOC	Ungood	goodthinkful
Ninth 3 Year Plan	Oldspeak	We are the dead.
Airstrip One	Refs Unperson	Prole's soong
Oceania	11th Edition of Newspeak Dictionary	Oranges and lemons…
Newspeak	'Razor blades'	Goldstein
War Is Peace	Facecrime	Unperson
Freedom Is Slavery	Artsem	Mutability of the Past
Ignorance Is Strength	Jus primae noctis	
Who Controls the Past…"		
"Oldspeak		

Book 1

Chapter I. (pp. 1-19, Signet Edition)

1. What are the features of Winston's day-to-day life? What do these features suggest?

2. Why is Winston so concerned with the *Thought Police*? Is the concept of *Thought Police* too far fetched? Explain.

3. What is the nature of privacy in the world of *1984*? Why do you think privacy is devalued?

4. What is ironic about *The Ministry of Love*? Is it really ironic, or is it natural to express 'love' in 'tough love' ways?

5. What is unusual about Winston's *telescreen*? What are the implications of this?

6. What are the 'legal' consequences of Winston possessing the diary?

7. What is Winston's concept of time?

8. What is significant about the way *the Proles* react to the film? How does Winston react? Is his reaction significant? Why?

9. What is Winston's reaction toward Julia when he first meets her? Why?

10. What are Winston's suspicions regarding O'Brien?

11. Who is Emmanuel Goldstein? What is he advocating that could cause such hysteria among the people of Oceania?

12. What are the Anti-Semitic implications of naming this 'enemy of the people' *Goldstein*?

13. How do the images behind Goldstein's voiceover propagandize his status as an 'enemy of the people'?

14. How do these *hate rallies* succeed on one level but fail on another level? Is this success and failure 'on purpose'? Explain, using what you know of the effects of *doublethink*.

15. Using Orwell's words, describe the 'hate' this rally summons.

16. How is Winston's 'transference of hate' toward Julia an example of *doublethink*?

17. Describe the 'falling action' of the *Two Minutes Hate*.

18. At this point, what happens between Winston and O'Brien?

19. Define *Thoughtcrime* and give an example of it from the book and a *thoughtcrime* you might commit if you lived in Oceania.

Chapter II. (20-29)

20. Who is Parsons?

21. What is disturbing to Winston about the Parson's children? To you?

22. What is the attraction the Parson's children have to 'the Spies'?

23. Describe Winston's dream. What is its significance?

24. Why is the end of the war bad news for Winston?

25. What are some of your own thoughts regarding the nature of this 'war' Winston laments?

26. What is the psychological significance of the weekly non-strategic bombing of London?

27. If *Big Brother* is everywhere, what is the only thing at this point Winston is sure he possesses?

28. While writing in his diary, Winston concedes that he is writing for 'the future.' What does this poetic-like salutation reveal about him and the time in which he lives?

29. In writing this, what does Winston realize?

Chapter III (29-35)

30. Describe Winston's dream about his family. Why are "Dreams a continuation of an intellectual life"?

31. What are Winston's thoughts on *tragedy*?

32. What is suggested by Winston's understanding of Shakespeare?

33. What can be inferred by Winston's memory of his family in the shelter of the Tube station during the Atomic War?

34. What is troubling to Winston about 'continuous war'?

35. Using Winston's words explain *doublethink*. How would you explain *doublethink* to a stranger?

36. What jars Winston from his contemplation of the origins of *Big Brother*?

Chapter IV. (36-47)

37. Translate (explain) the 'four slips of paper' on which Winston is focused.

38. What is Winston's job at the *Ministry of Truth*?

39. What is the ultimate 'truth' about what Winston is doing, which is worse than falsifying the past?

40. What kind of 'information' is produced for the proletariat (the Proles)? What is the hoped-for effect of this 'information'?

41. What is the 'intricate' message Winston has to re-render? Why is this tricky?

42. Why is Withers being 'purged' from history?

43. Who is Comrade Oglivie? Compare the mythology and reality of this character.

44. Oglivie's attitudes toward family and marriage suggest what other aspects of 'Orwellian' values?

45. What is Orwell suggesting by comparing Oglivie to Charlemagne and Caesar? Is this a 'satirical flourish'? Explain.

Chapter V & VI. (48-58)

48. Who is Symes and what does he find beautiful? What is the purpose of "cutting language down to the bone"?

49. What is meant by the 'beauty' of "vagueness and [the] useless shades of meaning"?

50. To what end is the narrowing of thought?

51. What do Syme and Winston think about the *Proles* and their humanity?

52. What does *orthodoxy* mean? How is it relevant to 'unthinking'?

53. What is *Duckspeak*? How is it significant to Winston's frustrations to understand things, literally and figuratively?

54. How is the *Chestnut Tree Café* significant to the idea of *orthodoxy* and 'saving stupidity'?

55. Orwell describes Parsons' handwriting as "the neat handwriting of the illiterate." How is this an accurate portrayal of how Parsons and people like him are unconscious because of their *orthodoxy*?

56. What story does Parsons tell about his children?

57. How does the revision of the chocolate ration suggest something deeper about this society's collective memory?

58. What are Winston's instincts about the past? Why is this called *ancestral memory?*

59. What is *Facecrime*?

Chapter VI. (58-63)

60. What is the aim of the party in regard to loyalty between men and women? Marriage? Sex? Why?

61. Why is Winston's wife, Katherine, referred to as the "human soundtrack"?

62. How does the encounter with the prostitute constitute *thoughtcrime?*

Chapter VII. (63-81)

63. Why does Winston feel that the only hope lies with the *Proles*?

64. What does the 'saucepan' incident reveal about the *Proles*? The *Lottery*? The 'old men in the pub'?

65. What is suggested by the "children's history textbook regarding 'the Revolution'"? What is meant by "mute protest in your own bones"?

66. Who are Jones, Aaronson, and Rutherford?

67. "He seemed to be breaking up before our eyes—like a mountain crumbling." To whom is Orwell referring? What is the reason for this description?

68. How does Winston arrive upon the Party's deceit?

69. What fundamental question consumes Winston after he discovers the 'how' of things?

70. "Freedom is the freedom to say that two plus two make four. If that is granted all else follows." What is the significance of Winston's realization?

Chapter VIII. (80-107)

71. Why did the Party discourage its members from having spare time? Do you see any parallels to this social fixation?

72. How is the *Lottery* a manifestation of another way of controlling the *Proles*?

73. In his confrontation with the Old Man in the pub, for what is Winston really searching? What did he get for his efforts?

74. Why is Winston fascinated by the coral glass paperweight?

75. Why does Winston compare the Old Man to an 'ant'? Apply this to history?

76. How does the 'present' test itself against the 'past'? How does an individual apply this 'test' to himself/herself.

77. What is the significance of the 'uselessness' of the paperweight?

78. Why does Winston think about "sitting by the fireside and the 'friendly ticking of the clock' "?

79. What was the fate of books written before 1960? Why this particular date?

80. What is the significance of the line "Oranges and Lemons…"?

81. Who is Mr. Charrington? What is his attitude towards Winston?

82. What happens when Winston 'meets' Julia again?

83. When O'Brien says, "We shall meet in the place where there is no darkness," why does he say this and how does this resonate with Winston?

End of Book 1

Something to Consider

The first book of *1984* is about power and powerlessness. We are introduced to ideas that seem impossible for one to accept, especially when we consider how much power we think we have over our own lives. Consider the idea that if you are attending school regularly and have the privilege of reading books and discussing ideas, you have an advantage over those who do not have these privileges. Recognizing these privileges gives you a sense of power over your own lives. Is the first sign of the erosion of power the decline of educational privileges? Is an indifference to one's education a surrendering to those who will use power against you, to rally your substance to their ends?

BOOK 2

Chapter I (108-120)

84. What is written on the note Julia passes to Winston? Explain this turnabout and its consequences, using what you already know about Winston.

85. Who is Ampleforth?

86. What effect does Julia squeezing Winston's hand have on him? How does Orwell's narrative expression—his writing—change?

Chapter II (120-130)

87. What happens during Winston and Julia's first 'get together'? How is this significant in terms of your understanding of the story up to this point?

88. What is the nature of Julia's attraction to Winston? What does she say that is significant to this nature? Explain the 'logic' of her attitude in terms of what they are experiencing in this society.

89. Describe the *Golden Country* and the significance of the 'flight of the thrush.'

90. What is the nature of Winston's attraction to Julia?

91. How is 'sex a political act'? When is it not a political act?

Chapter III (130-140)

92. What is suggested by Julia cautiousness? What is Julia's job, and in her characterization of it, how does she reveal more details about the state of Oceania and the Party's deception?

93. What is significant about Julia's 'affair'? What is meant by the phrase: "Break the rules and then stay alive all the same"?

94. Why can't Winston grasp the meaning of the Party's 'sexual Puritanism'? How does Julia answer the question regarding as to why 'the Party cannot bear you to like sex"?

95. Winston could have killed his wife Katherine, but didn't. Why?

96. Explain: "She would not accept it as a law of nature that the individual is always defeated."

97. How is Julia critical of Winston? Why does she contradict Winston when he says, "We are the dead?" Do you think she is justified in her criticisms? Explain.

Chapter IV (140-151)

98. Why does Winston insist he's pursuing 'folly'? What is the significance of the *Prole's song*?

99. What is the nature of Winston's 'jealousy'? How does it evolve? Why isn't there more of this kind of narrative substance in the novel?

100. How does Julia reveal her transformation from a Party functionary into an individual? Into a woman?

101. Why is 'normalcy' an act of rebellion? What artifacts in 'the room' newly indicate the presence of the 'extraordinary'? Explain this reversal.

102. Why does Winston fear rats?

103. The coral glass paperweight has an illusion for Winston. What is this illusion?

104. What does Winston say about the hard-mounted picture on the wall of his getaway flat? Knowing that great writers do not trivialize detail without meaning, what do you think Winston's observation means?

Chapter V (153-161)

105. What is the significance of Charrington in Winston's life, his relevance to memory, and to Winston's search for understanding the world around him?

106. Why is Goldstein "outside" of Julia's imagination?

107. What are Julia's thoughts on the 'War'?

108. What is meant by "History has stopped"? Is that possible? How?

109. What does Winston mean when says to Julia: "You are only a rebel from the waste down"? Why does she find this witty?

110. How does Winston understand 'the world view of Party'? What metaphorical analogy does he use to represent his understanding?

Chapter VI (161-164)

111. How does Winston come to meet with O'Brien?

112. What is O'Brien's assessment of Winston's work at the *Minitrue*?

113. What is an *unperson*? How does O'Brien indirectly acknowledge this idea?

114. How does Winston react to some of O'Brien's exchanges in the brief time they meet in the corridor?

115. Moving from "thoughts to words" and "from words to action," what excites Winston, but terrifies him as well?

Chapter VII (164-171)

116. One of the great forces of the novel is Winston's memory of his mother. What were the circumstance surrounding the end of Winston's childhood and the death of his mother?

117. Describe Winston's dream about his mother and its significance to the idea of love and 'private loyalties,' his guilt, and Winston's growing inner rebellion.

118. Why does Winston find hope with the Proles?

119. What will Julia **not** do to Winston? What is the significance of this in terms of limiting or allowing the mutability of a character? Consider Winston, Julia, and O'Brien.

120. What are the essential arguments between Winston and Julia in this chapter, and how do they reveal their respective core beliefs? On what idea do they agree?

Chapter VIII (171-183)

121. What is the state of Winston's mind when he and Julia meet O'Brien at the Ministry of Truth?

122. Try to translate O'Brien's dictated 'Newspeak' message into 'Oldspeak.' What is the Inner Party doing to the English Language?

123. Listing all of them, what is the most shocking aspect of O'Brien's privileges as an Inner Party member?

124. Julia's reaction to wine is telling. How so?

125. What beliefs of Winston does O'Brien confirm?

126. To what extent will Winston serve and sacrifice for the revolution, the Brotherhood?

127. What will Julia NOT do for the Brotherhood? What does she say? How does this distinguish her from all other characters? How do Winston and O'Brien react?

128. What does O'Brien say to his office servant, Martin? What about Martin makes Winston curious?

129. What is the idea behind Winston and Julia, and the Brotherhood, working in 'the dark'?

130. Why does Winston nearly worship O'Brien by the end of their meeting?

131. How does O'Brien describe *The Brotherhood* and the consequences of getting caught?

132. When O'Brien uses the adage, "We are the dead," it has a different intended meaning. Explain.

133. What is ironic about O'Brien suggesting a toast? To what does Winston want to raise a toast? Explain why this is so important.

134. What is the significance of O'Brien completing the poem Winston was trying to remember?

The following section is concerned with Emmanuel Goldstein *Theory and Practice of Oligarchical Collectivism*, otherwise known as 'the Book.' Some of the questions are difficult to answer as they try to draw theoretical responses to the theoretical premises Orwell expresses through Goldstein's 'illegal book.' To assist you, the questions are embedded in the text from *1984*, with key ideas abstracted from the text as well, drawing modern parallels to Goldstein's theories. There is an additional section that 'collects' these abstracts from 'the Book' in Section 18. These modern parallels are fluid and should be reconsidered with every subsequent reading of *1984*. They are also the opinion of this writer, based on research, but built around conceptions rooted in shared political assumptions with Orwell. These assumptions should be challenged at every turn.

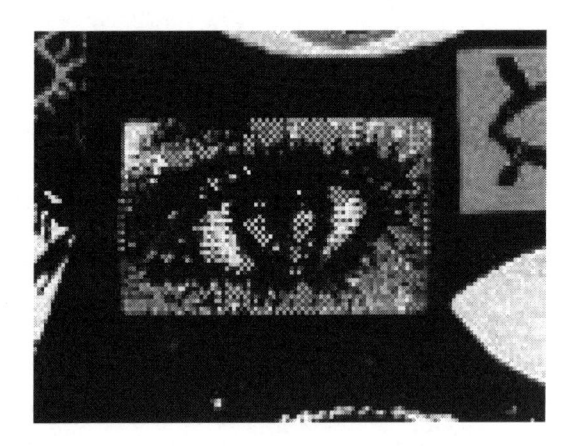

16. "THE BOOK"

Theory and Practice of Oligarchical Collectivism
By Emmanuel Goldstein

Strategically planted near the last third of the text, THE THEORY AND PRACTICE OF OLIGARCHICAL COLLECTIVISM BY EMMANUEL GOLDSTEIN is the book O'Brien gives to Winston in order to enlighten him about the true nature of the so-called revolution against Big Brother. It is at this point in the story where Winston and Julia feel confident that O'Brien is a member of The Brotherhood and that a breakthrough in the revolution is forthcoming. "The Book," as it is referred to in the text, is a chilling narrative about 'empirical truths' regarding the superstructure of the world, or the *realpolitik* behind the gruesome conditions present in Oceania and the other 'superstates.' It is a discourse on absolute power and reflects the very rationale for the book itself. Winston reads it while Julia sleeps, and his 'awakening' to all of Big Brother's deceits is plotted to draw in the awakening of readers to Orwell's dystopian conceits.

Because it is so purposefully devoid of rhetoric in its expression and assured in its convictions, some students and teachers skip over "The Book," as it is difficult and very time consuming to discuss, let alone understand. It is the wise student and teacher who invest time in this section of *1984*, as it brings context to many of the concepts Orwell allows to fit into his narrative without the benefit of explanation. "The Book" *is* his explanation. Orwell's experience as a soldier, prisoner, civil servant, student of literature and history, journalist, citizen and writer whose condemnation of propaganda is unrivaled, all come to bear on his theories of power. To short change this section is to experience the novel as half read.

The exposition in Chapter Nine sets up the reading of Goldstein's "Book" by revisiting the conditions under which Winston must live, focusing on the very irrationality of his own existence, the duplicity of living in a world in constant revision, and how his growing 'understanding' portends to approximate an informed reality.

Note: Orwell's plot narrative and Goldstein's *book* are interrupted below with 1) **textual questions** regarding the shifting dynamics of Winston's new realizations, and possibly yours; and 2) **annotations** and **observations** for the purposes of revealing parallel events that reflect today's world. [Reminder: The latter are collected together in a subsequent part of this guide.]

...from Nineteen Eighty-Four by George Orwell

Chapter 9

Winston was gelatinous with fatigue. Gelatinous was the right word. It had come into his head spontaneously. His body seemed to have not only the weakness of a jelly, but its translucency. He felt that if he held up his hand he would be able to see the light through it. All the blood and lymph had been drained out of him by an enormous debauch of work, leaving only a frail structure of nerves, bones, and skin. All sensations seemed to be magnified. His overalls fretted his shoulders, the pavement tickled his feet, even the opening and closing of a hand was an effort that made his joints creak.

He had worked more than ninety hours in five days. So had everyone else in the Ministry. Now it was all over, and he had literally nothing to do, no Party work of any description, until tomorrow morning. He could spend six hours in the hiding-place and another nine in his own bed. Slowly, in mild afternoon sunshine, he walked up a dingy street in the direction of Mr Charrington's shop, keeping one eye open for the patrols, but irrationally convinced that this afternoon there was no danger of anyone interfering with him. The heavy brief-case that he was carrying bumped against his knee at each step, sending a tingling sensation up and down the skin of his leg. Inside it was the book, which he had now had in his possession for six days and had not yet opened, nor even looked at.

On the sixth day of Hate Week, after the processions, the speeches, the shouting, the singing, the banners, the posters, the films, the waxworks, the rolling of drums and squealing of trumpets, the tramp of marching feet, the grinding of the caterpillars of tanks, the roar of massed planes, the booming of guns — after six days of this, when the great orgasm was quivering to its climax and the general hatred of Eurasia had boiled up into such delirium that if the crowd could have got their hands on the 2,000 Eurasian war-criminals who were to be publicly hanged on the last day of the proceedings, they would unquestionably have torn them to pieces — at just this moment it had been announced that Oceania was not after all at war with Eurasia. Oceania was at war with Eastasia. Eurasia was an ally.

Chapter IX

135. Why is Winston so exhausted? What are the events in Oceania that have confirmed Winston's suspicions about the state of things? What was the process of falsifying history? What surprised and impressed Winston?

136. What is meant by "sanity is not statistical"?

137. In describing the singing Prole woman, what does Winston mean when he says to Julia that the Prole woman has a "special kind of beauty."

138. This should not be a surprise to Winston, especially since his job is to revise historical records. However, the magnitude of this shifting allegiance should indicate to

> readers how pervasive revisionism is in the world of Big Brother. A major question is for what purpose does this enemy/alliance-trading serve the Inner Party? What does it say about the decay of individual and collective memory? Is it a natural result of brainwashing or a willingness to uncritically accept what authority prescribes? How do such large fabrications influence everyday half-truths, lies, deceptions and exaggerations?

There was, of course, no admission that any change had taken place. Merely it became known, with extreme suddenness and everywhere at once, that Eastasia and not Eurasia was the enemy. Winston was taking part in a demonstration in one of the central London squares at the moment when it happened. It was night, and the white faces and the scarlet banners were luridly floodlit. The square was packed with several thousand people, including a block of about a thousand schoolchildren in the uniform of the Spies. On a scarlet-draped platform an orator of the Inner Party, a small lean man with disproportionately long arms and a large bald skull over which a few lank locks straggled, was haranguing the crowd. A little Rumpelstiltskin figure, contorted with hatred, he gripped the neck of the microphone with one hand while the other, enormous at the end of a bony arm, clawed the air menacingly above his head. His voice, made metallic by the amplifiers, boomed forth an endless catalogue of atrocities, massacres, deportations, lootings, rapings, torture of prisoners, bombing of civilians, lying propaganda, unjust aggressions, broken treaties. It was almost impossible to listen to him without being first convinced and then maddened. At every few moments the fury of the crowd boiled over and the voice of the speaker was drowned by a wild beast-like roaring that rose uncontrollably from thousands of throats. The most savage yells of all came from the schoolchildren. The speech had been proceeding for perhaps twenty minutes when a messenger hurried on to the platform and a scrap of paper was slipped into the speaker's hand. He unrolled and read it without pausing in his speech. Nothing altered in his voice or manner, or in the content of what he was saying, but suddenly the names were different. Without words said, a wave of understanding rippled through the crowd. Oceania was at war with Eastasia! The next moment there was a tremendous commotion. The banners and posters with which the square was decorated were all wrong! Quite half of them had the wrong faces on them. It was sabotage! The agents of Goldstein had been at work! There was a riotous interlude while posters were ripped from the walls, banners torn to shreds and trampled underfoot. The Spies performed prodigies of activity in clambering over the rooftops and cutting the streamers that fluttered from the chimneys. But within two or three minutes it was all over. The orator, still gripping the neck of the microphone, his shoulders hunched forward, his free hand clawing at the air, had gone straight on with his speech. One minute more, and the feral roars of rage were again bursting from the crowd. The Hate continued exactly as before, except that the target had been changed.

> **139. Why does the arc of hysteria rise to distortion?** If we remember films of Adolph Hitler's speeches at Nuremburg, we see this arc as it begins slowly, first with resolve and contrition—an almost apology for the state of affairs that burdens him and the Fatherland. Then it rises to denigration and sloganeering, which masque any principle or

> conviction, relying less on substance than the rhythm of words. In the penultimate rise of his 'oratory,' his voice grows discordant, distorted, guttural; his gestures become animated, often wild, his arms and hands clutching some imaginary, wicked, nearly physically painful truth, now lost on a crowd who is more enraptured by his noise, their noise, rather than his message. All this said, why do people get lost in this kind of hysteria? Is it a form of mass or self-deception, or both? And why did the most savage yells come from the school children?

The thing that impressed Winston in looking back was that the speaker had switched from one line to the other actually in midsentence, not only without a pause, but without even breaking the syntax. But at the moment he had other things to preoccupy him. It was during the moment of disorder while the posters were being torn down that a man whose face he did not see had tapped him on the shoulder and said, 'Excuse me, I think you've dropped your brief-case.' He took the brief-case abstractedly, without speaking. He knew that it would be days before he had an opportunity to look inside it. The instant that the demonstration was over he went straight to the Ministry of Truth, though the time was now nearly twenty-three hours. The entire staff of the Ministry had done likewise. The orders already issuing from the telescreen, recalling them to their posts, were hardly necessary.

Oceania was at war with Eastasia: Oceania had always been at war with Eastasia. A large part of the political literature of five years was now completely obsolete. Reports and records of all kinds, newspapers, books, pamphlets, films, sound-tracks, photographs — all had to be rectified at lightning speed. Although no directive was ever issued, it was known that the chiefs of the Department intended that within one week no reference to the war with Eurasia, or the alliance with Eastasia, should remain in existence anywhere. The work was overwhelming, all the more so because the processes that it involved could not be called by their true names. Everyone in the Records Department worked eighteen hours in the twenty-four, with two three-hour snatches of sleep. Mattresses were brought up from the cellars and pitched all over the corridors: meals consisted of sandwiches and Victory Coffee wheeled round on trolleys by attendants from the canteen. Each time that Winston broke off for one of his spells of sleep he tried to leave his desk clear of work, and each time that he crawled back sticky-eyed and aching, it was to find that another shower of paper cylinders had covered the desk like a snowdrift, half-burying the speakwrite and overflowing on to the floor, so that the first job was always to stack them into a neat enough pile to give him room to work. What was worst of all was that the work was by no means purely mechanical. Often it was enough merely to substitute one name for another, but any detailed report of events demanded care and imagination. Even the geographical knowledge that one needed in transferring the war from one part of the world to another was considerable.

> 140. It is important for students to consider historical revisionism in their own time. For example, the attacks on 9/11 were factually attributed to terrorist cells located in Saudi Arabia and Afghanistan. However, after a brief, but effective incursion into Afghanistan, the response of the United states was to invade Iraq, which critics of this invasion said had nothing to do with 9/11. The drumbeat of war, the political force of nationalism

> masquerading as patriotism, and the need for revenge against terrorism itself, eventually defined Iraq as the true enemy of the USA. Polls taken years after the invasion indicate that a major portion of Americans still believe that Iraq was responsible for 9/11. Do we practice this historical duplicity in other ways? Economically? Institutionally?

By the third day his eyes ached unbearably and his spectacles needed wiping every few minutes. It was like struggling with some crushing physical task, something which one had the right to refuse and which one was nevertheless neurotically anxious to accomplish. In so far as he had time to remember it, he was not troubled by the fact that every word he murmured into the speakwrite, every stroke of his ink-pencil, was a deliberate lie. He was as anxious as anyone else in the Department that the forgery should be perfect. On the morning of the sixth day the dribble of cylinders slowed down. For as much as half an hour nothing came out of the tube; then one more cylinder, then nothing. Everywhere at about the same time the work was easing off. A deep and as it were secret sigh went through the Department. A mighty deed, which could never be mentioned, had been achieved. It was now impossible for any human being to prove by documentary evidence that the war with Eurasia had ever happened. At twelve hundred it was unexpectedly announced that all workers in the Ministry were free till tomorrow morning. Winston, still carrying the brief-case containing the book, which had remained between his feet while he worked and under his body while he slept, went home, shaved himself, and almost fell asleep in his bath, although the water was barely more than tepid.

> **141.** Critics of work in America protest how the working week has expanded beyond the traditional 40-hour workweek, a period fought for by individuals and unions and once ratified by government sympathy for the health of the working family, often jeopardized by industry's early exploitation of men, women, and children. With the collapse of unions, the working week slowly expanded—people working vast amounts of overtime, often without extra compensation or with a suppressed minimum wage, or people telecommuting from home and working during 'family' time. Americans complain of work exhaustion and show disinterest in anything but tuning out the problems of the world when they are in the 'sanctuary' of their own homes. Social problems often follow the worn out worker in the forms of domestic abuse, alcoholism, and the kinds of dispiriting resentment that sabotage the workplace itself. Studs Terkel's landmark book *Working* chronicles the triumph and tragedy of work in America and reveals how work itself is the very definition of citizenship. Do *1984* and the conditions under which the *Outer Party* labours, give us insight into how work enables the faceless authority of capitalism to exploit the working person? Challenge this assumption with the benefits we enjoy from living in a capitalist society.

With a sort of voluptuous creaking in his joints he climbed the stair above Mr Charrington's shop. He was tired, but not sleepy any longer. He opened the window, lit the dirty little oilstove and put on a pan of water for coffee. Julia would arrive presently: meanwhile there was the book. He sat down in the sluttish armchair and undid the straps of the brief-case.

A heavy black volume, amateurishly bound, with no name or title on the cover. The print also looked slightly irregular. The pages were worn at the edges, and fell apart, easily, as though the book had passed through many hands. The inscription on the title-page ran:

THE THEORY AND PRACTICE OF OLIGARCHICAL COLLECTIVISM
BY
EMMANUEL GOLDSTEIN

Winston began reading:

Chapter I

IGNORANCE IS STRENGTH

Throughout recorded time, and probably since the end of the Neolithic Age, there have been three kinds of people in the world, the High, the Middle, and the Low. They have been subdivided in many ways, they have borne countless different names, and their relative numbers, as well as their attitude towards one another, have varied from age to age: but the essential structure of society has never altered. Even after enormous upheavals and seemingly irrevocable changes, the same pattern has always reasserted itself, just as a gyroscope will always return to equilibrium, however far it is pushed one way or the other.

The aims of these groups are entirely irreconcilable . . .

142. Why does the pattern of 'the High, the Middle, and the Low" in dividing people, or social status, or nearly any typography, persist among institutional humankind? Doe it correspond to real divisions, or assigned divisions? If you fail a standardized test, but excel in creativity and at research and more complex forms of inquiry, are you shuttered to a lower division if that institution relies primarily on high stakes tests to determine achievement? Why do some intellectuals consider 'folk' music a lower form of musical expression, when it is known that most traditional 'classical' music—considered the highest form of music— borrows its themes from folk melodies? Why do we need to classify, quantify, and qualify?

#	Page	From *1984* (Signet Edition 1980)	MODERN PARALLELS
1	184	High, middle, low social groupings	Wealthy, middle class, welfare class; AP, Honors, College Prep, General, Vocational, etc.; Rural, suburban, urban;

			Ghetto, downtown, uptown; Amateur, dilettante, professional **OTHERS:**

Winston stopped reading, chiefly in order to appreciate the fact that he was reading, in comfort and safety. He was alone: no telescreen, no ear at the keyhole, no nervous impulse to glance over his shoulder or cover the page with his hand. The sweet summer air played against his cheek. From somewhere far away there floated the faint shouts of children: in the room itself there was no sound except the insect voice of the clock. He settled deeper into the arm-chair and put his feet up on the fender. It was bliss, it was eternity.

> **143. Is the privilege Winston feels when he is reading, the same privilege we feel when we can spend undistracted time doing something we actually want to do, not what others want us to do?**
>
> **144. While reading is illegal in the world of *Big Brother*, is this a privilege we covet in our own lives? Are we in danger of losing this privilege, or worse, in losing the riches that reading provides if we don't covet and encourage it? Beyond enjoyment, what are the riches of literacy?**

Suddenly, as one sometimes does with a book of which one knows that one will ultimately read and re-read every word, he opened it at a different place and found himself at Chapter III. He went on reading:

Chapter III

WAR IS PEACE

The splitting up of the world into three great super-states was an event which could be and indeed was foreseen before the middle of the twentieth century. With the absorption of Europe by Russia and of the British Empire by the United States, two of the three existing powers, Eurasia and Oceania, were already effectively in being. The third, Eastasia, only emerged as a distinct unit after another decade of confused fighting. The frontiers between the three super-states are in some places arbitrary, and in others they fluctuate according to the fortunes of war, but in general they follow geographical lines. Eurasia comprises the whole of the northern part of the European and Asiatic land-mass, from Portugal to the Bering Strait. Oceania comprises the Americas, the Atlantic islands including the British Isles, Australasia, and the southern portion of Africa. Eastasia, smaller than the others and with a less definite western frontier, comprises China and the countries to the south of it, the Japanese islands and a large but fluctuating portion of Manchuria, Mongolia, and Tibet.

145. Why is the concept of a 'high, middle, low' of things a permanent fixation in the way we order the world? Does it have something to do with ethnicity? Explain.

146. What makes one country a dominant country? What are the differences between *First*, *Second*, and *Third* world countries?

| 2 | 185 | Superstates: Oceania, Eurasia, Eastasia | Current superstates: The West (USA, Canada, Europe); The East: Russia/China; The Middle East: OPEC (oil producing nations in the Middle East) |

In one combination or another, these three super-states are permanently at war, and have been so for the past twenty-five years. War, however, is no longer the desperate, annihilating struggle that it was in the early decades of the twentieth century. It is a warfare of limited aims between combatants who are unable to destroy one another, have no material cause for fighting and are not divided by any genuine ideological difference. This is not to say that either the conduct of war, or the prevailing attitude towards it, has become less bloodthirsty or more chivalrous. On the contrary, war hysteria is continuous and universal in all countries, and such acts as raping, looting, the slaughter of children, the reduction of whole populations to slavery, and reprisals against prisoners which extend even to boiling and burying alive, are looked upon as normal, and, when they are committed by one's own side and not by the enemy, meritorious. But in a physical sense war involves very small numbers of people, mostly highly-trained specialists, and causes comparatively few casualties. The fighting, when there is any, takes place on the vague frontiers whose whereabouts the average man can only guess at, or round the Floating Fortresses which guard strategic spots on the sea lanes. In the centres of civilization war means no more than a continuous shortage of consumption goods, and the occasional crash of a rocket bomb which may cause a few scores of deaths. War has in fact changed its character. More exactly, the reasons for which war is waged have changed in their order of importance. Motives which were already present to some small extent in the great wars of the early twentieth century have now become dominant and are consciously recognized and acted upon.

147. What are the ramifications of *perpetual war*? Is *perpetual war* consigned to smaller countries in the modern age in the form of *civil war*? If so, why do *first* world superpowers get involved?

148. What are the consequences of hiring mercenary soldiers ("highly trained specialists") to accomplish the goals of a state military?

| 3 | 185 | Concept of perpetual war | Middle East; Former Soviet States; projected 100 years in Iraq and Afghanistan; South & North Korea; the Congo in Africa; Arab Spring; Israel & Palestine; 'terror' as a permanent enemy; water wars of the future |

4	186	Specialized soldiers	Mercenary soldiers in Iraq: Blackwater, C.A.C.I., KBR, Chilean mercenaries

To understand the nature of the present war — for in spite of the regrouping which occurs every few years, it is always the same war — one must realize in the first place that it is impossible for it to be decisive. None of the three super-states could be definitively conquered even by the other two in combination. They are too evenly matched, and their natural defences are too formidable. Eurasia is protected by its vast land spaces, Oceania by the width of the Atlantic and the Pacific, Eastasia by the fecundity and industriousness of its inhabitants. Secondly, there is no longer, in a material sense, anything to fight about. With the establishment of self-contained economies, in which production and consumption are geared to one another, the scramble for markets which was a main cause of previous wars has come to an end, while the competition for raw materials is no longer a matter of life and death. In any case each of the three super-states is so vast that it can obtain almost all the materials that it needs within its own boundaries. In so far as the war has a direct economic purpose, it is a war for labour power. Between the frontiers of the super-states, and not permanently in the possession of any of them, there lies a rough quadrilateral with its corners at Tangier, Brazzaville, Darwin, and Hong Kong, containing within it about a fifth of the population of the earth. It is for the possession of these thickly-populated regions, and of the northern ice-cap, that the three powers are constantly struggling. In practice no one power ever controls the whole of the disputed area. Portions of it are constantly changing hands, and it is the chance of seizing this or that fragment by a sudden stroke of treachery that dictates the endless changes of alignment.

All of the disputed territories contain valuable minerals, and some of them yield important vegetable products such as rubber which in colder climates it is necessary to synthesize by comparatively expensive methods. But above all they contain a bottomless reserve of cheap labour. Whichever power controls equatorial Africa, or the countries of the Middle East, or Southern India, or the Indonesian Archipelago, disposes also of the bodies of scores or hundreds of millions of ill-paid and hard-working coolies. The inhabitants of these areas, reduced more or less openly to the status of slaves, pass continually from conqueror to conqueror, and are expended like so much coal or oil in the race to turn out more armaments, to capture more territory, to control more labour power, to turn out more armaments, to capture more territory, and so on indefinitely. It should be noted that the fighting never really moves beyond the edges of the disputed areas. The frontiers of Eurasia flow back and forth between the basin of the Congo and the northern shore of the Mediterranean; the islands of the Indian Ocean and the Pacific are constantly being captured and recaptured by Oceania or by Eastasia; in Mongolia the dividing line between Eurasia and Eastasia is never stable; round the Pole all three powers lay claim to enormous territories which in fact are largely uninhabited and unexplored: but the balance of power always remains roughly even, and the territory which forms the heartland of each super-state always remains inviolate. Moreover, the labour of the exploited peoples round the Equator is not really necessary to the world's economy. They add nothing to the wealth of the world, since whatever they produce is used for purposes of war, and the object of waging a war is always to be in a better position in which to wage another war. By their labour the slave populations allow the tempo of continuous warfare to be speeded up. But if they did not exist, the structure of world society, and the process by which it maintains itself, would not be essentially different.

> **149.** As economies are built around investment and consumption, what are the positive and negative economic results of a 'war economy'?
>
> **150.** What are the consequences of a *perpetual war* if there are no absolute outcomes, territory that cannot be conquered, and no end to conflict for those at war?
>
> **151.** Right now we exist in a 'global economy,' for better or worse. What are the consequences for those countries that elect to pursue isolated and self-contained economies? What is the fallout from these isolated economies dealing with global interference or interests? How do states create 'slave labor' economies?
>
> **152.** Does this global economy put into motion large groups of workers who are 'disposable' laborers, like the 'coolies' to whom 'Goldstein' refers?

5	186-7	States cannot be conquered	M.A.D. (Mutual Assured Destruction): Official Nuclear policy between USA & Soviet Union during Cold War; still largely in effect; economy trumps diplomacy; predicable and unpredictable alliances
6	187	Self-contained economies;	Global market is backfiring; default of Greek, Euro economies = possible collapse of EU; Bank crash has had similar effect; we're about to AGAIN experience 'contracting' economies; banks too big to fail are now bigger than ever; no USA bankers have been jailed for wrecking world economy
7	187-8	Exploited economies	Africa, South America, American rural, Small Asian economies, workers of India and China; outsourcing; corporate tax incentives

The primary aim of modern warfare (in accordance with the principles of DOUBLETHINK, this aim is simultaneously recognized and not recognized by the directing brains of the Inner Party) is to use up the products of the machine without raising the general standard of living. Ever since the end of the nineteenth century, the problem of what to do with the surplus of consumption goods has been latent in industrial society. At present, when few human beings even have enough to eat, this problem is obviously not urgent, and it might not have become so, even if no artificial processes of destruction had been at work. The world of today is a bare, hungry, dilapidated place compared with the world that existed before 1914, and still more so if compared with the imaginary future to which the people of that period looked forward. In the early twentieth century, the vision of a future society unbelievably rich, leisured, orderly, and efficient — a glittering antiseptic world of glass and steel and snow-white concrete — was part of the consciousness of nearly every literate person. Science and technology were developing at a prodigious speed, and it seemed natural to assume that they would go on developing. This failed to happen, partly because of the impoverishment caused by a long series of wars and revolutions, partly because scientific and technical progress depended on the empirical habit of thought, which could not survive in a strictly regimented society. As a whole the world is more primitive today than it was fifty years ago. Certain backward areas have advanced, and various devices, always in some way connected with warfare and police espionage, have been developed, but experiment and invention have largely stopped, and the ravages of the atomic war of the nineteen-fifties have never been fully repaired. Nevertheless the dangers inherent in the machine are still there. From the moment when the machine first made its appearance it was clear to all thinking people that the need for human drudgery, and therefore to a great extent for human inequality, had disappeared. If the machine were used deliberately for that end, hunger, overwork, dirt, illiteracy, and disease could be eliminated within a few generations. And in fact, without being used for any such purpose, but by a sort of automatic process — by producing wealth which it was sometimes impossible not to distribute — the machine did raise the living standards of the average human being very greatly over a period of about fifty years at the end of the nineteenth and the beginning of the twentieth centuries.

153. What is a 'standard of living'? If a country is producing products for a war economy, and the war persists without end, why doesn't its 'standard of living' rise accordingly, as in the past? What forces depress the 'standard of living'? Why must the standard of living be constantly suppressed? What are the results of a society that cannot hope to advance?

154. Why is it impossible for the 'empirical habit of thought' to survive in a 'regimented society'?

155. Despite the machines and technologies needed to perpetuate war, why have 'experiment and invention' mostly stopped?

156. Why is it important for human drudgery to continue?

8	186	Shortage of consumption goods	Sporadic oil shortage affecting gas and petroleum by-products and energy costs; permanent fluctuation in gas prices; WHO predicts eventual shortage of fresh water
9	188	Standard of living	America's neglected infrastructure, it's declining institutions, it's debt, it's loss of political will and the trust of its citizenry— all are a result of our seemingly permanent war/military-based economy; corrupt financial institutions; monopolies; corporate media

| 10 | 188 | Regimented society | Expanded work week; uniform standards of learning; retail monopolies; telecom monopolies; religious coercion driving political policies; uniform substandard healthcare for the middle and low; narrowing of production; formulaic entertainment and leisure models; three strikes law and order mandates; obsession with sports and military |
| 11 | 188 | Experiment and invention | Religious ideals preempt medical research; science education through trial and analysis marginalized in standardized testing environment; space race conceded to other nations and private, for-profit corporations; loss of manufacturing base; dumbing down is cheered while intelligence is equated with elitism; personal media trumps mass media for efficacy and truth; mass corporate media |

But it was also clear that an all-round increase in wealth threatened the destruction — indeed, in some sense was the destruction — of a hierarchical society. In a world in which everyone worked short hours, had enough to eat, lived in a house with a bathroom and a refrigerator, and possessed a motor-car or even an aeroplane, the most obvious and perhaps the most important form of inequality would already have disappeared. If it once became general, wealth would confer no distinction. It was possible, no doubt, to imagine a society in which WEALTH, in the sense of personal possessions and luxuries, should be evenly distributed, while POWER remained in the hands of a small privileged caste. But in practice such a society could not long remain stable. For if leisure and security were enjoyed by all alike, the great mass of human beings who are normally stupefied by poverty would become literate and would learn to think for themselves; and when once they had done this, they would sooner or later realize that the privileged minority had no function, and they would sweep it away. In the long run, a hierarchical society was only possible on a basis of poverty and ignorance. To return to the agricultural past, as some thinkers about the beginning of the twentieth century dreamed of doing, was not a practicable solution. It conflicted with the tendency towards mechanization which had become quasi-instinctive throughout almost the whole world, and moreover, any country which remained industrially backward was helpless in a military sense and was bound to be dominated, directly or indirectly, by its more advanced rivals.

157. What is the relationship of wealth and equality to power and intelligence?

158. Goldstein suggests that when people learn to think for themselves, the privileged minority would serve no purpose. Explain.

12	186-7	Wealth and power	Citizens United allows corporations and wealthy individuals to give huge sums of money to causes and candidates who invariably work for their interests; wealth confers prestige; genuine, benign achievement and generosity are often mocked; only millionaires can run for Congress; private privileges triumph over the public good
13	187	Critical thinking	Standardized tests marginalize thinking; schools pursue rote learning; large numbers of students are warehoused to impede debate and exacerbate bad parenting outcomes;
15	188	Shortage of consumption goods	Sporadic oil shortage affecting gas and petroleum by-products and energy costs; permanent fluctuation in gas prices; WHO predicts eventual shortage of fresh water
16	187	Cheap (slave) labor	First world economies exploit third world countries for cheap labor and resources; outsourcing; West uneasy about flood of immigrants from third world countries; massive unemployment resulting (see Greece, Spain, England, Ireland, parts of USA)
17	189	Industrial machines: vision of society; wars and revolution permanently stalled progress	Arms race caused the collapse of Soviet Union; Cold Warrior mentality derailed US "peace" dividend, spending on environment, science, education, health care
18	190	Preservation of the hierarchical order of society is based on the perpetuation of poverty and ignorance	1% of the US population controls most of the wealth; the middle class has steadily declined over the past three decades; US has highest adult illiteracy rate, high school drop out rate, and infant mortality rate of most first world countries.

    Nor was it a satisfactory solution to keep the masses in poverty by restricting the output of goods. This happened to a great extent during the final phase of capitalism, roughly between 1920 and 1940. The economy of many countries was allowed to stagnate, land went out of cultivation, capital equipment was not added to, great blocks of the population were prevented from working and kept half alive by State charity. But this, too, entailed military weakness, and since the privations it inflicted were obviously unnecessary, it made opposition inevitable. The problem was how to keep the wheels of industry turning without increasing the real wealth of the world. Goods must be produced, but they must not be distributed. And in practice the only way of achieving this was by continuous warfare.

159. What advantage is achieved when unemployment and underemployment persist in an economy?

| 14 | 188 | Material surplus | The United States keeps enormous surpluses—military and usable goods and food—in large warehouses throughout the country, surpluses that would benefit its citizenry but remain in storage for no apparent reason other than to maintain market margins; farmers regularly destroy crops to sustain a high monetary yield in the market, despite how many Americans go hungry everyday; the corn and soybean surpluses have also led to the ruination of family farms here and abroad and have adulterated feed for farm animals, contributing to national health problems. |

The essential act of war is destruction, not necessarily of human lives, but of the products of human labour. War is a way of shattering to pieces, or pouring into the stratosphere, or sinking in the depths of the sea, materials which might otherwise be used to make the masses too comfortable, and hence, in the long run, too intelligent. Even when weapons of war are not actually destroyed, their manufacture is still a convenient way of expending labour power without producing anything that can be consumed. A Floating Fortress, for example, has locked up in it the labour that would build several hundred cargo-ships. Ultimately it is scrapped as obsolete, never having brought any material benefit to anybody, and with further enormous labours another Floating Fortress is built. In principle the war effort is always so planned as to eat up any surplus that might exist after meeting the bare needs of the population. In practice the needs of the population are always underestimated, with the result that there is a chronic shortage of half the necessities of life; but this is looked on as an advantage. It is deliberate policy to keep even the favoured groups somewhere near the brink of hardship, because a general state of scarcity increases the importance of small privileges and thus magnifies the distinction between one group and another. By the standards of the early twentieth century, even a member of the Inner Party lives an austere, laborious kind of life. Nevertheless, the few luxuries that he does enjoy his large, well-appointed flat, the better texture of his clothes, the better quality of his food and drink and tobacco, his two or three servants, his private motor-car or helicopter — set him in a different world from a member of the Outer Party, and the members of the Outer Party have a similar advantage in comparison with the submerged masses whom we call 'the proles'. The social atmosphere is that of a besieged city, where the possession of a lump of horseflesh makes the difference between wealth and poverty. And at the same time the consciousness of being at war, and therefore in danger, makes the handing-over of all power to a small caste seem the natural, unavoidable condition of survival.

160. What happens when a state dedicates its labor to a war economy?

161. How does *perpetual war* impede social and cultural progress?

162. Why is the preservation of a hierarchical society dependent on poverty, ignorance, and the hardship of the middle and low populace?

19	191	Essential act of war is to waste products of human labor (e.g. 'floating fortress'=100 cargo ships)	US military wastes 100's of millions on Osprey helicopter (doesn't fly); F-22 fighter ($133 million each) & B1 bomber (1$ billion each) not suitable for current wars. Cost of one B1 bomber= 25-35 new schools
20	191	The psychology of the 'scarcity of small privileges'	In the West we are always told to be thankful for what we have, no matter how bad or expensive things get
21	192	Keeping the elite in power provides stability for society during war	G.W. Bush, Barack Obama (Iraq War, Afghanistan War), R.M. Nixon (Vietnam War), F.D. Roosevelt (WWII), A. Lincoln (Civil War) ran on this premise

    War, it will be seen, accomplishes the necessary destruction, but accomplishes it in a psychologically acceptable way. In principle it would be quite simple to waste the surplus labour of the world by building temples and pyramids, by digging holes and filling them up again, or even by producing vast quantities of goods and then setting fire to them. But this would provide only the economic and not the emotional basis for a hierarchical society. What is concerned here is not the morale of masses, whose attitude is unimportant so long as they are kept steadily at work, but the morale of the Party itself. Even the humblest Party member is expected to be competent, industrious, and even intelligent within narrow limits, but it is also necessary that he should be a credulous and ignorant fanatic whose prevailing moods are fear, hatred, adulation, and orgiastic triumph. In other words it is necessary that he should have the mentality appropriate to a state of war. It does not matter whether the war is actually happening, and, since no decisive victory is possible, it does not matter whether the war is going well or badly. All that is needed is that a state of war should exist. The splitting of the intelligence which the Party requires of its members, and which is more easily achieved in an atmosphere of war, is now almost universal, but the higher up the ranks one goes, the more marked it becomes. It is precisely in the Inner Party that war hysteria and hatred of the enemy are strongest. In his capacity as an administrator, it is often necessary for a member of the Inner Party to know that this or that item of war news is untruthful, and he may often be aware that the entire war is spurious and is either not happening or is being waged for purposes quite other than the declared ones: but such knowledge is easily neutralized by the technique of DOUBLETHINK. Meanwhile no Inner Party member wavers for an instant in his mystical belief that the war is real, and that it is bound to end victoriously, with Oceania the undisputed master of the entire world.

> 163. What is the psychology behind product scarcity and the desperate appreciation of small privileges?
>
> 164. How does war function as political security for those in power?
>
> 165. What is the 'mental hysteria' created by *perpetual war*? How are patriotism and nationalism confused by this hysteria?

| 22 | 192 | The mental hysteria of the Inner & Outer Party in service of war ("duckspeak") | Patriotism, Nationalism is cultivated mostly among the middle class to support invasion of Iraq; Congressmen shouted down by Tea Partiers at Town meetings |

All members of the Inner Party believe in this coming conquest as an article of faith. It is to be achieved either by gradually acquiring more and more territory and so building up an overwhelming preponderance of power, or by the discovery of some new and unanswerable weapon. The search for new weapons continues unceasingly, and is one of the very few remaining activities in which the inventive or speculative type of mind can find any outlet. In Oceania at the present day, Science, in the old sense, has almost ceased to exist. In Newspeak there is no word for 'Science'. The empirical method of thought, on which all the scientific achievements of the past were founded, is opposed to the most fundamental principles of Ingsoc. And even technological progress only happens when its products can in some way be used for the diminution of human liberty. In all the useful arts the world is either standing still or going backwards. The fields are cultivated with horse-ploughs while books are written by machinery. But in matters of vital importance — meaning, in effect, war and police espionage — the empirical approach is still encouraged, or at least tolerated. The two aims of the Party are to conquer the whole surface of the earth and to extinguish once and for all the possibility of independent thought. There are therefore two great problems which the Party is concerned to solve. One is how to discover, against his will, what another human being is thinking, and the other is how to kill several hundred million people in a few seconds without giving warning beforehand. In so far as scientific research still continues, this is its subject matter. The scientist of today is either a mixture of psychologist and inquisitor, studying with real ordinary minuteness the meaning of facial expressions, gestures, and tones of voice, and testing the truth-producing effects of drugs, shock therapy, hypnosis, and physical torture; or he is chemist, physicist, or biologist concerned only with such branches of his special subject as are relevant to the taking of life. In the vast laboratories of the Ministry of Peace, and in the experimental stations hidden in the Brazilian forests, or in the Australian desert, or on lost islands of the Antarctic, the teams of experts are indefatigably at work. Some are concerned simply with planning the logistics of future wars; others devise larger and larger rocket bombs, more and more powerful explosives, and more and more impenetrable armour-plating; others search for new and deadlier gases, or for soluble poisons capable of being produced in such quantities as to destroy the vegetation of whole continents, or for breeds of disease germs immunized against all possible antibodies; others strive to produce a vehicle that shall bore its way under the soil like a submarine under the water, or an aeroplane as independent of its base as a sailing-ship; others explore even remoter possibilities such as focusing the sun's rays through lenses suspended thousands of kilometres away in space, or producing artificial earthquakes and tidal waves by tapping the heat at the earth's centre.

166. In *1984's* 'Newspeak Dictionary' there is no word for science. According to 'the Book' why is there no advancement in science or in learning? How is this beneficial to an oligarchical society? How does this preserve the three-tiered hierarchy?

167. In our own culture today, how has science suffered? Why is it easier for a populace to understand emotions more than logic and facts?

168. What are the two fundamental aims of the Party?

169. How does constant activity and 'business' serve the aims of these two goals?

170. How is one of the goals an extension of 20th Century genocide?

23	193	Science and speculative learning only advance in the cause of war; Newspeak has no word for 'science'	US, Russia, China dedicate their greatest minds and scientists to building weapons of mass destruction; We reduce scientists to nerds; we counter scientific theory with ideas like 'creationism' and "intelligent design"; we underfund science despite its benefits in health and industry
24	193	"Reading minds"	Continuous polling, profiling, invasion of privacy through Internet commerce, Facebook (etc.), creation of formulaic entertainment, GPS cell phone monitoring—all indicate a knowledge of people's politics, tastes, opinions, and where they go and how they spend money and time
25	193	Killing millions	Countries in the West, Russia, China, Israel, Pakistan, India, and North Korea have the capacity to kill large populations quickly; other countries as well have biological and chemical weapons that can accomplish mass slaughter

But none of these projects ever comes anywhere near realization, and none of the three super-states ever gains a significant lead on the others. What is more remarkable is that all three powers already possess, in the atomic bomb, a weapon far more powerful than any that their present researches are likely to discover. Although the Party, according to its habit, claims the invention for itself, atomic bombs first appeared as early as the nineteen-forties, and were first used on a large scale about ten years later. At that time some hundreds of bombs were dropped on industrial centres, chiefly in European Russia, Western Europe, and North America. The effect was to convince the ruling groups of all countries that a few more atomic bombs would mean the end of organized society, and hence of their own power. Thereafter, although no formal agreement was ever made or hinted at, no more bombs were dropped. All three powers merely continue to produce atomic bombs and store them up against the decisive opportunity which they all believe will come sooner or later. And meanwhile the art of war has remained almost stationary for thirty or forty years. Helicopters are more used than they were formerly, bombing planes have been largely superseded by self-propelled projectiles, and the fragile movable battleship has given way to the almost unsinkable Floating Fortress; but otherwise there has been little development. The tank, the submarine, the torpedo, the machine gun, even the rifle and the hand grenade are still in use. And in spite of the endless slaughters reported in the Press and on the telescreens, the desperate battles of earlier wars, in which hundreds of thousands or even millions of men were often killed in a few weeks, have never been repeated.

171. During the Cold War, the United States and the Soviet Union embraced a foreign and military policy of 'mutually assured destruction' (MAD). How are Orwell's 'superstates' a reflection of this policy? Why?

172. Why is 'conventional war' the practical choice for 'perpetual war'?

26	194	All superstates possess atomic bombs as a means of stability **WAR IS PEACE**	US, Russia, China, France, England, India, Pakistan, Israel possess nuclear weapons, yet we worry about more nations possessing them when only a few bombs could destabilize the world
27	195	**Conventional weapons are the practical choices for perpetual war; yet the bulk of labor goes into creating weapons of immense mass destruction, which go unused**	Iraq and Afghanistan are conventional wars requiring conventional weapons, but we spend trillions of dollars worth on advanced weaponry that we cannot use in these theatres, often depriving ground troops of protective gear to help them

None of the three super-states ever attempts any manoeuvre which involves the risk of serious defeat. When any large operation is undertaken, it is usually a surprise attack against an ally. The strategy that all three powers are following, or pretend to themselves that they are following, is the same. The plan is, by a combination of fighting, bargaining, and well-timed strokes of treachery, to acquire a ring of bases completely encircling one or other of the rival states, and then to sign a pact of friendship with that rival and remain on peaceful terms for so many years as to lull suspicion to sleep. During this time rockets loaded with atomic bombs can be assembled at all the strategic spots; finally they will all be fired simultaneously, with effects so devastating as to make retaliation impossible. It will then be time to sign a pact of friendship with the remaining world-power, in preparation for another attack. This scheme, it is hardly necessary to say, is a mere daydream, impossible of realization. Moreover, no fighting ever occurs except in the disputed areas round the Equator and the Pole: no invasion of enemy territory is ever undertaken. This explains the fact that in some places the frontiers between the super-states are arbitrary. Eurasia, for example, could easily conquer the British Isles, which are geographically part of Europe, or on the other hand it would be possible for Oceania to push its frontiers to the Rhine or even to the Vistula. But this would violate the principle, followed on all sides though never formulated, of cultural integrity. If Oceania were to conquer the areas that used once to be known as France and Germany, it would be necessary either to exterminate the inhabitants, a task of great physical difficulty, or to assimilate a population of about a hundred million people, who, so far as technical development goes, are roughly on the Oceanic level. The problem is the same for all three super-states. It is absolutely necessary to their structure that there should be no contact with foreigners, except, to a limited extent, with war prisoners and coloured slaves. Even the official ally of the moment is always regarded with the darkest suspicion. War prisoners apart, the average citizen of Oceania never sets eyes on a citizen of either Eurasia or Eastasia, and he is forbidden the knowledge of foreign languages. If he were allowed contact with foreigners he would discover that they are creatures similar to himself and that most of what he has been told about them is lies. The sealed world in which he lives would be broken, and the fear, hatred, and self-righteousness on which his morale depends might evaporate. It is therefore realized on all sides that however often Persia, or Egypt, or Java, or Ceylon may change hands, the main frontiers must never be crossed by anything except bombs.

> **173. Why are these perpetual wars fought be the superstates staged on neutral or disputed territories and not in any of the three superstates?**
>
> **174. Why are xenophobia and isolationism prominent features of 'perpetual war'?**

| 28 | 196 | Staged war theatres | The Middle East; the former Soviet Blocs; Africa, some countries in South America, are all now or were at one time theatres of war waged by one of the three current superstates |

| 29 | 196 | Contact with foreigners is prohibited; xenophobia is encouraged, as is isolationism | During times of international military and economic stress, the West practices xenophobia, authors anti-immigration legislation, and oppresses its minorities |

Under this lies a fact never mentioned aloud, but tacitly understood and acted upon: namely, that the conditions of life in all three super-states are very much the same. In Oceania the prevailing philosophy is called Ingsoc, in Eurasia it is called Neo-Bolshevism, and in Eastasia it is called by a Chinese name usually translated as Death-Worship, but perhaps better rendered as Obliteration of the Self. The citizen of Oceania is not allowed to know anything of the tenets of the other two philosophies, but he is taught to execrate them as barbarous outrages upon morality and common sense. Actually the three philosophies are barely distinguishable, and the social systems which they support are not distinguishable at all. Everywhere there is the same pyramidal structure, the same worship of semi-divine leader, the same economy existing by and for continuous warfare. It follows that the three super-states not only cannot conquer one another, but would gain no advantage by doing so. On the contrary, so long as they remain in conflict they prop one another up, like three sheaves of corn. And, as usual, the ruling groups of all three powers are simultaneously aware and unaware of what they are doing. Their lives are dedicated to world conquest, but they also know that it is necessary that the war should continue everlastingly and without victory. Meanwhile the fact that there IS no danger of conquest makes possible the denial of reality which is the special feature of Ingsoc and its rival systems of thought. Here it is necessary to repeat what has been said earlier, that by becoming continuous war has fundamentally changed its character.

In past ages, a war, almost by definition, was something that sooner or later came to an end, usually in unmistakable victory or defeat. In the past, also, war was one of the main instruments by which human societies were kept in touch with physical reality. All rulers in all ages have tried to impose a false view of the world upon their followers, but they could not afford to encourage any illusion that tended to impair military efficiency. So long as defeat meant the loss of independence, or some other result generally held to be undesirable, the precautions against defeat had to be serious. Physical facts could not be ignored. In philosophy, or religion, or ethics, or politics, two and two might make five, but when one was designing a gun or an aeroplane they had to make four. Inefficient nations were always conquered sooner or later, and the struggle for efficiency was inimical to illusions. Moreover, to be efficient it was necessary to be able to learn from the past, which meant having a fairly accurate idea of what had happened in the past. Newspapers and history books were, of course, always coloured and biased, but falsification of the kind that is practised today would have been impossible. War was a sure safeguard of sanity, and so far as the ruling classes were concerned it was probably the most important of all safeguards. While wars could be won or lost, no ruling class could be completely irresponsible.

175. In 'the Book' Orwell categorizes the three 'superstates' via these philosophies: *Ingsoc*, *Neo-Bolshevism*, and *Death Worship*. What are the differences?

169. How does 'war everlasting without victory' reshape reality?

30	196-7	Prevailing superstate philosophies: **Oceania: INSOC** **Eurasia: Neo-Bolshevism** **Eastasia: Death Worship** (people would rather die than be conquered; they	Prevailing superstate philosophies: **West: Capitalism;** **Russo/Sino: Socialist/Marxist /Capitalism;** **OPEC: Monarchical /Theocratic Petro-Capitalism;** **North Korea, Taliban, Al Qaeda, ISIS, Boko Haram: Cultural Fanaticism: Suicide**

| | | would die a "thousand deaths" for their leader= Hierarchies preserved | bombers
=Hierarchies preserved (North Korea) |

But when war becomes literally continuous, it also ceases to be dangerous. When war is continuous there is no such thing as military necessity. Technical progress can cease and the most palpable facts can be denied or disregarded. As we have seen, researches that could be called scientific are still carried out for the purposes of war, but they are essentially a kind of daydreaming, and their failure to show results is not important. Efficiency, even military efficiency, is no longer needed. Nothing is efficient in Oceania except the Thought Police. Since each of the three super-states is unconquerable, each is in effect a separate universe within which almost any perversion of thought can be safely practised. Reality only exerts its pressure through the needs of everyday life — the need to eat and drink, to get shelter and clothing, to avoid swallowing poison or stepping out of top-storey windows, and the like. Between life and death, and between physical pleasure and physical pain, there is still a distinction, but that is all. Cut off from contact with the outer world, and with the past, the citizen of Oceania is like a man in interstellar space, who has no way of knowing which direction is up and which is down. The rulers of such a state are absolute, as the Pharaohs or the Caesars could not be. They are obliged to prevent their followers from starving to death in numbers large enough to be inconvenient, and they are obliged to remain at the same low level of military technique as their rivals; but once that minimum is achieved, they can twist reality into whatever shape they choose.

The war, therefore, if we judge it by the standards of previous wars, is merely an imposture. It is like the battles between certain ruminant animals whose horns are set at such an angle that they are incapable of hurting one another. But though it is unreal it is not meaningless. It eats up the surplus of consumable goods, and it helps to preserve the special mental atmosphere that a hierarchical society needs. War, it will be seen, is now a purely internal affair. In the past, the ruling groups of all countries, although they might recognize their common interest and therefore limit the destructiveness of war, did fight against one another, and the victor always plundered the vanquished. In our own day they are not fighting against one another at all. The war is waged by each ruling group against its own subjects, and the object of the war is not to make or prevent conquests of territory, but to keep the structure of society intact. The very word 'war', therefore, has become misleading. It would probably be accurate to say that by becoming continuous war has ceased to exist. The peculiar pressure that it exerted on human beings between the Neolithic Age and the early twentieth century has disappeared and been replaced by something quite different. The effect would be much the same if the three super-states, instead of fighting one another, should agree to live in perpetual peace, each inviolate within its own boundaries. For in that case each would still be a self-contained universe, freed forever from the sobering influence of external danger. A peace that was truly permanent would be the same as a permanent war. This — although the vast majority of Party members understand it only in a shallower sense — is the inner meaning of the Party slogan: WAR IS PEACE.

176. 'The Book' suggests that 'when war is continuous, it is not dangerous.' Explain.

177. What is the essential goal of 'the ruling class waging war against its own subjects'?

| 31 | 198 | When war is continuous it is not dangerous | Except to our soldiers, how dangerous is the War in Iraq/Afghanistan to most Americans? |
| 32 | 199 | War is waged by the ruling group against its own subjects to keep society intact: WAR IS PEACE | Terrorist threat levels keep us on our toes; we tolerate inflated energy prices, despite "defeating" an oil-rich nation. Yet, we are safe. WAR IS PEACE |

Winston stopped reading for a moment. Somewhere in remote distance a rocket bomb thundered. The blissful feeling of being alone with the forbidden book, in a room with no telescreen, had not worn off. Solitude and safety were physical sensations, mixed up somehow with the tiredness of his body, the softness of the chair, the touch of the faint breeze from the window that played upon his cheek. The book fascinated him, or more exactly it reassured him. In a sense it told him nothing that was new, but that was part of the attraction. It said what he would have said, if it had been possible for him to set his scattered thoughts in order. It was the product of a mind similar to his own, but enormously more powerful, more systematic, less fear-ridden. The best books, he perceived, are those that tell you what you know already. He had just turned back to Chapter I when he heard Julia's footstep on the stair and started out of his chair to meet her. She dumped her brown tool-bag on the floor and flung herself into his arms. It was more than a week since they had seen one another.

'I've got THE BOOK,' he said as they disentangled themselves.

'Oh, you've got it? Good,' she said without much interest, and almost immediately knelt down beside the oil stove to make the coffee.

They did not return to the subject until they had been in bed for half an hour. The evening was just cool enough to make it worth while to pull up the counterpane. From below came the familiar sound of singing and the scrape of boots on the flagstones. The brawny red-armed woman whom Winston had seen there on his first visit was almost a fixture in the yard. There seemed to be no hour of daylight when she was not marching to and fro between the washtub and the line, alternately gagging herself with clothes pegs and breaking forth into lusty song. Julia had settled down on her side and seemed to be already on the point of falling asleep. He reached out for the book, which was lying on the floor, and sat up against the bedhead.

'We must read it,' he said. 'You too. All members of the Brotherhood have to read it.'

'You read it,' she said with her eyes shut. 'Read it aloud. That's the best way. Then you can explain it to me as you go.'

The clock's hands said six, meaning eighteen. They had three or four hours ahead of them. He propped the book against his knees and began reading:

> 178. How does the bomb ('steamer') going off in the distance reinforce some of what Winston is reading?
>
> 179. Can you guess why Julia seems indifferent to Winston possessing the book?
>
> 180. What is the significance of Winston noticing the singing Prole laundry woman?

Chapter I

IGNORANCE IS STRENGTH

Throughout recorded time, and probably since the end of the Neolithic Age, there have been three kinds of people in the world, the High, the Middle, and the Low. They have been subdivided in many ways, they have borne countless different names, and their relative numbers, as well as their attitude towards one another, have varied from age to age: but the essential structure of society has never altered. Even after enormous upheavals and seemingly irrevocable changes, the same pattern has always reasserted itself, just as a gyroscope will always return to equilibrium, however far it is pushed one way or the other

'Julia, are you awake?' said Winston.

'Yes, my love, I'm listening. Go on. It's marvellous.'

He continued reading:

The aims of these three groups are entirely irreconcilable. The aim of the High is to remain where they are. The aim of the Middle is to change places with the High. The aim of the Low, when they have an aim — for it is an abiding characteristic of the Low that they are too much crushed by drudgery to be more than intermittently conscious of anything outside their daily lives — is to abolish all distinctions and create a society in which all men shall be equal. Thus throughout history a struggle which is the same in its main outlines recurs over and over again. For long periods the High seem to be securely in power, but sooner or later there always comes a moment when they lose either their belief in themselves or their capacity to govern efficiently, or both. They are then overthrown by the Middle, who enlist the Low on their side by pretending to them that they are fighting for liberty and justice. As soon as they have reached their objective, the Middle thrust the Low back into their old position of servitude, and themselves become the High. Presently a new Middle group splits off from one of the other groups, or from both of them, and the struggle begins over again. Of the three groups, only the Low are never even temporarily successful in achieving their aims. It would be an exaggeration to say that throughout history there has been no progress of a material kind. Even today, in a period of decline, the average human being is physically better off than he was a few centuries ago. But no advance in wealth, no softening of manners, no reform or revolution has ever brought human equality a millimetre nearer. From the point of view of the Low, no historic change has ever meant much more than a change in the name of their masters.

> **181. How is the 'attempted' movement of classes into another, 'better' class, an illusion perpetuated by the high class?**
>
> **182. How do the middle and high class help each other in perpetuating the permanent poverty of the low?**

33	200	Drudgery of the low	Unemployment, underemployment, lack of skills, and poor education allow people to remain in a lower class?
34	201	Permanence of the low	Minorities in every culture seem to remain poor and exploited; poverty impedes lack of access to progress

By the late nineteenth century the recurrence of this pattern had become obvious to many observers. There then rose schools of thinkers who interpreted history as a cyclical process and claimed to show that inequality was the unalterable law of human life. This doctrine, of course, had always had its adherents, but in the manner in which it was now put forward there was a significant change. In the past the need for a hierarchical form of society had been the doctrine specifically of the High. It had been preached by kings and aristocrats and by the priests, lawyers, and the like who were parasitical upon them, and it had generally been softened by promises of compensation in an imaginary world beyond the grave. The Middle, so long as it was struggling for power, had always made use of such terms as freedom, justice, and fraternity. Now, however, the concept of human brotherhood began to be assailed by people who were not yet in positions of command, but merely hoped to be so before long. In the past the Middle had made revolutions under the banner of equality, and then had established a fresh tyranny as soon as the old one was overthrown. The new Middle groups in effect proclaimed their tyranny beforehand. Socialism, a theory which appeared in the early nineteenth century and was the last link in a chain of thought stretching back to the slave rebellions of antiquity, was still deeply infected by the Utopianism of past ages. But in each variant of Socialism that appeared from about 1900 onwards the aim of establishing liberty and equality was more and more openly abandoned. The new movements which appeared in the middle years of the century, Ingsoc in Oceania, Neo-Bolshevism in Eurasia, Death-Worship, as it is commonly called, in Eastasia, had the conscious aim of perpetuating UNfreedom and INequality. These new movements, of course, grew out of the old ones and tended to keep their names and pay lip-service to their ideology. But the purpose of all of them was to arrest progress and freeze history at a chosen moment. The familiar pendulum swing was to happen once more, and then stop. As usual, the High were to be turned out by the Middle, who would then become the High; but this time, by conscious strategy, the High would be able to maintain their position permanently.

The new doctrines arose partly because of the accumulation of historical knowledge, and the growth of the historical sense, which had hardly existed before the nineteenth century. The cyclical movement of history was now intelligible, or appeared to be so; and if it was intelligible, then it was alterable. But the principal, underlying cause was that, as early as the beginning of the twentieth century, human equality had become technically possible. It was still true that men were not equal in their native talents and that functions had to be specialized in ways that favoured some individuals against others; but there was no longer any real need for class distinctions or for large differences of wealth. In earlier ages, class distinctions had been not only inevitable but desirable. Inequality was the price of civilization. With the development of machine production, however, the case was altered. Even if it was still necessary for human beings to do different kinds of work, it was no longer necessary for them to live at different social or economic levels. Therefore, from the point of view of the new groups who were on the point of seizing power, human equality was no longer an ideal to be striven after, but a danger to be averted. In more primitive ages, when a just and peaceful society was in fact not possible, it had been fairly easy to believe it. The idea of an earthly paradise in which men should live together in a state of brotherhood, without laws and without brute labour, had haunted the human imagination for thousands of years. And this vision had had a certain hold even on the groups who actually profited by each historical change. The heirs of the French, English, and American revolutions had partly believed in their own phrases about the rights of man, freedom of speech, equality before the law, and the like, and have even allowed their conduct to be influenced by them to some extent. But by the fourth decade of the twentieth century all the main currents of political thought were authoritarian. The earthly paradise had been discredited at exactly the moment when it became realizable. Every new political theory, by whatever name it called itself, led back to hierarchy and regimentation. And in the general hardening of outlook that set in round about 1930, practices which had been long abandoned, in some cases for hundreds of years — imprisonment without trial, the use of war prisoners as slaves, public executions, torture to extract confessions, the use of hostages, and the deportation of whole populations — not only became common again, but were tolerated and even defended by people who considered themselves enlightened and progressive.

183. When Orwell intimates that 'history is cyclical, intelligible, and therefore alterable,' what is he suggesting in light of the fact that history is written by the conquerors?

184. How is Orwell's allusion to 'an earthly paradise lost' a violation of basic human rights?

185. How and why have "imprisonment without trial, the use of war prisoners as slaves, public executions, torture to extract confessions, the use of hostages, and the deportation of whole populations" emerged in late 20th & early 21st centuries?

| 35 | 203 | History is cyclical, therefore | History is written by the victors; history is |

		intelligible, therefore alterable	forgotten by those who don't study it; Americans know less history every year that passes; school history textbooks avoid anything critical of the conquering nation's sins of war and colonialism.
36	204	**Earthly paradise as a promise is a lost hope**	**Year after year, human rights—an emblem of civil paradise—disappear more and more as the planet becomes destabilized by war, terrorism, and environmental catastrophe. We favor security over rights; without rights, security is an illusion.**
37	204	**Human rights abuses**	**Chain gangs in the South; terrorist and nation-state beheadings, stonings and mass executions; child abductions; waterboarding; immigrant issues in many Western countries; rape culture; persecution of women**

It was only after a decade of national wars, civil wars, revolutions, and counter-revolutions in all parts of the world that Ingsoc and its rivals emerged as fully worked-out political theories. But they had been foreshadowed by the various systems, generally called totalitarian, which had appeared earlier in the century, and the main outlines of the world which would emerge from the prevailing chaos had long been obvious. What kind of people would control this world had been equally obvious. The new aristocracy was made up for the most part of bureaucrats, scientists, technicians, trade-union organizers, publicity experts, sociologists, teachers, journalists, and professional politicians. These people, whose origins lay in the salaried middle class and the upper grades of the working class, had been shaped and brought together by the barren world of monopoly industry and centralized government. As compared with their opposite numbers in past ages, they were less avaricious, less tempted by luxury, hungrier for pure power, and, above all, more conscious of what they were doing and more intent on crushing opposition. This last difference was cardinal. By comparison with that existing today, all the tyrannies of the past were half-hearted and inefficient. The ruling groups were always infected to some extent by liberal ideas, and were content to leave loose ends everywhere, to regard only the overt act and to be uninterested in what their subjects were thinking. Even the Catholic Church of the Middle Ages was tolerant by modern standards. Part of the reason for this was that in the past no government had the power to keep its citizens under constant surveillance. The invention of print, however, made it easier to manipulate public opinion, and the film and the radio carried the process further. With the development of television, and the technical advance which made it possible to receive and transmit simultaneously on the same instrument, private life came to an end. Every citizen, or at least every citizen important enough to be worth watching, could be kept for twenty-four hours a day under the eyes of the police and in the sound of official propaganda, with all other channels of communication closed. The possibility of enforcing not only complete obedience to the will of the State, but complete uniformity of opinion on all subjects, now existed for the first time.

> 186. Explain 'new aristocracy' in terms of the 'managerial society' of bureaucrats.
>
> 187. What kinds of adjustments did the new tyrannies have to make to advance absolute power?
>
> 188. What is the goal of constant surveillance beyond the obvious lack of privacy? What are modern versions of the 'surveillance state'?

38	205	The Managerial Society: bureaucracy is the new aristocracy	Corporate cosmology triumphs over government: profit over people; corporate power over human progress; uniformity over diversity; centralization over localization. Accountants, lawyers, stock analysts, bankers are the new guardians of humanity.
39	205	Constant surveillance	Traffic video control, credit card info, Facebook (etc.), email, on-demand, cell phone monitoring, street monitoring, toll booth monitoring, drone spying, NSA (Snowden)

After the revolutionary period of the fifties and sixties, society regrouped itself, as always, into High, Middle, and Low. But the new High group, unlike all its forerunners, did not act upon instinct but knew what was needed to safeguard its position. It had long been realized that the only secure basis for oligarchy is collectivism. Wealth and privilege are most easily defended when they are possessed jointly. The so-called 'abolition of private property' which took place in the middle years of the century meant, in effect, the concentration of property in far fewer hands than before: but with this difference, that the new owners were a group instead of a mass of individuals. Individually, no member of the Party owns anything, except petty personal belongings. Collectively, the Party owns everything in Oceania, because it controls everything, and disposes of the products as it thinks fit. In the years following the Revolution it was able to step into this commanding position almost unopposed, because the whole process was represented as an act of collectivization. It had always been assumed that if the capitalist class were expropriated, Socialism must follow: and unquestionably the capitalists had been expropriated. Factories, mines, land, houses, transport — everything had been taken away from them: and since these things were no longer private property, it followed that they must be public property. Ingsoc, which grew out of the earlier Socialist movement and inherited its phraseology, has in fact carried out the main item in the Socialist programme; with the result, foreseen and intended beforehand, that economic inequality has been made permanent.

But the problems of perpetuating a hierarchical society go deeper than this. There are only four ways in which a ruling group can fall from power. Either it is conquered from without, or it governs so inefficiently that the masses are stirred to revolt, or it allows a strong and discontented Middle group to come into being, or it loses its own self-confidence and willingness to govern. These causes do not operate singly, and as a rule all four of them are present in some degree. A ruling class which could guard against all of them would remain in power permanently. Ultimately the determining factor is the mental attitude of the ruling class itself.

After the middle of the present century, the first danger had in reality disappeared. Each of the three powers which now divide the world is in fact unconquerable, and could only become conquerable through slow demographic changes which a government with wide powers can easily avert. The second danger, also, is only a theoretical one. The masses never revolt of their own accord, and they never revolt merely because they are oppressed. Indeed, so long as they are not permitted to have standards of comparison, they never even become aware that they are oppressed. The recurrent economic crises of past times were totally unnecessary and are not now permitted to happen, but other and equally large dislocations can and do happen without having political results, because there is no way in which discontent can become articulate. As for the problem of over-production, which has been latent in our society since the development of machine technique, it is solved by the device of continuous warfare (see Chapter III), which is also useful in keying up public morale to the necessary pitch. From the point of view of our present rulers, therefore, the only genuine dangers are the splitting-off of a new group of able, under-employed, power-hungry people, and the growth of liberalism and scepticism in their own ranks. The problem, that is to say, is educational. It is a problem of continuously moulding the consciousness both of the directing group and of the larger executive group that lies immediately below it. The consciousness of the masses needs only to be influenced in a negative way.

189. What is *collectivism*? Why is it necessary to the 'totalitarian state'?

190. What are the effects of 'permanent economic inequality'? What modern examples exemplify these effects?

191. Why do the masses—the Proles—never revolt in *1984*? The mass protests against the Vietnam War were largely fueled by conscription—the draft. When the draft was abolished, why were Americans reluctant to mass protest against another war—The Iraq War? When the world economy collapsed in 2007-8, why were there no sustained mass protests against the forces—Wall Street and the multi-national banks—that caused the collapse? What were the nature, success and/or failure of The Occupy Movement?

| 40 | 206 | Abolition of private property (collectivism); permanent economic inequality | Massive foreclosures, Wall Street bail outs; permanent national debt; America is the greatest debtor nation of all time; |
| 41 | 207 | Masters never revolt | As Americans are not asked to sacrifice, to save, to do really anything but consume, Americans have not protested this war despite its economic drain; the masses cannot understand the implications of this |

			as they are not educated in the nuances of war and its effects on commerce

Given this background, one could infer, if one did not know it already, the general structure of Oceanic society. At the apex of the pyramid comes Big Brother. Big Brother is infallible and all-powerful. Every success, every achievement, every victory, every scientific discovery, all knowledge, all wisdom, all happiness, all virtue, are held to issue directly from his leadership and inspiration. Nobody has ever seen Big Brother. He is a face on the hoardings, a voice on the telescreen. We may be reasonably sure that he will never die, and there is already considerable uncertainty as to when he was born. Big Brother is the guise in which the Party chooses to exhibit itself to the world. His function is to act as a focusing point for love, fear, and reverence, emotions which are more easily felt towards an individual than towards an organization. Below Big Brother comes the Inner Party. Its numbers limited to six millions, or something less than 2 per cent of the population of Oceania. Below the Inner Party comes the Outer Party, which, if the Inner Party is described as the brain of the State, may be justly likened to the hands. Below that come the dumb masses whom we habitually refer to as 'the proles', numbering perhaps 85 per cent of the population. In the terms of our earlier classification, the proles are the Low: for the slave population of the equatorial lands who pass constantly from conqueror to conqueror, are not a permanent or necessary part of the structure.

In principle, membership of these three groups is not hereditary. The child of Inner Party parents is in theory not born into the Inner Party. Admission to either branch of the Party is by examination, taken at the age of sixteen. Nor is there any racial discrimination, or any marked domination of one province by another. Jews, Negroes, South Americans of pure Indian blood are to be found in the highest ranks of the Party, and the administrators of any area are always drawn from the inhabitants of that area. In no part of Oceania do the inhabitants have the feeling that they are a colonial population ruled from a distant capital. Oceania has no capital, and its titular head is a person whose whereabouts nobody knows. Except that English is its chief LINGUA FRANCA and Newspeak its official language, it is not centralized in any way. Its rulers are not held together by blood-ties but by adherence to a common doctrine. It is true that our society is stratified, and very rigidly stratified, on what at first sight appear to be hereditary lines. There is far less to-and-fro movement between the different groups than happened under capitalism or even in the pre-industrial age. Between the two branches of the Party there is a certain amount of interchange, but only so much as will ensure that weaklings are excluded from the Inner Party and that ambitious members of the Outer Party are made harmless by allowing them to rise. Proletarians, in practice, are not allowed to graduate into the Party. The most gifted among them, who might possibly become nuclei of discontent, are simply marked down by the Thought Police and eliminated. But this state of affairs is not necessarily permanent, nor is it a matter of principle. The Party is not a class in the old sense of the word. It does not aim at transmitting power to its own children, as such; and if there were no other way of keeping the ablest people at the top, it would be perfectly prepared to recruit an entire new generation from the ranks of the proletariat. In the crucial years, the fact that the Party was not a hereditary body did a great deal to neutralize opposition. The older kind of Socialist, who had been trained to fight against something called 'class privilege' assumed that what is not hereditary cannot be permanent. He did not see that the continuity of an oligarchy need not be physical, nor did he pause to reflect that hereditary aristocracies have always been short-lived, whereas adoptive organizations such as the Catholic Church have sometimes lasted for hundreds or thousands of years. The essence of oligarchical rule is not father-to-son inheritance, but the persistence of a certain world-view and a certain way of life, imposed by the dead upon the living. A ruling group is a ruling group so long as it can nominate its successors. The Party is not concerned with perpetuating its blood but with perpetuating itself. WHO wields power is not important, provided that the hierarchical structure remains always the same.

All the beliefs, habits, tastes, emotions, mental attitudes that characterize our time are really designed to sustain the mystique of the Party and prevent the true nature of present-day society from being perceived. Physical rebellion, or any preliminary move towards rebellion, is at present not possible. From the proletarians nothing is to be feared. Left to themselves, they will continue from generation to generation and from century to century, working, breeding, and dying, not only without any impulse to rebel, but without the power of grasping that the world could be other than it is. They could only become dangerous if the advance of industrial technique made it necessary to educate them more highly; but, since military and commercial rivalry are no longer important, the level of popular education is actually declining. What opinions the masses hold, or do not hold, is looked on as a matter of indifference. They can be granted intellectual liberty because they have no intellect. In a Party member, on the other hand, not even the smallest deviation of opinion on the most unimportant subject can be tolerated.

192. What are the new personifications and icons of *Big Brother*?

193. What are the new versions of *Inner Party, Outer Party,* and *Proles*?

194. What groups are currently ostracized from the mainstream and are often considered a threat to social stability?

195. How is 'intellectual liberty' threatened, according to Goldstein? How is it threatened today?

42	208	Big Brother	The President? God? TV? The Automobile? The Internet? Who or What is Big Brother?
43	209	Inner / Outer Party membership built around orthodoxy;	Social hierarchies are built around status and education; orthodoxies based on tribal loyalties. What are student hierarchies? Are they cliques? Honors classes? Sports? Drama? Band? Other? What are some American hierarchies?
		Those who are militantly opposed or discontent are ostracized	Minorities, gays, nerds, liberals, hippies—are they ostracized in America? In schools? Churches? States?
44	210	Intellectual liberty is not	Superfluousness of opinions; blogs;

| | | liberating if there is no intellect | disrespect for language, reading, scholarship (high stakes testing); emotional opinions trump thoughtful, fact based debates |

A Party member lives from birth to death under the eye of the Thought Police. Even when he is alone he can never be sure that he is alone. Wherever he may be, asleep or awake, working or resting, in his bath or in bed, he can be inspected without warning and without knowing that he is being inspected. Nothing that he does is indifferent. His friendships, his relaxations, his behaviour towards his wife and children, the expression of his face when he is alone, the words he mutters in sleep, even the characteristic movements of his body, are all jealously scrutinized. Not only any actual misdemeanour, but any eccentricity, however small, any change of habits, any nervous mannerism that could possibly be the symptom of an inner struggle, is certain to be detected. He has no freedom of choice in any direction whatever. On the other hand his actions are not regulated by law or by any clearly formulated code of behaviour. In Oceania there is no law. Thoughts and actions which, when detected, mean certain death are not formally forbidden, and the endless purges, arrests, tortures, imprisonments, and vaporizations are not inflicted as punishment for crimes which have actually been committed, but are merely the wiping-out of persons who might perhaps commit a crime at some time in the future. A Party member is required to have not only the right opinions, but the right instincts. Many of the beliefs and attitudes demanded of him are never plainly stated, and could not be stated without laying bare the contradictions inherent in Ingsoc. If he is a person naturally orthodox (in Newspeak a GOODTHINKER), he will in all circumstances know, without taking thought, what is the true belief or the desirable emotion. But in any case an elaborate mental training, undergone in childhood and grouping itself round the Newspeak words CRIMESTOP, BLACKWHITE, and DOUBLETHINK, makes him unwilling and unable to think too deeply on any subject whatever.

A Party member is expected to have no private emotions and no respites from enthusiasm. He is supposed to live in a continuous frenzy of hatred of foreign enemies and internal traitors, triumph over victories, and self-abasement before the power and wisdom of the Party. The discontents produced by his bare, unsatisfying life are deliberately turned outwards and dissipated by such devices as the Two Minutes Hate, and the speculations which might possibly induce a sceptical or rebellious attitude are killed in advance by his early acquired inner discipline. The first and simplest stage in the discipline, which can be taught even to young children, is called, in Newspeak, CRIMESTOP. CRIMESTOP means the faculty of stopping short, as though by instinct, at the threshold of any dangerous thought. It includes the power of not grasping analogies, of failing to perceive logical errors, of misunderstanding the simplest arguments if they are inimical to Ingsoc, and of being bored or repelled by any train of thought which is capable of leading in a heretical direction. CRIMESTOP, in short, means protective stupidity. But stupidity is not enough. On the contrary, orthodoxy in the full sense demands a control over one's own mental processes as complete as that of a contortionist over his body. Oceanic society rests ultimately on the belief that Big Brother is omnipotent and that the Party is infallible. But since in reality Big Brother is not omnipotent and the party is not infallible, there is need for an unwearying, moment-to-moment flexibility in the treatment of facts. The keyword here is BLACKWHITE. Like so many Newspeak words, this word has two mutually contradictory meanings. Applied to an opponent, it means the habit of impudently claiming that black is white, in contradiction of the plain facts. Applied to a Party member, it means a loyal willingness to say that black is white when Party discipline demands this. But it means also the ability to BELIEVE that black is white, and more, to KNOW that black is white, and to forget that one has ever believed the contrary. This demands a continuous alteration of the past, made possible by the system of thought which really embraces all the rest, and which is known in Newspeak as DOUBLETHINK.

196. The presence of the *Thought Police* in *1984* is ominous and something to be dreaded by Oceania's citizens. Are there equivalent 'thought police'-type forces functioning in our present society or our personal lives? How do they actually 'orchestrate' thought?

197. If one thing is certain about human nature, it is that our private emotional universes are difficult for others to navigate. How does the Party stifle certain private emotions in Oceania? Why? Where are emotions, if any, directed? Why?

198. What is *crimestop*? Why is it safer to be stupid? What are examples of 'protective stupidity' in our own culture?

199. What is *blackwhite*? How does it benefit the Party? What are some of the issues today that can be filtered through the concept of *blackwhite*?

45	210	The Thought Police	Helicopter parents, jealous friends, nosey neighbors, pollsters, invasive media
46	211	No private emotions	No mood swings; no down time; no sadness; no excessive silliness; need to join; need to bend to peers; need to imitate
47	212	Crimestop: "protective stupidity"	Personal dumbing down; underachievement a point of pride; settling for a passing grade; resenting smart people; shaping opinions through emotion and not facts; using force and hysteria to convey authority; following orders without questions; giving in to routines
48	212	Blackwhite: believing a complete lie	79% of Americans believed in 2003 that Iraq was involved in 9/11; poor people drag down the economy; immigrants steal our jobs

The alteration of the past is necessary for two reasons, one of which is subsidiary and, so to speak, precautionary. The subsidiary reason is that the Party member, like the proletarian, tolerates present-day conditions partly because he has no standards of comparison. He must be cut off from the past, just as he must be cut off from foreign countries, because it is necessary for him to believe that he is better off than his ancestors and that the average level of material comfort is constantly rising. But by far the more important reason for the readjustment of the past is the need to safeguard the infallibility of the Party. It is not merely that speeches, statistics, and records of every kind must be constantly brought up to date in order to show that the predictions of the Party were in all cases right. It is also that no change in doctrine or in political alignment can ever be admitted. For to change one's mind, or even one's policy, is a confession of weakness. If, for example, Eurasia or Eastasia (whichever it may be) is the enemy today, then that country must always have been the enemy. And if the facts say otherwise then the facts must be altered. Thus history is continuously rewritten. This day-to-day falsification of the past, carried out by the Ministry of Truth, is as necessary to the stability of the regime as the work of repression and espionage carried out by the Ministry of Love.

The mutability of the past is the central tenet of Ingsoc. Past events, it is argued, have no objective existence, but survive only in written records and in human memories. The past is whatever the records and the memories agree upon. And since the Party is in full control of all records and in equally full control of the minds of its members, it follows that the past is whatever the Party chooses to make it. It also follows that though the past is alterable, it never has been altered in any specific instance. For when it has been recreated in whatever shape is needed at the moment, then this new version IS the past, and no different past can ever have existed. This holds good even when, as often happens, the same event has to be altered out of recognition several times in the course of a year. At all times the Party is in possession of absolute truth, and clearly the absolute can never have been different from what it is now. It will be seen that the control of the past depends above all on the training of memory. To make sure that all written records agree with the orthodoxy of the moment is merely a mechanical act. But it is also necessary to REMEMBER that events happened in the desired manner. And if it is necessary to rearrange one's memories or to tamper with written records, then it is necessary to FORGET that one has done so. The trick of doing this can be learned like any other mental technique. It is learned by the majority of Party members, and certainly by all who are intelligent as well as orthodox. In Oldspeak it is called, quite frankly, 'reality control'. In Newspeak it is called DOUBLETHINK, though DOUBLETHINK comprises much else as well.

DOUBLETHINK means the power of holding two contradictory beliefs in one's mind simultaneously, and accepting both of them. The Party intellectual knows in which direction his memories must be altered; he therefore knows that he is playing tricks with reality; but by the exercise of DOUBLETHINK he also satisfies himself that reality is not violated. The process has to be conscious, or it would not be carried out with sufficient precision, but it also has to be unconscious, or it would bring with it a feeling of falsity and hence of guilt. DOUBLETHINK lies at the very heart of Ingsoc, since the essential act of the Party is to use conscious deception while retaining the firmness of purpose that goes with complete honesty. To tell deliberate lies while genuinely believing in them, to forget any fact that has become inconvenient, and then, when it becomes necessary again, to draw it back from oblivion for just so long as it is needed, to deny the existence of objective reality and all the while to take account of the reality which one denies — all this is indispensably necessary. Even in using the word DOUBLETHINK it is necessary to exercise DOUBLETHINK. For by using the word one admits that one is tampering with reality; by a fresh act of DOUBLETHINK one erases this knowledge; and so on indefinitely, with the lie always one leap ahead of the truth. Ultimately it is by means of DOUBLETHINK that the Party has been able — and may, for all we know, continue to be able for thousands of years — to arrest the course of history.

All past oligarchies have fallen from power either because they ossified or because they grew soft. Either they became stupid and arrogant, failed to adjust themselves to changing circumstances, and were overthrown; or they became liberal and cowardly, made concessions when they should have used force, and once again were overthrown. They fell, that is to say, either through consciousness or through unconsciousness. It is the achievement of the Party to have produced a system of thought in which both conditions can exist simultaneously. And upon no other intellectual basis could the dominion of the Party be made permanent. If one is to rule, and to continue ruling, one must be able to dislocate the sense of reality. For the secret of rulership is to combine a belief in one's own infallibility with the Power to learn from past mistakes.

It need hardly be said that the subtlest practitioners of DOUBLETHINK are those who invented DOUBLETHINK and know that it is a vast system of mental cheating. In our society, those who have the best knowledge of what is happening are also those who are furthest from seeing the world as it is. In general, the greater the understanding, the greater the delusion; the more intelligent, the less sane. One clear illustration of this is the fact that war hysteria increases in intensity as one rises in the social scale. Those whose attitude towards the war is most nearly rational are the subject peoples of the disputed territories. To these people the war is simply a continuous calamity which sweeps to and from over their bodies like a tidal wave. Which side is winning is a matter of complete indifference to them. They are aware that a change of overlordship means simply that they will be doing the same work as before for new masters who treat them in the same manner as the old ones. The slightly more favoured workers whom we call 'the proles' are only intermittently conscious of the war. When it is necessary they can be prodded into frenzies of fear and hatred, but when left to themselves they are capable of forgetting for long periods that the war is happening. It is in the ranks of the Party, and above all of the Inner Party, that the true war enthusiasm is found. World-conquest is believed in most firmly by those who know it to be impossible. This peculiar linking-together of opposites — knowledge with ignorance, cynicism with fanaticism — is one of the chief distinguishing marks of Oceanic society. The official ideology abounds with contradictions even when there is no practical reason for them. Thus, the Party rejects and vilifies every principle for which the Socialist movement originally stood, and it chooses to do this in the name of Socialism. It preaches a contempt for the working class unexampled for centuries past, and it dresses its members in a uniform which was at one time peculiar to manual workers and was adopted for that reason. It systematically undermines the solidarity of the family, and it calls its leader by a name which is a direct appeal to the sentiment of family loyalty. Even the names of the four Ministries by which we are governed exhibit a sort of impudence in their deliberate reversal of the facts. The Ministry of Peace concerns itself with war, the Ministry of Truth with lies, the Ministry of Love with torture and the Ministry of Plenty with starvation. These contradictions are not accidental, nor do they result from ordinary hypocrisy; they are deliberate exercises in DOUBLETHINK. For it is only by reconciling contradictions that power can be retained indefinitely. In no other way could the ancient cycle be broken. If human equality is to be for ever averted — if the High, as we have called them, are to keep their places permanently — then the prevailing mental condition must be controlled insanity.

But there is one question which until this moment we have almost ignored. It is: WHY should human equality be averted? Supposing that the mechanics of the process have been rightly described, what is the motive for this huge, accurately planned effort to freeze history at a particular moment of time?

Here we reach the central secret. As we have seen. the mystique of the Party, and above all of the Inner Party, depends upon DOUBLETHINK But deeper than this lies the original motive, the never-questioned instinct that first led to the seizure of power and brought DOUBLETHINK, the Thought Police, continuous warfare, and all the other necessary paraphernalia into existence afterwards. This motive really consists . . .

> **200.** Why is Winston's job at the Ministry of Truth essential for the Party? How do we today 'revise' the past to fit our concept of the future?
>
> **201.** What does Orwell mean by 'the mutability of the past'? How can we assign this mutability today?
>
> **203.** *Doublethink* is an overwhelming concept in *1984*. How is this a form of 'mental cheating'? What are some examples of *doublethink* today? Explain the consequence of your examples.

49	212	Alteration of the past	Swift Boat Veterans for Truth lie about Kerry's service in Vietnam; G.W. Bush lies about own service record; Clinton lies about sex; Reagan creates myth of 1950's—"Morning in America"—the good old days. The Truth: McCarthyism, Cold War, high unemployment, Jim Crow Laws, white flight from the cities, rise of military industrial complex, TV begins dumbing down America
50	213	Mutability of the past	Our history fades when people don't read, journalists don't report news, people become incurious about the past, people do not debate ideas, people do not stand up for justice (e.g. Florida election of 2000)

52	214	**War Is Peace Freedom Is Slavery Ignorance Is Strength**	**Our missiles are called "Peacemakers"; one former president—the most powerful position in the world—was ignorant of world history, was a 'C' student, was proud of being incurious; our freedoms are defined by the fruits of our labor, even if our labor spends us into debt and servitude.**
51	214	**Doublethink: mental cheating**	**Some pro-life adherents support death penalty; we hold dear family values, yet our divorce rate is over 50%, there's a marriage penalty tax, families have to pay fees for children to be involved in after school activities because communities do not want to share in the tax burden that, spread out, could easily support these activities**

Winston became aware of silence, as one becomes aware of a new sound. It seemed to him that Julia had been very still for some time past. She was lying on her side, naked from the waist upwards, with her cheek pillowed on her hand and one dark lock tumbling across her eyes. Her breast rose and fell slowly and regularly.

'Julia.'

No answer.

'Julia, are you awake?'

No answer. She was asleep. He shut the book, put it carefully on the floor, lay down, and pulled the coverlet over both of them.

He had still, he reflected, not learned the ultimate secret. He understood HOW; he did not understand WHY. Chapter I, like Chapter III, had not actually told him anything that he did not know, it had merely systematized the knowledge that he possessed already. But after reading it he knew better than before that he was not mad. Being in a minority, even a minority of one, did not make you mad. There was truth and there was untruth, and if you clung to the truth even against the whole world, you were not mad. A yellow beam from the sinking sun slanted in through the window and fell across the pillow. He shut his eyes. The sun on his face and the girl's smooth body touching his own gave him a strong, sleepy, confident feeling. He was safe, everything was all right. He fell asleep murmuring 'Sanity is not statistical,' with the feeling that this remark contained in it a profound wisdom.

204. In his play *Enemy of the People*, writer Henrik Ibsen said that the 'majority is always wrong' and that it takes fifty years for the majority to catch up with minority opinions and insights. What does he mean? Give examples. When Winston professes "Being in a minority, even a minority of one, did not make you mad," is he reinforcing Ibsen's idea? Are fringe intellects necessary to a citizenry? Why? If so, why do we often treat the fringe, the loner, as a stranger and often as an enemy of the people?

Return to regular story text...

17. Continuation of Regular Reading Comprehension Questions: Book 3

Chapter X (223-231)

205. What is Winston's essential question after reading these portions of 'the Book'?

206. What are Winston's observations regarding the Prole woman singing and hanging laundry?

207. Even though the song she sings was written by a machine (*the Versfiicator*), how is it relevant to Winston and how is it cruelly ironic?

208. What does Julia say to Winston when he reminds her of 'the thrush that sang to us'? How does that impact Winston's assessment of who and what are dead?

209. Winston and Julia are arrested by the *Thought Police* after the Winston reads the first twenty or so pages of 'the Book.' How do they discover Winston and Julia's 'deceit'?

210. How does the phrase "We are the dead" become a self-fulfilling prophecy—something they knew was inevitable?

211. Why is it in perfect context to the Party to have Charrington operate an antiques store?

212. What surprises you about the behavior of the *Thought Police* and Mr. Charrington?

Chapter I (234-248)

213. What are the differences between Party prisoners and regular prisoners?

214. Describe the first stages of Winston's initial incarceration.

215. How does O'Brien replace Julia as an object of Winston's concentrated affection? In light of this, what does Winston mean when he claims his love for Julia is a fact, like arithmetic, and he would not betray her?

216. Describe this "place of no darkness."

217. What was Ampleforth's crime?

218. Explain Parsons' crime and the absurdity of the accusation against him.

219. To what extent does Bumstead 2713 want to avoid Room 101?

220. What will Winston willingly do for Julia?

221. What is the significance of O'Brien's first words to Winston?

222. What is the process O'Brien uses to reduce Winston's humanity?

223. How is O'Brien simultaneously Winston's interrogator, tormentor, protector, friend? Why is this a grand deception and to what effect does he deceive Winston?

224. Is Winston's "disease," as O'Brien refers to it, a virtue? Explain. What bit of information does Winston hold onto to attest to the Party's deceit?

225. A much quoted maxim from *1984*—"Who controls the past controls the future; who controls the present, controls the past"—is often considered a paradox. Explain this maxim in real terms, giving examples from the book or from modern life.

226. What is O'Brien's explanation for 'reality'?

227. Why does Winston believe that O'Brien is not the one who is making him suffer?

228. Why does Winston love O'Brien unconditionally?

229. What are O'Brien's views on posterity rising up against the Party?

230. What is "negative obedience"? What does O'Brien mean when he says, "We will make the brain perfect then we will blow it out"?

231. Why is Winston 'oppressed' by his own intellectual inferiority?

232. What is the ultimate goal of the Party?

233. After the torture machine is switched off, O'Brien allows Winston to ask him questions. What are those questions? What are the answers? How are O'Brien's answers 'more' than answers?

234. What will remain an unsolved riddle?

235. What are the three stages of Winston's 'reintegration'?

236. What key question eludes Winston?

237. What is the nature of power, according to O'Brien?

238. How does one exert power over another?

239. What devastating image does O'Brien use to characterize the future of humankind?

240. What is the real use of Goldstein's 'heresies'?

241. What is Winston's penultimate rebellious thought?

242. They both admit to betraying each other immediately. We know the party used rats to get to Winston. How did the party get to Julia? What is the evidence of this?

235. What is the difference in their 'betrayals'? Why is this significant?

236. For whom does Winston have heartfelt affection? Why?

Something for Students to Consider

"It is in adolescence that most of us grasp that life—our own life—is a problem to be solved, that a set of personal unknowns must now be factored together with the frightening variables of experience. The future suddenly appears—it is the space upon which the answers will be inscribed." — Sven Birkerts, *The Gutenberg Elegies: The Fate of Reading in an Electronic Age*

Admittedly there are a lot of questions here and, therefore, a lot to consider. However, I believe there are an unlimited number of questions a student could pursue after reading *1984*. The goal of any good read is to do a deep read. This is the "interiority" of reading Birkerts suggests. The best questions explore an interior understanding and not a numbered list of exterior comprehension questions or even questions posed by a teacher. This interior understanding consists of the questions posed by the reader unsatisfied with the exterior drive to meaning. And this interior understanding is linked to the "frightening variables of experience." How do your experiences line up with the characters form *1984*. How are Orwell's ideas urgent for you and your world?

18. Comparison/Contrast: Emmanuel Goldstein's "Theory & Practice of Oligarchichal Collectivism"

Students and teachers who get through "The Book" will need to see its value, not just in terms of understanding Orwell's full narrative import, but to see how many of 'Goldstein's ideas' have significant modern parallels. Giving context to the contemporary world we live in gives even greater value to this reading experience and assures students that ideas are permanent and are worthy of their consideration. Students can apply the 'Principles of Ingsoc' directly to their own school experience, as many learning institutions have similar authoritarian structures where accountability is elusive and the individual is marginalized.

The following comparison-contrast representations are collected together to accommodate a discussion of Orwell's ideas and how they apply today. I cherry pick the fundamental points of "The Book," locate them in the Signet Edition (1980), and provide, in theory, modern parallels and contexts for Goldstein's assumptions. It would be interesting for students and teachers to add, update, and give macro and micro contexts to the points provided.

COLLECTED: Comparison/Contrast: Emmanuel Goldstein's "Theory & Practice of Oligarchichal Collectivism"

#	Page	From *1984* (Signet Edition 1980)	MODERN PARALLELS
1	184	High, middle, low social groupings	Wealthy, middle class, welfare class; AP, Honors, College Prep, General, Vocational, etc.; Rural, suburban, urban; Ghetto, downtown, uptown; Amateur, dilettante, professional OTHERS:
2	185	Superstates: Oceania, Eurasia, Eastasia	**Current superstates:** The West (USA, Canada, Europe); The East: Russia/China; The Middle East: OPEC (oil producing nations in the Middle East)
3	185	Concept of	Middle East; Former Soviet States;

		perpetual war	projected 100 years in Iraq and Afghanistan; South & North Korea; the Congo in Africa; Arab Spring; Israel & Palestine; 'terrorism' as a permanent enemy; future 'water wars'
4	186	Specialized soldiers	Mercenary soldiers in Iraq: Blackwater, C.A.C.I., KBR, Chilean mercenaries
5	186-7	States cannot be conquered	==M.A.D.== (Mutual Assured Destruction): Official Nuclear policy between USA & Soviet Union during Cold War; still largely in effect; economy trumps diplomacy; predictable and unpredictable alliances
6	187	Self-contained economies;	Global market is backfiring; default of Greek, Euro economies = possible collapse of EU; Bank crash has had similar effect; we're about to AGAIN experience 'contracting' economies; banks too big to fail are now bigger than ever; no USA bankers have been jailed for wrecking world economy
7	187-8	Exploited economies	Africa, South America, American rural, Small Asian economies, workers of India and China; outsourcing; corporate tax incentives
8	186	Shortage of consumption goods	Sporadic oil shortage affecting gas and petroleum by-products and energy costs; ==permanent fluctuation in gas prices==; WHO predicts ==eventual shortage of fresh water==
9	188	Standard of living	America's neglected infrastructure, it's declining institutions, it's debt, it's loss of political will and the trust of its citizenry— all are a result of our seemingly permanent war/military-based economy; corporate financial institutions; corporate media
10	188	Regimented society	Expanded work week; uniform standards of learning; retail monopolies; telecom monopolies; religious coercion driving political policies; uniform substandard healthcare for the middle and low; narrowing of production; formulaic entertainment and leisure models; three strikes law and order mandates; obsession with sports and military
11	188	Experiment and invention	==Religious ideals preempt medical research==; science education through trial and analysis marginalized in standardized testing environment; space race conceded to other nations and private, for-profit corporations; loss of manufacturing base; dumbing down

			is cheered while intelligence is equated with elitism; personal media trumps mass media for efficacy and truth; corporate mass media
12	186-7	Wealth and power	Citizens united allows corporations and wealthy individuals to give huge sums of money to causes and candidates who invariably work for their interests; wealth confers prestige; genuine, benign achievement and generosity are often mocked; only millionaires can run for Congress; private privileges triumph over the public good
13	187	Critical thinking	Standardized tests marginalize thinking; schools pursue rote learning; large numbers of students are warehoused to impede debate and exacerbate bad parenting outcomes
14	188	Material surplus	The United States keeps enormous surpluses—military and usable goods and food—in large warehouses throughout the country, surpluses that would benefit its citizenry but remain in storage for no apparent reason other than to maintain market margins; farmers regularly destroy crops to sustain a high monetary yield in the market, despite how many Americans go hungry everyday; the corn and soybean surpluses have also led to the ruination of family farms here and abroad and have adulterated feed for farm animals, contributing to national health problems.
15	188	Shortage of consumption goods	Sporadic oil shortage affecting gas and petroleum by-products and energy costs; permanent fluctuation in gas prices; WHO predicts eventual shortage of fresh water
16	187	Cheap (slave) labor	First world economies exploit third world countries for cheap labor and resources; outsourcing; West uneasy about flood of immigrants from third world countries; massive unemployment resulting (see Greece, Spain, England, Ireland, parts of USA)
17	189	Industrial machines: vision of society; wars and revolution	Arms race caused the collapse of Soviet Union; Cold Warrior mentality derailed US "peace" dividend, spending on environment, science, education, health care

		permanently stalled progress	
18	190	Preservation of the hierarchical order of society is based on the perpetuation of poverty and ignorance	1% of the US population controls most of the wealth; the middle class has steadily declined over the past three decades; US has highest adult illiteracy rate, high school drop out rate, and infant mortality rate of most first world countries.
19	191	Essential act of war is to waste products of human labor (e.g. 'floating fortress'=100 cargo ships)	US military wastes 100's of millions on Osprey helicopter (doesn't fly); F-22 fighter ($133 million each) & B1 bomber (1$ billion each) not suitable for current wars. Cost of one B1 bomber= 25-35 new schools
20	191	The psychology of the 'scarcity of small privileges'	In the West we are always told to be thankful for what we have, no matter how bad or expensive things get
21	192	Keeping the elite in power provides stability for society during war	G.W. Bush, Barack Obama (Iraq War, Afghanistan War), R.M. Nixon (Vietnam War), F.D. Roosevelt (WWII), A. Lincoln (Civil War) ran on this premise
22	192	The mental hysteria of the Inner & Outer Party in service of war ("duckspeak")	Patriotism, Nationalism is cultivated mostly among the middle class to support invasion of Iraq; Congressmen shouted down by Tea Partiers at Town meetings
26	194	All superstates possess atomic bombs as a means of stability WAR IS PEACE	US, Russia, China, France, England, India, Pakistan, Israel possess nuclear weapons, yet we worry about more nations possessing them when only a few bombs could destabilize the world
27	195	Conventional weapons are the practical choices for perpetual war; yet the bulk of labor goes into creating weapons of immense mass destruction, which go unused	Iraq and Afghanistan are conventional wars requiring conventional weapons, but we spend trillions of dollars worth on advanced weaponry that we cannot use in these theatres, often depriving ground troops of protective gear to help them
23	193	Science and speculative learning only advance in the cause of war; Newspeak has no word for 'science'	US, Russia, China dedicate their greatest minds and scientists to building weapons of mass destruction; We reduce scientists to nerds; we counter scientific theory with ideas like 'creationism' and "intelligent design"; we underfund

Focus Study Guide for George Orwell's *1984*

			science despite its benefits in health and industry
24	193	"Reading minds"	Continuous polling, profiling, invasion of privacy through Internet commerce, Facebook (etc.,), creation of formulaic entertainment, GPS cell phone monitoring—all indicate a knowledge of people's politics, tastes, opinions, and where they go and how they spend money and time
25	193	Killing millions	Countries in the West, Russia, China, Israel, Pakistan, India, and North Korea have the capacity to kill large populations quickly; other countries as well have biological and chemical weapons that can accomplish mass slaughter
28	196	Staged war theatres	The Middle East; the former Soviet Blocs; Africa, some countries in South America, are all now or were at one time theatres of war waged by one of the three current superstates
29	196	Contact with foreigners is prohibited; xenophobia is encouraged, as is isolationism	During times of international military and economic stress, the West practices xenophobia, authors anti-immigration legislation, and oppresses its minorities
30	196-7	Prevailing superstate philosophies: Oceania: INSOC Eurasia: Neo-Bolshevism Eastasia: Death Worship (people would rather die than be conquered; they would die a "thousand deaths" for their leader =Hierarchies preserved	Prevailing superstate philosophies: West: Capitalism; Russo/Sino: Socialist/Marxist /Capitalism; OPEC: Monarchical /Theocratic Petro-Capitalism; North Korea, Taliban, Al Qaeda, ISIS, Boko Haram: Cultural Fanaticism: Suicide bombers =Hierarchies preserved (North Korea)
31	198	When war is continuous it is not dangerous	Except to our soldiers, how dangerous is the War in Iraq/Afghanistan to most Americans?
32	199	War is waged by the ruling group against	Terrorist threat levels keep us on our toes; we tolerate inflated energy prices, despite

Edward Morneau

Focus Study Guide for George Orwell's *1984*

		its own subjects to keep society intact: WAR IS PEACE	"defeating" an oil-rich nation. Yet, we are safe. WAR IS PEACE
33	200	Drudgery of the low	Unemployment, underemployment, lack of skills, and poor education allow people to remain in a lower class?
34	201	Permanence of the low	Minorities in every culture seem to remain poor and exploited; poverty impedes lack of access to progress
35	203	History is cyclical, therefore intelligible, therefore alterable	History is written by the victors; history is forgotten by those who don't study it; Americans know less history every year that passes; school history textbooks avoid anything critical of the conquering nation's sins of war and colonialism
36	204	Earthly paradise as a promise is a lost hope	Year after year, human rights—an emblem of civil paradise—disappear more and more as the planet becomes destabilized by war, terrorism, and environmental catastrophe. We favor security over rights; without rights, security is an illusion.
37	204	Human rights abuses	Chain gangs in the South; terrorist and nation-state beheadings, stonings and mass executions; child abductions; waterboarding; immigrant issues in many Western countries; rape culture; persecution of women
38	205	The Managerial Society: bureaucracy is the new aristocracy	Corporate cosmology triumphs over government: profit over people; corporate power over human progress; uniformity over diversity; centralization over localization. Accountants, lawyers, stock analysts, bankers are the new guardians of humanity.
39	205	Constant surveillance	Traffic video control, credit card info, Facebook (etc.), email, on-demand, cell phone monitoring, street monitoring, toll booth monitoring, drone spying, NSA (Snowden)
40	206	Abolition of private property (collectivism); permanent economic inequality	Massive foreclosures, Wall Street bail outs; permanent national debt; America is the greatest debtor nation of all time

98   Edward Morneau

Focus Study Guide for George Orwell's *1984*

41	207	Masters never revolt	As Americans are not asked to sacrifice, to save, to do really anything but consume, Americans have not protested this war despite its economic drain; the masses cannot understand the implications of this as they are not educated in the nuances of war and its effects on commerce
42	208	Big Brother	The President? God? TV? The Automobile? The Internet? Who or What is Big Brother?
43	209	Inner / Outer Party membership built around orthodoxy; Those who are militantly opposed or discontent are ostracized	Social hierarchies are built around status and education; orthodoxies based on tribal loyalties. What are student hierarchies? Are they cliques? Honors classes? Sports? Drama? Band? Other? What are some American hierarchies? Minorities, gays, nerds, liberals, hippies—are they ostracized in America? In schools? Churches? States?
44	210	Intellectual liberty is not liberating if there is no intellect	Superfluousness of opinions; blogs; disrespect for language, reading, scholarship (high stakes testing); emotional opinions trump thoughtful, fact based debates
45	210	The Thought Police	Helicopter parents, jealous friends, nosey neighbors, pollsters, invasive media
46	211	No private emotions	No mood swings; no down time; no sadness; no excessive silliness; need to join; need to bend to peers; need to imitate
47	212	Crimestop: "protective stupidity"	Personal dumbing down; underachievement a point of pride; settling for a passing grade; resenting smart people; shaping opinions through emotion and not facts; using force and hysteria to convey authority; following orders without questions; giving in to routines
48	212	Blackwhite: believing a complete lie	79% of Americans believed in 2003 that Iraq was involved in 9/11; poor people drag down the economy; immigrants steal our jobs
49	212	Alteration of the past	Swift Boat Veterans for Truth lie about Kerry's service in Vietnam; G.W. Bush lies about own service record; Clinton lies about sex; Reagan creates myth of 1950's—"Morning in America"—the good old days. The Truth: McCarthyism, Cold War, high unemployment, Jim Crow Laws, white flight from the cities, rise of military industrial

50	213	Mutability of the past	complex, TV begins dumbing down America — *climate change not covered by BBC*
			Our history fades when people don't read, journalists don't report news, people become incurious about the past, people do not debate ideas, people do not stand up for justice (e.g. Florida election of 2000)
51	214	Doublethink: mental cheating	Some pro-life adherents support the death penalty; we hold dear family values, yet our divorce rate is over 50%, there's a marriage penalty tax, families have to pay fees for children to be involved in after school activities because communities do not want to share in the tax burden that, spread out, could easily support these activities
52	214	War Is Peace Freedom Is Slavery Ignorance Is Strength	Our missiles are called "Peacemakers"; our former president—the most powerful position in the world—was ignorant of world history, was a 'C' student, was proud of being incurious; our freedoms are defined by the fruits of our labor, even if our labor spends us into debt and servitude.

Something to Consider

As mentioned before, the above comparisons of Orwell's *realpolitik* to our own contemporary state of political and institutional affairs are highly debatable and should be discussed outside of the forums of state and national paranoia and reactionary polemics (Cable TV, Blogs, Shock Radio, etc.). The distinctions demand a sobering and rational dialogue. These parallels are ever changing, but conform to permanent aspects of human nature. To understand these dynamics on a most human level, we should locate these parallels within a smaller context, like a municipality or a school or a team. The roots of fascism and the abuses of power begin as nearly invisible movements within a small group of people and grow like pathogens among large groups until they are institutionalized for the many. At the heart of these abuses is the willingness of the people who are victimized by them to be bystanders to the growing threat of fascism. This willingness grows from indifference and ignorance and is largely informed by the marginalization of culture, the declining habits of reading and literacy, and the desire to be left alone.

Is the desire to be left alone a result of the world collapsing on the individual? When O'Brien intimates that the individual is dead—the single cell is irrelevant—is this Orwell's way of predicting the end of individual freedom? Is this a natural destiny or a political destiny? Is it a response to the ageless difficulty of organizing the human race into peaceful tribes and nations?

Anthropologists argue that human beings, like all biological entities, are primarily territorial. Goldstein (Orwell) writes that territory is no longer the goal of waring nations, and that conquering lands is no longer the object of macro aggression. It can be argued that the new economies and trade agreements of the late 20th century and early 21st century are the new 'territories' that instigate civil wars and nation-to-nation aggressions. The marketplace is the new territory. Is this where power resides? If so, where do ordinary individuals find themselves in this political and economic matrix? Are soldiers and consumers the commodities of marketplace aggression?

Author, journalist, and media commentator Thomas Hartman traces the dissatisfaction many Americans have with government to the deliberate marginalization of government through deregulation and corporate lobbying, meaning that subtracting government protections and incentives from our daily lives make government inefficient. And when this inefficiency trickles into the life of the average citizen, the monolithic forces that degraded government in the first place blame government for its own failures, denying any role in this failure. What is left is the nearly incomprehensible cycle of blame and disrepair, leaving the average citizen powerless to do anything about it except to vote for those who wind up perpetuating the same cycle of blame and disrepair by convincing us through propaganda that they are the only ones who can fix things.

Is this what Orwell is predicting?

19. Assessment: Book I

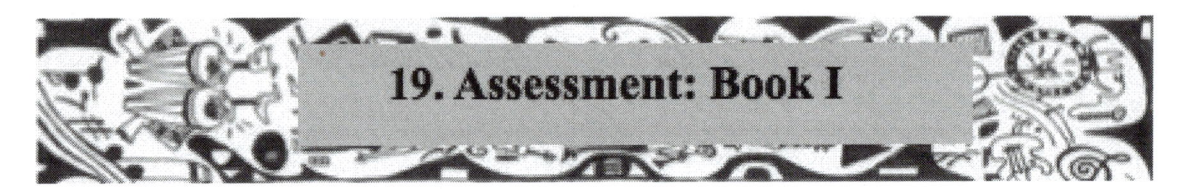

Feel Free to Copy

I. Basic Term Identification: Multiple Choice:

1. **The language of Oceania is** A) Oldspeak B) Newspeak C) Doublespeak D) Duckspeak

2. **Winston works at The Minstry of** A) Truth B) Love C) Plenty D) Peace

3. **England is now called** A) Oceania B) Eurasia C) Airstrip One D) the Golden Country

4. A) Ingsoc B) Oldspeak C) Verificator D) Doublethink **is Newspeak for English Socialism.**

5. **Winston uses this to re-record the past:** A) Versificator B) Novel Writing Machines C) Speakwrite Machines D) Duckspeak

6. *1984* **takes place in what superstate?** A) Oceania B) Eastasia C) Eurasia D) Africa

7. **Parson's children belong to** A) Physical Jerks B) Sports Committee C) Anti-Sex League D) The Spies.

8. A) Ignorance Is Strength B) Doubkethink C) Thoughtcrime D) Oldspeak **is the doublespeak slogan than justifies illiteracy.**

9. **'Minipax' means, or is an example of, ALL of the following, EXCEPT**: A) Doublethink B) Pornosec C) INGSOC D) Ministry of Peace

10. **The name given to inferior products suggesting something they achieve but do not is** A) hate B) doubleplusgood C) Victory D) Overfullfilment

11. A) Pornosec B) Novel Writing Machines C) Speakwrite Machines D) Versificator **produces the literature for the masses.**

12. **The Ministry of Truth's** A) Spies B) Anti-Sex League C) Pornosec D) Victory **mansions is where sex-driven literature is manufactured.**

13. **What is the statistical propaganda reference that reinforces the success of INGSOC and the Party.** A) 9th Three Year Plan B) Victory C) Ministry of Plenty D) Overfullfilment

14. **ALL of the following are a constant presence in the lives of Outer Party members, EXCEPT**: A) Telescreens B) Golden Country C) Big Brother D) Overfullfilment Announcements

15. A) Room 101 B) Ministry of Peace C) Oceania D) Golden Country **is the place Winston thinks he will meet O'Brien—"in a place where there is no darkness."**

16. **Which of the following examples of doublethink justifies war?**
    A) War Is Peace B) "the book" C) Hate Week D) Thoughtcrime

17. A) Ninth 3 Year Plan B) Victory Gin C) Overfullfilment D) **is a slippery term suggesting that one has a surplus when one really has a shortage.**

18. **Julia belongs to which of the following organizations?** A) Pornosec B) Novel Writing Division C) The Spies D) Anti-Sex League

19. **Winston believes all hope lies with …** A) The Proles B) Emmanuel Goldstein C) The Brotherhood D) Big Brother

20. A) Facecrime B) Thoughtcrime C) Hatecrime D) Physical Jerks **is the essential crime that contained all other crimes in itself.**

II. True (A) or False (B)

21. George Orwell wrote *1984* as a prophecy. B

22. When Winston first saw Julia, he was immediately attracted to her. B

23. The Party encourages marriage, family, prayer and devotion to friends. B

24. The Proles are not obligated to have telescreens in their apartments. B

25. Winston bought the coral embedded in glass mostly because of its uselessness. A

III. Multiple Choice

26. **Who is the "alleged" author of "the book," which is outlawed by the Party?**
    A. Oglivie B. Syme C. Goldstein D. Charrington

27. **What is the regularly scheduled event that Party members are required to attend to show their devotion to Big Brother and the Party?**
    A) Physical Jerk Hour B) Hate Week C) Ministry Prayer D) Spies Outings

28. **Who first accuses Winston of being a thought criminal?**
    A. Julia B. O'Brien C. Syme D. The Parsons children

29. **At first, Winston wants to believe he's writing his diary to the future, but by the end of Book I, he believes he's writing it for**
    A. Charrington B. Julia C. O'Brien D. Katherine

30. What was the name of the new war hero that Winston uses to replace Withers, who was "vaporized" from history? A. Rutherford B. Oglivie C. Jones D. Aaronson

31. Preferring solitude, or busying yourself with non-party activities, is the act of committing which thoughtcrime?
    A. speakwrite   B. ownself   C. refs unperson   D. memoryholing

32. What character is editing the 11th Edition of the Newspeak Dictionary?
    A. Parsons   B. Syme   C. Charrington   D. Winston

33. Winston is desperate to remember a time when things where different, and his instincts suggests such a time. He calls this…
    A. ancestral memory   B. oldspeak   C. derivative memory   D. facecrime

34. Who did Winston bump into leaving the Prole area? A) O'Brien B) Julia C) Parsons D) Syme

35. What was given to Winston at this juncture? A) "the book" B) slip of paper C) Copy of *Newspeak Dictionary* D) Winston's diary

III. Essays: 30 Points Each: Choose One: Free Write:

1. Choose and write about two of the topics listed in the above CONCEPT/MOTIF BANK. Consider their relationship to each other in terms of commonalities, cause and effect, or contrasts. Choose these CONCEPTS carefully, as you will continue developing this topic on future assessments, after which you will be asked to formalize your freewriting into an essay. You must turn this freewrite in at the end of this class.

2. In 1949, George Orwell used his experience writing about and witnessing *fascism* in Europe and *totalitarianism* in the Soviet Union and China, and consequently wrote *1984* as a warning to the future. The future has done a poor job of heeding Orwell's warning. Some of the above concepts are political, social and cultural realities in many parts of the world today, including the USA. Choose a concept and argue for or against its practice. Give examples to back up your assertion.

3. Choose two questions from the objective portion of the assessment and challenge the possibility that there could be more than one correct answer. Be sure to compare and contrast the probable answers by bringing context to this probability and citing examples from the text.

20. Assessment: Book I: ANSWERS

I. Basic Term Comprehension: Multiple Choice:	II. True (A) or False (B)
1. B) Newspeak	21. FALSE (B)
2. A) Truth	22. FALSE (B)
3. C) Airstrip One	23. FALSE (B)
4. A) Ingsoc	24. TRUE (A)
5. C) Speakwrite Machines	25. TRUE (A)
6. A) Oceania	
7. D) The Spies	**III. Multiple Choice**
8. A) Ignorance Is Strength	26. C. Goldstein
9. D) Ministry of Peace	27. B) Hate Week
10. C) Victory	28. D. The Parsons Children
11. Novel Writing Machines	29. C. O'Brien
12. C) Pornosec.	30. B. Oglivie
13. A) Ninth's 3 Year Plan	31. B. ownself
14. B) Golden Country	32. B. Syme
15. D) Golden Country	33. A. ancestral memory
16. A) War Is Peace	34. B) Julia
17. C) Overfullfilment	35. B) slip of paper
18. D) Anti-Sex League	
19. A) The Proles	
20. B) Thoughtcrime	

Focus Study Guide for George Orwell's *1984*

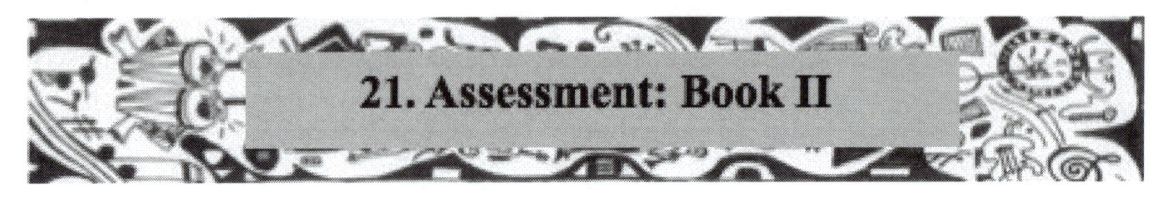

21. Assessment: Book II

Feel Free to Copy

Multiple Choice

1. "I Love You" is written on the note Julia slips into Winston's hand in their chance meeting in the tunnel between their respective ministries. From what you know at this point, which of the following is the wrong inference concerning this exchange?

   A. Winston is surprised, as he was sure she hated him and he hated her
   B. Winston believes Julia is a member of the Brotherhood
   C. Julia is trying to trap him and turn him in to the Thought Police.
   D. Winston has been planning on murdering Julia after his encounter with her at the last Hate Week rally.

2. To plan for their first afternoon away in the country, Julia and Winston had arranged to meet

   A. at the Minipax Cafeteria
   B. at a Hate Week Rally
   C. at "a place where there was no darkness"
   D. at Charrington's Junk Shop in the Proletarian Sector

3. Julia was attracted to Winston for all of the following reasons EXCEPT:
   A. She intuitively knew he was against the Party
   B. There was something about Winston's face
   C. She knew for a fact Winston was willing to join Goldstein
   D. She was good at spotting people who don't belong.

4. Winston was attracted to Julia for all of the following reasons EXCEPT
   A. She was pure and certain of her virtue.
   B. She was impure.
   C. She was full of undifferentiated desire
   D. was promiscuous (over-sexed)

5. Who "would not accept it as a law of nature that the individual is always defeated"?   A. Winston B. Julia C. O'Brien D. Katherine

Focus Study Guide for George Orwell's *1984*

6. *It was only an 'opeless fancy, / It passed like an Ipril dye, / But a look an' a word an' the dreams they stirred / They 'ave stolen my 'eart awye!* This piece was all of th following things EXCEPT:
    A. a popular song for the masses to sing
    B. composed on the *versificator*
    C. is alluring to Winston because of the way the prole sang it
    D. Julia's favorite son

7. Julia smuggled all of the following items into Charrington's apartment EXCEPT:
    A. coffee B. a gun C. jam D. women's clothes and makeup

8. When Julia says of the picture of St. Clemens Church hanging in Charrington's apartment—"I bet that picture' got bugs behind it," Orwell is giving us a nifty bit of
    A. allusion B. foreshadowing C. personification D. gross-out imagery

9. The political theories of Emmanuel Goldstein and the whole idea of revolution itself were outside whose imagination?
    A. Winston's B. Julia's C. Ampleforth's D. Parsons'

10. When Winston visits O'Brien at his apartment, O'Brien exercises all of the following privileges before Winston EXCEPT:
    A. The drinking of wine
    B. The shutting off the telescreen volume
    C. The writing of notes before the telescreen
    D. The passing of the book

11. Winston dreams about his mother, who represents a loss that he cannot reconcile. He is particular tortured by which of the following memories:
    A. stealing his starving sister's chocolate ration
    B. refusing to help his mother out when the Party took his father
    C. watching rats devour his mother and sister and not doing anything to stop them
    D. not caring what happened to them after they disappeared

12. In observing the Proles, Winston saw firsthand that their loyalty was to each other; their care was for each other; their loyalty was not to a country, or a flag, or an idea, but to a person. This is the opposite of
    A. patriotism B. nationalism C. primitivism D. crimespeak

13. Winston has a deeply felt fear of
    A. open spaces B. snakes C. premature burial D. rats

14-20: TRUE (A) or FALSE (B)

14. Despite the note's contents, Winston's loathing of Julia only increased, as he feared she was either a spy for the Party or an actual operative of the Thought Police.

15. Despite whatever feelings he had, his very first desire was to be alone.

16. Despite her behavior, Winston felt that Julia did not understand the Party's sexual Puritanism, as she still was a member of the Anti-Sex League.

17. Julia believed that Winston's idea that the endless wars were just to keep people frightened was naïve and that the wars were all around them and were as real as the drudgery of their lives that went into supporting these wars.

18. When Winston accuses Julia of being "only a rebel from the waist down," she mocks him and calls him a dreamer and a morbid man who is too full of doubt to make a difference.

19. O'Brien confirms Winston's belief that the Revolution and Emmanuel Goldstein exist.

20. In front of O'Brien and Julia, Winston confesses to every crime of revolution he is bout to commit.

Review of Terms:

21. **Any manner of possessing this is a Thoughtcrime**:
    A. Ownlife   B. Oldspeak   C. Child Hero   D. Memory Hole

22. **Winston disposes history through:**
    A. Memory Hole   B. Duckspeak   C. Versificator   D. ArtSem

23. A. PornoSec   B. Duckspeak   C. ArtSem   D. INGSOC
    is a 'dialect' of doublespeak, according to Winston.

24. **This is the highest individual status achievement of The Spies:**
    A. Brotherhood   B. Ownlife   C. Child Hero   D. Overfullfilment

25. **A reference to language before it was purged of meaning is**
    A. Newspeak   B. Doublespeak   C) Duckspeak   D) Oldspeak

Essays: Choose One: 25 Points Each: Free Write

1. Choose two questions from the objective portion of the assessment and challenge the possibility that there could be more than one correct answer. Be sure to compare and contrast the probable answers by bringing context to this probability and citing examples from the text.

2. If you chose the first essay from the previous assessment, continue to work on and refine your essay. Be sure to create context for your argument and cite examples from the text to support your assertions.

3. What is the nature of love between Winston and Julia. At what point do we learn that Julia is more committed to her relationship with Winston than he is with her? Who is witness to this remarkable expression of loyalty, and what are the probable consequences to Julia? In terms of Winston and Julia evolving into true revolutionaries against Big Brother, why is hers a complete revolution? In answering this, why does Winston's commitment to the revolution fall short, despite his willingness to do anything to destroy Big Brother?

4. One of he first things that female Holocaust prisoners did when they were liberated from the concentration camps was to wash their clothes and hair and apply rouge and lipstick. For some this was even more important than eating. Why? What is the significance of Julia getting made up and wearing a dress for Winston? When we compare the urgent preference for the Holocaust survivors to Julia's looking for a lost aspect of her, what is being suggested about the state of affairs in Oceania, especially for women?

22. Assessment Book II: ANSWERS

Multiple Choice:

1. D
2. B
3. C
4. A
5. B
6. D
7. B
8. B
9. B
10. D
11. A
12. A
13. D

True / False

14. B-False
15. A-True
16. B-False
17. B-False
18. B-False
19. A-True
20. A-True

Review Terms:

21. A
22. A
23. B
24. C
25. D

23. Assessment: Whole Book:

Feel Free to Copy

Part One (10 Points Each):

Choose THREE concepts from the list below. Explain anything you know about the concept, its context to the story and relevance to a character.

Hate week	War Is Peace	Golden Country
Thoughtcrime	Doublethink	Proles
Big Brother	Anti Sex League	Facecrime
Ministry of Love	The Spies	Crimestop
Newspeak		Blackwhite

Part Two (20 Points): Match Goldstein's "book" with the following modern parallels.

1:_____   2:_____   3:_____   4:_____   5:_____

1	Preservation of the hierarchical order of society is based on the perpetuation of poverty and ignorance	A	Our history fades when people don't read, journalists don't report news, people become incurious about the past, people do not debate ideas, people do not stand up for justice.
2	Earthly paradise as a promise is a lost hope	B	Corporate cosmology triumphs over government: profit over people; corporate power over human progress; uniformity over diversity; centralization over localization. Accountants, lawyers, stock analysts, bankers are the new guardians of humanity.
3	The Managerial Society: bureaucracy is the new aristocracy	C	Superfluousness of opinions; blogs; disrespect for language, reading, scholarship (high stakes testing); emotional opinions trump thoughtful, fact based debates
4	Intellectual liberty is not liberating if there is no intellect	D	Year after year, human rights—an emblem of civil paradise—disappear more and more as the planet becomes destabilized by war, terrorism, and environmental catastrophe. We favor security over rights; without rights, security is an illusion.
5	Mutability of the past	E	1% of the US population controls most of the wealth; the middle class has steadily declined over the past three decades; US has highest adult illiteracy rate and high school drop out rate, and infant mortality rate of first world countries.

Part Three (20 Points Each):

Choose TWO of the follow short essay questions—one from the **odd** numbers and one from the **even** numbers, and answer them as thoughtfully as you can.

1. How is *1984* a novel about love?
2. How does *1984* use irony to establish truth?
3. How is *1984* a novel about memory?
4. How does *1984* use time to tell us its story?
5. How is *1984* a feminist novel?
6. How does *1984* use myth to propel its story?
7. How is *1984* a novel about rebellion?
8. How does *1984* use artifact to give detail to its story?
9. How is *1984* a novel about language?
10. How does *1984* use atmosphere and setting to tell its story?

Part 4: Mixed: 30 Points

1. "Under the spreading chestnut tree _____."

_____ 2. According to O'Brien, what is "the worst thing in the world."

_____ 3. Before O'Brien delivers Winston to Room 101, he betrays his love for Julia to himself, but will not give O'Brien the satisfaction of telling him no matter how much O'Brien tortures him.   A. True B. False

_____ 4. _____ 5. _____ 6.
are the THREE stages of re-integration, according to O'Brien.

_____ 7. Winston believes ALL of the following will defeat O'Brien and the Party EXCEPT: A. life B. human spirit C. the Proles D. love

8. What image does O'Brien suggest represents the future of the human race?
_____

9. What is O'Brien's response to Winston when he allows him to ask some questions, the specific question—"Does Big Brother exist in the way I exist?"
_____

10-11. "Who controls the past, controls the _____; who controls the present controls the _____." (Think about this!!!)

_____ 12. Winston feels that the Prole woman singing that machine-written song has a "special kind of beauty. " Julia feels the same way. A. True B. False

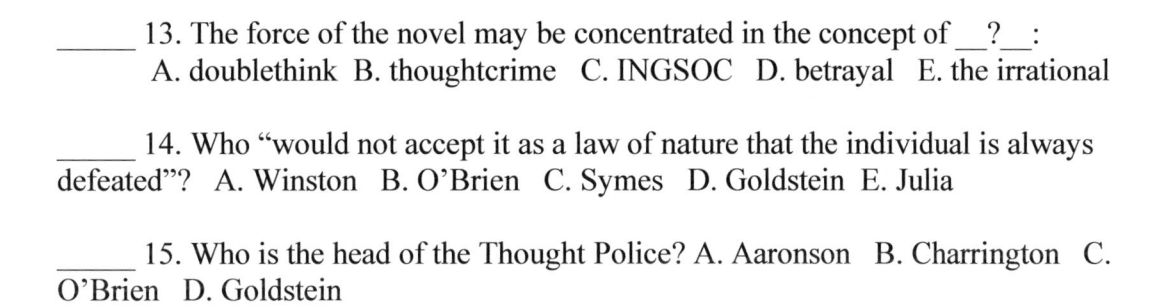

_____ 13. The force of the novel may be concentrated in the concept of __?__:
A. doublethink B. thoughtcrime C. INGSOC D. betrayal E. the irrational

_____ 14. Who "would not accept it as a law of nature that the individual is always defeated"? A. Winston B. O'Brien C. Symes D. Goldstein E. Julia

_____ 15. Who is the head of the Thought Police? A. Aaronson B. Charrington C. O'Brien D. Goldstein

Whole Book Assessment Alternatives

Consider the student who has mastered the information and some and the broader concepts and implications of *1984* and allow her to explore deeper aspects of Orwell's dystopian novel. The following topics are suggestions requiring imagination and / or some research.

1. It must have been shattering for Winston when O'Brien revealed that he took part of writing Goldstein's manifesto. The double irony of this sabotages Winston's last hope for any truth in the world of Big Brother. We, the reader, also feel betrayed because we go into literature and history with a hope that what we read has an unimpeachable quality of truth and speculation. Throughout the world, and even in the United States, the authorship of literature and history sometimes has fraudulent intentions. A few southern states in America downplay their role in resisting the abolition the slavery and adjust their textbooks accordingly. China heavily censors the Internet, while North Korea forbids it altogether, choosing many aspects of Orwell's blueprint to consolidate and maintain power through propaganda. North Koreans live in misery, but are told they live in paradise. The dichotomy is achievable when authority is corrupt. It would be of interest to the student to explore these hypocrisies, as this dichotomy is not isolated to totalitarian regimes, but is practiced in otherwise altruistic democratic institutions, like schools, for instance. For example, 'school pride' is a rallying point for students, but on what achievements is this pride based? School sports are a source of pride, but is this pride located in victories at the expense of sportsmanship?

2. In *1984* privacy is impossible. Is privacy a core concern for Americans? Why do so many in *1984* find solace in Big Brother, despite its constant oppression? Do we as Americans choose security over privacy? Are we in danger of compromising basic rights so the larger desire to remain safe is guaranteed? How is this an illusion, according to those who argue against this arrangement?

3. How is *1984* an attack on institutions that we still regard as sacred and viable? Do these institutions deserve to be attacked, as they are part of a larger hypocrisy? For example, Big Brother forbids family because loyalty to family compromises loyalty to Big Brother. Let's change terms: Work forbids family because loyalty to family compromises loyalty to one's career.

24. Assessment: Whole Book: ANSWERS

Part Two (20 Points):

1:E   2:D   3:B   4:C   5:A

Part 4: Mixed: 30 Points

1. "I SOLD YOU AND YOU SOLD ME."

2. ROOM 101

3. B

4. LEARNING

5. UNDERSTANDING

6. ACCEPTANCE

7. D

8. "A BOOT STAMPING ON A HUMAN FACE FOREVER"

9. "YOU DON'T EXIST"

10. PRESENT

11. FUTURE

12. B

13. D

14. E

15. B

25. Assessment 4: Codes, Nationalism/Patriotism, Michael Radford's Adaptation of *1984*:

Feel Free to Copy

Part I: Objective.

1. All the following codes pertain to the dystopian sub genre EXCEPT:
   A) The masses are oppressed
   B) There must be blind obedience to authority
   C) Police are disorganized and part of a counter rebellion
   D) Minorities are persecuted

2. In Michael Radford's adaptation of George Orwell's *1984*, the concept of *doublethink* is central to all of the following ideas EXCEPT:
   A) Ministry of Truth   B) Victory Cigarettes   C) Ninth Three Year Plan
   D) Anti-Sex League   E) The Spies

3. Winston Smith realizes what Big Brother is doing but wants to know why he is doing it. As a result part of his search for truth lies with all of the following EXCEPT: A) the past B) the Brotherhood   C) Julia   D) the Proles   E) O'Brien

4. All the following codes pertain to the dystopian sub genre EXCEPT:
   A) The use of terror and torture are instruments of order
   B) Books are banned or burned, or both
   C) Civil and human rights are eliminated
   D) The consumption of alcohol, drugs and pornography is forbidden

5. The endless public address announcements emanating from the Ministry of Plenty have the effect of
   A) discouraging Oceania's citizens from getting their hopes up
   B) assuring the citizens that the economy is rolling along fine
   C) educating the citizens about the economy
   D) assuring Winston that he is doing a good job.

6. The main object of hate during Two Minutes Hate and Hate Week is
A) the war B) foreigners C) language and its potential for propaganda D) Goldstein

7. Julia is the force behind Winston obtaining the secret "Book."   A) True B) False

8. It is in the Ministry of A) Truth B) Love C) Peace or D) Plenty **where Winston and Julia are tortured and forced to confess their crimes against Big Brother.**

9. All the following codes pertain to the dystopian sub genre EXCEPT:
   A) Language is corrupted, convoluted, misused, & reduced
   B) The presence of an enemy is necessary, whether real or fictional
   C) Religion is either eliminated or amplified to extremes
   D) Society consists of only one persecuted class of people

10. Who says "the destruction of words is a beautiful thing," suggesting that with that destruction the last vestiges of *thoughtcrime* will be cleansed from the language?
   A) Syme B) Goldstein C) Julia D) Parsons E) Winston

11. Winston says that if the answer lies anywhere it is with
   A) the Thought Police B) The Proles C) Julia
   D) the remembrance of his mother E) the Golden Country

12. By meeting secretly in the proletariat area, Julia and Winston are committing
   A) Anti-Sex B) *doublespeak* C) *duckspeak* D) *thoughtcrime*

13. All of the following are examples of *doublethink*, EXCEPT:
   A. freedom is slavery B) ignorance is strength C) war is peace
   D) Oceania is permanently at war with Eastasia E) Winston's fear of rats

14. All the following codes pertain to the dystopian sub genre EXCEPT:
   A) The establishment of authority borders on the semi-divine
   B) There is a constant conflict between the inner world and outer world
   C) People never had so good, though things have never been worse
   D) Technology always advances and rises to defeat dystopian exploitation

15. Even members of the Inner Party are forbidden to turn off the Telescreens.
   A) True B) False

16. The Novel Writing Machines produce WHAT for the Proles in order to keep them content and semi-literate? A) pornography B) poetry C) religious parables D) statistics

17. Julia does not love Winston and only desires him physically. A) True B) False

18. Winston's fear of rats is based on
   A) an irrational fear B) his mother and sister were eaten by rats
   C) his apartment is full of rats D) he knows they carry disease

19. Winston's job at the Ministry of truth is to A) catalogue the news B) revise and falsify history C) edit information for *mini-plenty* D) assist in the elimination of words

20. O'Brien admits to authoring parts of "The Book." A) True B) False

Part II: Essays: Short

1. When O'Brien calls Winston, "The last man," what does he mean? In thinking about this, for what reason does Orwell invent Winston's character? Why does O'Brien seem to take special interest in breaking him down?
2. How is Julia a counter weight to Winston? How does she represent a different set of values? What is her function in the story and her unique challenge to dystopia?
3. How does Oceania use technology to keep its citizens under compete control and to get then to enthusiastically support a dystopia that keeps them in misery and destitution?
4. How is Radford's film design a reflection of dystopian ideals?
5. The last maxim in the book, not mentioned in the film, is: *God Is Power*. How is this the most perfect representation of *doublethink*?

III. Essays: Longer Free Writes

Using the articles on Nationalism and Patriotism, discuss the differences, giving modern examples of each and citing how one or the other, or both, reflect *1984*.

1. *1984* was a warning to the future about the dangers of fascism and totalitarianism to free forms of government. One student suggested that the kind of extreme dystopian ruination occurring in *1984* could never be visited upon our democracy. Is he right? Are there already critical dystopian parallels in America that mirror *1984*?

2. Why does O'Brien mean about Winston not existing. Why do the Inner Party and its minions want to warp reality for the citizens of Oceania? Give examples of how this warping effect gives the Party more power.

3. The term *rubblescape* was invented to describe the *mise en scene* (What is 'put upon stage') in Michael Radford's adaptation of *1984*. When we look around our own communities, is there a growing *rubblecape* to our surroundings? What causes this and why is there such rural, suburban, and urban neglect? How does living in a *rubblescape* impact our own personal spaces?

4. How close do the performances of John Hurt as Winston, Suzanna Hamilton as Julia, and Richard Burton as O'Brien, represent Orwell's original vision? What scenes best deliver the oppression and terror of *1984*? How effective are the minor characters in delivering Orwell's subtexts?

5. Review the codes of nationalism and patriotism. Which aspects of *1984* are extreme examples of nationalism? Which ones could be mistaken for patriotism?

26. Assessment on Codes, Nationalism/Patriotism, Michael Radford's Adaptation of *1984*: ANSWERS

Part I: Objective.	
1. C	11. B
2. D	12. D
3. C	13. E
4. D	14. D
5. B	15. B
6. D	16. A
7. B	17. B
8. B	18. B
9. D	19. B
10. A	20. A

27. Formal Essay Assignments / Options

Below are a number of essay topics. Each should be composed using a thoroughly realized argument regarding Orwell's text and any signed critical sources you can find on the subject of your discussion. You are required to cite passages from the book and sources to substantiate your arguments. You are to set this up according to your school's style sheet. You must also use proper citations and referencing for Orwell's text and any other texts you use for this paper. The standard five-paragraph **rubric*** applies, though you may use more than three examples to argue your point. I strongly urge you to do so.

Options:

1. Compare / Contrast the private rebellions of Julia and Winston against the Party. Citing the text, what views of the Party do they share, with what views are they in conflict, and what is the nature of their respective rebellions?

2. How is O'Brien a totally original figure in literature? As we see him through Winston's eyes, are you surprised by the full range of his capacities to think beyond Winston's probing assessment of the inner workings of the Party? What surprises you?

3. On your test I asked you to briefly write about two of the following:

   1. How is *1984* a novel about love?
   2. How is *1984* a novel about language?
   3. How is *1984* a novel about memory?
   4. How is *1984* a novel about rebellion?
   5. How is *1984* a feminist novel?

As # 4 (in the box above) is covered in # 1 of this essay assignment, I'd like you to choose EITHER 1,2,3, or 5 as an essay topic and significantly expand on your ideas, using the text for support and refining your general thoughts into specific thoughts in your argument.

4. Read Kurt Vonnegut's short story "Harrison Bergeron."

(https://archive.org/stream/HarrisonBergeron/Harrison%20Bergeron_djvu.txt).

Compare Vonnegut's vision to Orwell's, noting the differences in how each defines the individual. Give equal weight to what happens to the protagonists in each story. What parallel lessons do Orwell and Vonnegut convey to you?

5. One of the most complex incidents in the book concerns Winston's response to O'Brien, his torturer: "He had never loved him so deeply as at this moment, and not merely because he stopped the pain. [...] O'Brien had tortured him to the edge of lunacy, and in a little while, it was certain, he would send him to his death. It made no difference. In some sense that went deeper than friendship, they were intimates…"(252). How would you describe the personal and/or political psychology behind Winston's feelings in this moment? You may want to do a little research on this, or talk to one of your psych teachers for some insight.

6. Are there some elements in the world of *1984* that seem to you so farfetched, so much the product of Orwell's own irrational fear and perhaps hysteria, that they cannot be justified even as extreme versions of an historical possibility? You could help yourself here by finding articles critical of Orwell's book—scholars who scoff at Orwell's vision. If you bring them into your argument, be sure to add your arguments and disagreements.

7. One of the most precious elements of western society is often said to be the concept of the self, the sense of uniqueness and individuality that people cherish. How does the Party obliterate the individual in Oceania?

8. Orwell uses the diary, the coral paperweight, the old rhyme, the Prole's song, and a number of apparently trivial objects symbolically throughout the story. What does he mean to suggest through these symbols? How do they contribute to the pathos of the story?

9. How do the two figures, Big Brother and Emmanuel Goldstein—figures that actually don't exist in the flesh—function in the novel? In what ways do they maintain a hold over the people, and how does their shadowiness as political leaders contribute to this hold?

10. Why does the party look upon sexuality as a threat to its domination? How does it nevertheless exploit the natural sex drives of its citizens? Where does Julia fit into this amalgam? How is she a protest against the sexual mores of Big Brother? How is Winston a collaborator to these mores?

11. Explain Orwell's concept of *doublethink* and how it applies to the book and the Party's goals, using examples from the book. Then Google *doublethink* and refer to at least three modern examples of *doublethink* in American political culture within the last ten years. Draw some conclusions about the function of political language.

12. Why is it necessary for the Party to have control over the past by remanufacturing it? For what end does it do this and by what process does it shape reality? (Be sure to account for O'Brien's explanations for reality, as well as Goldstein's rationale for altering the past.)

13. If it is vitally important for the Party to obliterate the individual, why is it equally important for the Party to separate people from each other and all the things that constitute joy, love, making love, family, trust, peace, tenderness and having time to one self? Give example of why these things are dangerous to the party.

14. Consider the codes of fascism located elsewhere in the guide. How is *1984* a blueprint for fascism? Be sure to use specific examples from the text. Expand this analysis by pinpointing aspects of fascism that exist in our own society. What institutions have exacerbated or fought to curtail movements toward fascism in America today?

15. Is there redemption in this novel? Widely criticized as dark and hopeless, is it possible to locate some abstractions of redemption in *1984*? Is there love beyond the 'love of Big Brother'? Consider all you know about Julia.

16. As a reader, what is the sequence of illuminations you experienced about any given concept explored throughout the book? For example, new realizations about the power of language may have provided for you a deeper respect for language itself. Or the propaganda of Orwell's concept of 'supply and demand' may have given you insight into how politics of fiscal prosperity often create illusions about economic quality, availability, success, failure, obfuscation, thrift or waste. Other illuminations regard the manufacturing of history, the vitality of human institutions, the value of memory, and so on.

28. General Five Paragraph Rubric

I. **Introductory Paragraph**: includes **key information** (author, title, dates); **motivator** (e.g., anecdotal relevance) and **expertise** (establishing your knowledge and voice); stating your **thesis**; and providing at least **three supporting arguments.**

II—IV. **Supporting Paragraphs** include key points, testimony and citations, your clarifications and arguments in your own voice, usually formal.

V. **Conclusion**: Not just a reiteration of your thesis or its supporting elements, but a **reflection** of the meaning of your argument expressed in a broader context that gives **your work** relevance apart from what testimony you have used to make the argument.

NOTE: There are several models of **Introductory** and **Concluding Paragraphs** throughout this book.

*****ALSO:** The goal of any good writer is to liberate oneself from structures that inhibit **argument, voice, audience, style,** and any other expressive attribute one wants to develop in writing. **The Five Paragraph** structure exists to organize ideas on a fundamental and clear level. An analogy is a jazz pianist practicing formal scales before reassembling them into her own unique expression.

29. Samples of the Motivator & the Conclusion

Often, there are two areas of composition with which students struggle: the *introductory motivator* and the *conclusion*.

The *motivator* is where the writer "motivates" the reader to read on, to trust the writer's expertise regarding the subject matter beyond the focused argument, and to establish the writer's voice and conviction before revealing the essence of the argument.

MOTIVATOR

The following is the opening *motivator* for an essay about the role of memory in *1984*:

Memory makes our lives unique. Remembrance defines time and helps us build our lives in the present and helps us plan for the future. The past is fixed and teaches us of our successes and failures. Without memory we would wander aimlessly like the dumbest animal, using only our instincts to survive. We'd have to invent ways of survival everyday. We could never develop as a species. Remembrance creates the complex ideas of emotion and allows us to look toward to the things we long for and hopefully forget the things we regret. All human effort, all art and literature, embrace memory, but no more so in the darkest way than George Orwell's *1984*. *1984* is a novel about the destruction of memory. In this novel, memory suffers at the hands of those who want to falsify history, deny people the beauty of remembrance, and change reality itself for goals of absolute power. Through this destruction we see its greater value.

The writer establishes some universal truths, reflections, and assertions about memory before introducing his focus: ***1984* is a novel about the destruction of memory.** He follows this with three ways he will explore this thesis: **In this novel, memory suffers at the hands of those who want to falsify history, deny people the beauty of remembrance, and change reality itself for goals of absolute power.** In his reading and study, he has a variety of sections from *1984* to develop his argument:

1. Falsifying history: Ministry of Truth, Ninth 3 Year Plan, Newspeak Dictionary

2. Denying the beauty of remembrance: Winston's love for Julia, Winston's search of the past through the Proles, his remembrance of the Truth (Aaronson, Jones, etc.)

3. Changing reality: Ministry of Information's *revisionist* nature; Torture (2+2=5), betrayal of Julia, "I Love Big Brother

He ends the motivator with a larger reflection, which should be the basis of his conclusion: **Through this destruction we see its greater value.**

CONCLUSION

The *conclusion* is not merely a reiteration of the thesis, but a final reflection that finishes off the main argument with some elegance of thought, identifying the larger significance of Orwell's intentions through the isolated thesis of the role of memory in the novel:

Orwell's intentions are rather large in *1984*. In the end Winston's fate is the realization of O'Brien's bitter estimation of what's in store for the human race. If fate is a forward projection as something we cast into the future—perhaps the hope that life will be better—Orwell lets us down. How he doesn't let us down, though, is through Winston's struggle—the struggle of every hero, no matter if he succeeds or fails, to discover something about truth. The truth revealed by Orwell through Winston is that memory of even the tiniest, most tender details of life, makes up life, and therefore makes up memory. As we catalogue our experiences, we set the score for our futures by reaching back to the notes of our past. As discordant as O'Brien's soulless quest for power is, we must know that it is bleak and meaningless and futureless. Though Winston is defeated, we remember the joys of his little remembrances, the simple touches between him and Julia, and the hope that the past did mean something, no matter how much O'Brien wants to corrupt it.

On the following pages we explore more fundamental ideas on organizing one's thoughts to write about *1984*, or any work of literature that calls out for literary investigation, including samples deconstructing the relationship of the **Introductory Paragraph** to the **Body (Supporting) Paragraphs;** an exploration of a **Freewrite Essay** where the writer is somewhat liberated from the hard structures of formal analysis; a novel approach to **Formal and Collaborative Research;** and **Freewrite** and **Structured Research** models for writing about film, utilizing film vocabularies to inform student writing.

30. Sample: Introduction & Body

In *1984* George Orwell uses his own form of *doublethink* to give meaning to the novel. As life consists of dualities—up and down, good and bad, joy and sorrow, for example, Orwell loads his story with powerful contrasting themes. He actually hits one over the head with meaning and examples of *doublethink,* such as the slogans "War Is Peace," "Freedom Is Slavery," and "Ignorance Is Strength," until one either gets it or doesn't. If one gets it, the concept of "meaning" is shredded; if one doesn't get it, a different kind of "meaning" persists and the novel as a concept is lost on the reader. What isn't lost, though, are the smaller themes that give a meaning quite the opposite of what Orwell may have intended. And these are located in odd places and moments. **In the story, the uselessness embedded in the coral paperweight he finds in the Prole section of Oceania; the quiet, uneventful moments he spends with Julia; and Winston's own obsession with the large Prole woman, point to a *doubletheme*, have you, that shadows the dark, obvious themes in *1984*.**	**Thesis** up front (underlined for our purposes here) **Motivators**: Knowledge of Orwell's book reveals writer's awareness of Orwell's world and persistence in forcing an argument based on this knowledge. **Supporting Statements** (boldface).
Winston is curious about many items in Mr. Charrington's Junk Shoppe, but one item in particular caught his attention: "It was a heavy lump of glass…[a] pink convoluted object that recalled a rose or a sea anemone. […] 'It's a beautiful thing,' said Winston" (95). When Julia asked him what it was, he confessed that he didn't know but we remember that he bought it "because of its apparent uselessness" (96). This is an odd comment, but appropriate for a man whose every movement as an Outer Party member is scrutinized for its usefulness to the Inner Party. Winston sees something refreshing in the coral paperweight's meaninglessness, as if owning something without value could somehow lessen the burden and oppression in his own life. In a strange way, this is Winston's form of rebellion. It's his own way of applying *doublethink* against The Party: "Anything old, and for that matter anything beautiful, was always vaguely suspect"(96). And so on… [The subsequent parts of the thesis— **the quiet, uneventful moments he spends with Julia; and Winston's own obsession with the large Prole woman**—need to be developed to complete the Body of the essay.]	This is the **first developmental paragraph** (Body: development of **the uselessness embedded in the coral paperweight he finds in the Prole section of Oceania**). The first quote breaks up a longer quote from the book using an ellipsis […]. A bracketed ellipsis indicates separation in text. Unbracketed ellipsis signifies separation in a statement. A bracketed term indicates the writer added a word for grammatical clarification. The single quotation marks are required because double quotation marks are used to begin the citation. In a longer citation (five lines or more), In a longer citation (five lines or more), you would indent, isolate, and separate, and not use double quotation marks you would not use double quotation marks; therefore quotations within the citation would require double quotation marks.

124   Edward Morneau

31. Sample Freewrite for Orwell's *1984*.

Concept: Doublethink

The concept of *doublethink* is used prominently as a driving force in George Orwell's *1984*. In theory, it is the ability to make useless two ideas by simultaneously equating their opposites with each other. The main slogans of Orwell's Oceania society are examples of this: *War is Peace, Freedom is Slavery,* and *Ignorance is Strength.* Each term is set against the other, thus cancelling all meaning for both terms. As there is no meaning, there is no significance to the term. As it is now meaningless, it no longer exists and is not worthy of thought or discussion. Therefore a conversation about the evils of war when it is defined as "peace" cannot take place. And because it is a *thoughtcrime* to challenge anything in the world of *Big Brother*, no debate is possible. War becomes a rigid truth in a society of total lies.

An example of this kind of *doublethink* today exists in our understanding of health care. *The Affordable Health Care Act,* when explained carefully to anyone who will listen, is supported by a majority of Americans. Basically, this legislation allows for 43 million uninsured to have access to health care. Who wouldn't support that? It prevents insurance companies from denying insurance to anyone who has pre-existing conditions. Again, a good idea since so many families go bankrupt paying out-of-pocket for catastrophic illnesses because they are refused insurance. It provides several options and subsidies for those people who cannot afford insurance, taking the strain off of a health care system that drives costs up for the rest of us; and it helps small businesses afford to give their employees proper health care benefits if they so choose. When explained this way, most people think it's a good step in the right direction to solve one of America's most serious problems.

Let's employ a little *doublethink* here: When some politicians and members of the media began to call *The Affordable Health Care Act* **Obamacare,** support for this new law reversed itself. Why? It was still the same legislation, but now that it was associated with a President who some intensely dislike, the legislation suffered as a result. It was referred to as a socialist scam because it was born out of government. Well, almost all national progress is born out of government *of the people*—Social Security, Medicare, Medicaid, the US Military, the US Highway System, the Internet—hardly anything of merit doesn't have its kernel of funding or support without the people (our taxes, the government). So why is Obamacare so poisonous? Could it be that he is Black? Is it possible that some very powerful Americans still do not like Black people? Is it possible that racism of this kind still persists in this country? If most people support the principles of *The Affordable Health Care Act*, why do they reject these very same principles when they are under the name of *Obamacare?* This is the trick of *doublethink*. This trick negates the content of the act and focuses on the prejudices that are conjured by the word *Obama,* thus cancelling out the merits of the act. Pure *doublethink*.

In fact almost everything this President does is a casualty of *doublethink,* which leads me to believe that George Orwell's *1984* is alive and well in 2012. For example, let's look at the two wars America has been engaged in for the past decade.

In many ways the wars in Iraq and Afghanistan are like the wars Oceania is waging against Eurasia and Eastasia. In *1984* the citizens don't really know who they truthfully are fighting because The Ministry of Truth can change the enemy at any given time. What we do know and learn from *Goldstein's book* is that Oceania is at perpetual war—a war without end. A *war without end* effectively keeps Oceania's citizens in a constant state of fear, loyal to and thankful for strong leadership, accepting of poverty as sacrifice for the war effort, and a workforce dedicated to building weapons instead of things that could actually make life better.

Since 9/11, America's two wars have really been a war against terror. Terror is an idea that has no national boundaries. It is waging war against an idea. For the past ten years the war against terror has been located in Iraq and Afghanistan. The Iraq war is strategically over, but we still continue to fight in Afghanistan. Terrorism, however, is sponsored in many other countries, such as Pakistan, Syria and Iran, to name just three. Terrorism is most closely associated with Muslim nations who resent America's presence among their nations, so, in theory: 1) There's no end to where terrorism can spring up. In this way, war with an idea can continue forever. 2) Like Oceania's war with a shifting enemy where there are a limited number of casualties, America's terrorist wars have taken its toll on only Americans (and their families) who have volunteered to fight for their country and innocent nationals—the rest of us have directly sacrificed very little. 3) Our standard of living has declined each year since the beginning of these wars. 4) Challenging one war president, Bush, was considered treasonous; challenging another, Obama, however, is considered fair because we are now tired of war, though he started neither—pure doublethink!]. 5) Our middle class protest against poverty and unemployment, somewhat represented by the Occupy Movement, has been discouraged on the streets and in the media, suggesting that these Americans have nobody to blame except themselves for their economic situation, and that everyone has to sacrifice during hard times; 6) and while much of our entitlement programs (Medicare, Medicaid, Head Start, Education, EPA, etc.) that help people out are suffering from drastic cuts, we continue to build resources for our military while our nation suffers massive infrastructure problems, including not having enough money to build schools, hospitals, repair bridges and highways, and exploring energy alternatives and ecological systems for clean living.

Another Orwellian parallel is how the economy is explained to Americans. The financial collapse came about because Wall Street was allowed to gamble money that did not actually exist and build up debt, insure itself against this debt until the very insurance companies could not cover the damages that were certain to occur because of this debt. As a result, the markets collapsed, especially housing, which is the backbone of the economy. In *1984* it appears there is no housing except for slums, so there is no tax base. Today, with massive foreclosures and layoffs, the tax base further shrinks as does the economy and, and as a result, jobs become scarce. No jobs, no taxpayers. No taxes, no consumers. In a consumer society, even less tax is collected, so the burden is put on those who do have jobs and do own property to float the economy. If the burden is lifted from those with the most money, the burden on the middleclass is even greater. Then their disposable income shrinks and the economy does not grow. This creates a recession, at worst a depression. *1984's* Oceania is in a constant state of depression because they have no economy, because they have no tax base, because they have no middle class—everyone is poor. If the current conditions continue to worsen in The West, the state of *1984* may be our state.

You should notice that this 'freewrite' requires less structure, as the gravitational pull of the five-paragraph paper is resisted and a more natural flow of argument and ideas takes place above the stoic structure of expository writing. This kind of composition is motivated by an **attitude** towards the subject matter and an awareness that an **audience** is more important than the structure of the argument. As it almost borders on a polemic, the 'freewrite' liberates the writer and reader to scaffold expression and comprehension organically, almost the way we engage in improvised arguments, with just enough emotion and rhetoric to give life to the argument, but not too much emotion to drown it in sentiment and hyperbole.

32. First Draft Rubric

√+ = Excellent   √ = Adequate   √- = Inadequate

CONTENT: **SPECIFIC COMMENT:**

_____Motivator: _____

_____Thesis Statement: _____

_____Supporting Statements: _____

_____Text Support: _____

_____Balance between support & your ideas / argument: _____

_____

_____Conclusion: _____

WRITING / EXPRESSION: √+ = Excellent   √ = Adequate   √- = Inadequate

_____Coherence / Clarity _____

_____Mechanics _____

_____Organization _____

COMMENTS: _____

_____

_____

_____

_____

Preliminary Grade =   Content_____ / Expression_____

33. First Draft Rubric MODEL

√+ = Excellent   √ = Adequate   √- = Inadequate

CONTENT: **SPECIFIC COMMENT:**

__√-__ Motivator: *Establish why the reader should be interested, establish your expertise*

__√+__ Thesis Statement: *Excellent thesis; it has power and purpose; allude to it in your motivator*

__√__ Supporting Statements: *Good key points, but you could provide some more explanation*

__√-__ Text Support: *Need to draw more from the text and your experts*

__√__ Balance between support & your ideas / argument: *Lot of potential here, but you should provide more of your voice and integrate your experts, giving your argument more authority*

__√-__ Conclusion: *Your conclusion should reflect a larger lesson and leave the reader satisfied*

WRITING / EXPRESSION

__√__ Coherence / Clarity: *Provide transitions between supporting paragraphs; vary your sentence lengths. Most of your essay is very clear but lacks balance between you and your sources.*

__√__ Mechanics: *Proofread for errors in punctuation and fragments*

__√__ Organization: *The organization is there, but you need to refine your content.*

COMMENTS: *This essay has a lot of potential. You are organized and this organization makes what you have flow. You need to provide balance between the expression of your argument and the supporting expertise of your scholarly sources. This will give your essay balance. Your writing is clear, but please provide transitions between your supporting arguments, as well as refine your conclusion so it is not just a repetition of your thesis paragraph. Good job, so far. PROOFREAD!*

Preliminary Grade: Content   B- / Expression: B

34. Formal and Collaborative Approach to Research

One goal of the research paper is to get students to move from citing one text in order to support a narrow assertion regarding that text, to gathering a variety of insights from multiple sources in order to advance a more sophisticated thesis that features multiple, broader, and detailed assertions. In short, to get the novice thinker to borrow insights from established thinkers to argue a position.

Another goal is to get students to stop stealing these insights and calling them their own. The only way to do this is for the teacher to be familiar with the limited stream of insights available to the students for a given project. Knowing the material puts teachers in the position of spending more time on helping students integrate borrowed insights and teaching the methodology of quoting, summarizing, paraphrasing, and formatting instead of policing students on content.

By providing students with enough research to facilitate choice in cultivating a variety of assertions, students will feel less locked in to a topic. Sure, letting them choose their own high interest topic is ideal, but because so few students can tell the difference between a legitimate, scholarly source and a caffeine-addled blogger twittering unsubstantiated opinions about nothing, papers pretending to substance suffer an early web-infected death.

This doesn't mean that great research isn't available on the web, but it does mean that the teacher simply has to limit it or that teacher will go insane. Whether print or web based, here is an example of how to remedy this situation.

Δ Here are a number of **scholarly articles** on George Orwell's *1984*:

- Irving Howe, "The Fiction of Anti-Utopia"
- Philip Rahv, "The Unfuture of Utopia"
- Isaac Rosenfeld, "Decency and Death"
- Isaac Deutscher, "*1984*—The Mysticism of Cruelty"
- Irving Howe, "*1984*: History as Nightmare"
- Eric Fromm, "Afterword on *1984*"
- Samuel Sillen, "Maggot of the Month"
- James Walsh, "George Orwell"
- Lionel Trilling, "George Orwell and the Politics of Truth"
- Philip Rieff, "George Orwell and the Post Liberal Imagination"
- Betrand Russell, "George Orwell"
- Aldous Huxley, "A Footnote about 1984"
- T.R. Fyvel, "A Writer's Life"

Δ Here are **short works** dealing with concepts of totalitarianism and privacy:
- Richard Lowenthal, "Our Peculiar Hell"
- Hannah Arendt, "Ideology and Terror: A Novel Form of Government"
- William Lutz, "No One Died in Tiananmen Square"
- Reed Karaim, "The Invasion of Privacy"

Δ Here are some **corresponding works** by Orwell that may be of interest to those supernaturally ambitious students:
- "Why I Write"
- "Politics and the English Language"
- "Freedom and Happiness"

Δ Here are some **parallel dystopian texts** for those students who have a very deep and critically thoughtful appreciation for dystopian literature and love to read and write about it:

- *Brave New World* by Aldous Huxley
- *We* by Eugene Zamyatin
- *Erewhon* by Samuel Butler
- *This Perfect Place* by Ira Levin
- *Anthem* by Ayn Rand
- *Fahrenheit 451* by Ray Bradbury
- *Year Nine* by Cyril Connolly
- *The Revolution Betrayed* by Leon Trotsky
- *The Handmaid's Tale* by Margaret Atwood

All the above **scholarly articles** are available on the web. The best way to deal with this material is for the students to form cooperative groups and report on one or two articles, depending on the size of the class. This cultivates the skills of summarizing, paraphrasing, and bulleting ideas contained in the source. When done correctly, this handy summation gives those students who did not read the article some idea about the content of that article. It's best if a teacher models this. For example, in my reading of James Walsh's essay "George Orwell," the writer's criticisms of Orwell and *1984* can be summarized thusly:

- Orwell has a neurotic and depressing obsession with socialism itself;
- Orwell understands neither communism nor capitalism
- Orwell is fixated on intellectually vague ideas about propaganda, inquisition and torture;
- Orwell despises the working class;
- Orwell's low opinion of human dignity is an affront to those who stood up to European forms of fascism;

- Orwell "borrowed" much of *1984* from *We* by Eugene Zamyatin and does so artlessly;
- Orwell's own health compromises his confidence as an artist in telling an original story
- Orwell's war experience embittered him and clouded his political objectivity;
- Walsh is a defender of communism as a viable form of social organization;
- Orwell's book is not so much a warning but a "shriek" to instill irrational fear in the masses through a monolithic mass media;
- *1984* as a book thrives on hatred and distrust;
- Walsh thinks Orwell's book will fade and disappear.

Obviously this guy hates the book. Justifiably, Walsh has been largely discredited since the publication of his critique in 1956, especially by Christopher Hitchens (see *Why Orwell Matters*), but he does make a few interesting points and provides fodder for research. Any number of thesis topics can be generated from this one article alone:

George Orwell's *1984*...

- presents a political vision of the world that largely ignores human dignity.
- is more of a personal expression of humanity's failure to find the political means of civilized behavior than a coherent analysis of the failure of its current systems.
- is the natural reaction a jaundiced writer would have to the horrors of war.
- is not an original vision of the future, but has its roots in existing totalitarian societies.
- is ultimately a book that gives up on the ordinary person, which is a betrayal of history.
- is alarmist literature and discredits liberalism in the worst way possible.

When these bulleted encapsulations are posted for the students, kids have a bank of ideas from which to draw. With the teacher's help they begin to see patterns and how some articles, for instance, have shared criticism's of Orwell's grasp of politics; or how Orwell, because of his own misanthropy, writes off the working class; or how Orwell's vision has been realized in our media-saturated society. Multiply this by the number of articles, and students have a significant pool of insight and expertise from which to draw, covering a wide range of themes represented by the book, demonstrating the value of this book in the pantheon of great literature. Inevitably, this leads to appreciation and applied scholarship. This is where the arc of teaching bends to the student, but also reveals how the student must sit on the shoulders of giants to sustain a purposeful belief and argument about an engaging work of literature (or about anything worthwhile until they become that expert, that giant).

The Steps

1. Class reads a core work

    A. Student annotates text while reading
    B. Decides areas of interest (character, structure, theme, language, etc.)
    C. In class discussions of book, student raises profoundly selfish questions regarding these areas (I call this unleashing the *student Id*.)
    D. Teacher models the above (while suppressing out-of-control *teacher Id*)

2. Student participates in cooperative reading of the limited research provided by the teacher on Web or in hard copy form

    A. Student (or group) summarizes article(s) and presents bulleted points
    B. Other students engage "experts" in Q & A discussion (exercising more *student Id*)
    C. Students have access to all summarized articles
    D. Teacher models the above

3. Student refines topic based on interest and corresponding available research; teacher conferences and assists

4. Student then proceeds through established departmental steps

    A. Controlling Purpose/ Thesis Statement
    B. Research Questions
    C. Working Bibliography
    D. Working Note Cards
    E. Topic Outline
    F. Works Cited Page
    G. Final Note Cards
    H. Drafting
    I. Final Draft

I believe with this controlled research approach the task of writing a research paper will be less onerous. All the traditional, established steps above will feel less threatening. I think we should be very clear about the "Controlling Purpose" and encourage peer editing through every step. Lots of teachers think note cards are a waste, but in my experience it seems the kids who are better-organized fork over their note cards with glee. And they are the ones who sing and dance when the grades come out.

Something to Consider

Before embarking on a research project, remember that pursuing an argument through research is the highest form of scholarship. Standardized tests may be able to assess the memory of content and reinforce some critical thinking skills, but serous writing supported through research is the ultimate test of a student's learning. That said, I encourage you to take the following seriously:

1. Know that hard, but fruitful work is ahead of you.

2. Be certain to write about something of which you have some knowledge.

3. Be prepared to rely on organization to acquire more knowledge and move your project forward.

4. Recognize that your interest in the subject is equal to the support you need to pursue to illuminate this interest.

5. Trust your sources, but only when they are valid, expert, factual or speculatively profound, articulate and honest.

6. Never write from the top of your head; always partition your thoughts and the thoughts of others as if you are collecting evidence. There is no form of writing more dependent on writing as the **last step**. Research is all organization and thinking in its initial stages.

7. You can never have too much information.

8. Write down full bibliographical sources according to whatever **style sheet** you are using in your school. This will save you a lot of time when you finalize your paper.

9. This is your argument, your paper: Never let your sources overwhelm your input, which is to **clarify, shape,** and give **resonance** to your argument and their testimony.

10. Engage in discovery. You'll learn something, and even better, you'll add to the knowledge of the world.

35. Introduction to Dystopian Film

Film is relatively young compared to written literature. Most conversations about film automatically build comparative-contrast elements into an argument about film because genres are driven by a popular appreciation that demands more films of the same genre be made. For better or worse, the cycle of a genre that once captivated the popular imagination usually spends itself out of favor by relying on tired and predictable formulas. For example, the Western once had broad appeal, but fell from popularity until the works of Sergio Leone, Clint Eastwood, Sam Fuller and Quentin Tarantino reinvigorated the genre by blurring the lines of what constituted heroes and villains. Revisionism feeds off of the grey areas of moral complexity, and the more comfortable a public becomes with its cultural, political, and social inconsistencies, the more myths and legends are revisited and reassessed along artistic lines. The once black and white moral dimensions of the Wild West eventually fell into doubt, as society understood that America grew out of both an altruistic, utopian vision, as well as unrelenting violence, lawlessness, greed, genocide, and the questionable moral calamites of Manifest Destiny.

Dystopian film is no different than any genre. Growing out of the tired genre of early cinematic science fiction, the speculative film genre matured into looking more deeply into the conditions of technology, authority, law and order, and literacy itself to create a challenge to the utopian ideals that have obsessed the great thinkers of history.

Like dystopian literature, dystopian film explores the same codes, repeated here:

- Authority is corrupt
- The masses are oppressed
- There must be blind obedience to authority
- A faceless, well-equipped police state enforces laws
- Minorities are persecuted
- The use of terror and torture are instruments of order
- There are no governmental checks and balances
- Civil and human rights are eliminated
- Free movement is suspended
- Books are banned or burned, or both
- Language is corrupted, convoluted, misused, reduced
- Propaganda and brainwashing techniques are used
- The consumption of alcohol, drugs and pornography is encouraged or tolerated
- The presence of an enemy is necessary, whether real or fictional
- The concentration of power is in the hands of a few
- Society is divided into a caste system
- There is a calculated dissemination of money

- Religion is either eliminated or amplified to extremes
- The establishment of authority borders on the semi-divine
- There is a constant conflict between the inner world and outer world
- People never had it so good, though things have never been worse.

Acknowledging these codes is similar to acknowledging that worthwhile literature and film explore ideas that remain powerful because they are a permanent part of the grey area of human experience. In writing about dystopian film, these codes should constitute the essence of any discussion about this genre. In the following essay sample, the codes are invoked as each story and analysis pursues a larger thesis about the idea of dystopia in concert with the ideal of utopia. This reflects on the comparison contrast structure that is essential to discussing literature and film.

Something to Consider

Before writing about dystopian film, read film reviews authored by writers who use comparison-contrast critiques to convey the major points they are trying to express. By doing this they reinforce and redefine concepts and codes about the genre itself, as well as discover fault lines in the way a particular film fails to invigorate the genre. For example, the most profitable film up to this time is James Cameron's *Avatar*. Its success is built largely upon the special world he created through thousands of special effects. In this regard he reinvigorated a market already replete with special effects blockbusters. However, nearly every serious criticism of *Avatar* hinges on the story itself, which is stuffed with tired clichés, predictable performance trajectories, and motifs adapted from too many other films to consider Cameron's work an original vision of cinema. In many ways this shimmering view of an ecological future threatened by ecological tyranny is sabotaged by dull formulas.

When writers point these things out, note the language they use to identify visual and aural aspects of how film succeeds or fails. Film has its own language and requires a writer to have knowledge of it to be constructively critical. Film is also literature, so those codes of storytelling still matter when considering the whole effect and meaning of film.

36. Free Write: Paradise Lost: Sample Essays

Here are some questions for the ages: Why do peace and paradise on Earth elude us? Why do killing and violence persist? Why do lies and propaganda triumph over truth and reason? Why is faith in each other desecrated by doubt and mistrust? Here are some possible answers for the ages: We kill great individuals because weak individuals cannot look upon perfection. We believe in rumors, gossip, small talk and lies because thoughtfulness and knowledge are too difficult, and a casual relationship with the truth is just so much easier. We accept fantasy because we are unprepared for reality. Faith and reason cannot reconcile with each other and that is why we look upon each other with deep suspicion in matters of both. We are spies in a hemisphere of our own insecurities, and forever we will be at the blunt end of mistrust.

We are first and foremost animals, yet we are animals with brains; however, like animals, this does not make us less territorial and less inclined to search for security. It is our obsession with territorial security that precludes paradise and utopia. This is not new, even for a young country like America.

During The American Expansion under Thomas Jefferson, our third president had to communicate via coded language in his correspondence with Lewis Meriwether (of Lewis & Clarke) in order to address the territorial needs of the newly formed nation, so worried was he about being betrayed by foreign interlopers—particularly the British, who coveted continental territories. This deception was necessary in reshaping the very size of The United States, particularly with the acquisitions of the Louisiana Purchase and the Oregon Territory. Without this deception it would be difficult to know what kinds of border securities the new state would have to protect and what kind of limitations we would have as a nation (Rockwell). This may be one of the first instances of an American response to a foreign surveillance culture in action.

Today, America pursues a similar, but ultra-high tech intrusion into the lives of those who may be enemies of the state through drone surveillance, called Vanguard Defense. The dystopian aspect of this security measure is the potential of the spy state turning on its own citizens: "The prospect of cheap, small, portable flying video surveillance machines threatens to eradicate existing practical limits on aerial monitoring and allow for pervasive surveillance, police fishing expeditions, and abusive use of these tools in a way that could eventually eliminate the privacy Americans have traditionally enjoyed in their movements and activities" (ACLU). Indeed, in Seattle, the city council has reconsidered recent purchases of mini-drones to assist them in police offshore border surveillance. Anti-drone critics fear this newest incursion of the spying culture. Again, the ACLU:

> The American Civil Liberties Union of Washington says if society is not vigilant, new technology can outpace public policy. 'Police drones give government unprecedented abilities to engage in surveillance of people's activities,' says the ACLU's Doug Honig. 'Our elected officials need to adopt laws controlling law enforcement use of this new technology, or it will control

us.' The article goes onto to refer to the ominous presence of Big Brother's growing influence in American culture as new technologies erode our privacy in the name of keeping us safe (Thomas).

We should remember Ben Franklin's famous adage: "Those who would give up essential liberty to purchase a little temporary safety, deserve neither liberty nor safety." George Orwell's "Big Brother" is the embodiment of monolithic nationalism modeled more on fascism and totalitarianism than socialism. Orwell's experience in The Spanish Civil War taught him that the concentration of power in the hands of the corporate state betrays socialism and lays the groundwork for the creation of the *super state*, which is designed to crush dissent, rebellion, and therefore the individual. The superstate's goal is to keep its citizens maximally ignorant, in constant fear and terror, and to brainwash and propagandize them into believing their lives are fulfilled; and only by total allegiance to the superstate will such security and comfort persist.

In fact, the idea of safety and security are ideals polluted by comfort and ignorance. The dreamed-of perfect society—utopia—is built around safety and security; the realization of this ideal is impossible the more comfortable we get. The more comfortable we get the less skeptical and vigilante we become, the less curious we are, the more narrow our broader communal concerns are, the more we covet security and safety at any cost. We even pay out this cost in essential freedoms and the very comforts and privileges we covet. Every piece of dystopian literature and dystopian film spells this out in frightening detail.

37: Structured Research Essay on Dystopian Film

A Visual Trashing: Film & Dystopia

Any formal essay about film requires acknowledging specific introductory elements.

- Name the films
- Name the dates when these films were released
- Name the directors of these films
- Name prominent actors who give some shape to the story
- Divulge your thesis statement—the argument—clearly and convincingly
- Provide qualifying statements—motivators, contexts, ideas—anything that gives substance to your interest, knowledge and authority
- Divulge the key supporting arguments that shape your main argument.

Sample Introduction:

Dystopia, or anti-utopia, is a social state in which society has lost its ability to bring people together in any hopeful way. A dystopian society dehumanizes its members, marginalizes the majority for the benefit of the few, almost always enslaves fringe groups, and brutally punishes and discourages the brave souls who challenge authority and attempt to bring order and justice back to society.

Dystopian literature (and film) is a subgenre of science fiction and satire. Plato's *Republic* is the original source of Western utopian political thought, which was systematized and further explored by Sir Thomas More in his book *Utopia,* written during the bloody reign of Henry the Eighth.

Both Plato and More present a political and social vision of how society could organize itself for the benefit of all its citizens and allow them to thrive and grow as individuals, as citizens, and as collective members of society. War, poverty, ignorance and corruption are eradicated by diplomacy, shared wealth, education and mutual trust. The most imaginative conceptions of the utopian state are *Atlantis* and *The Garden of Eden*, where humankind is one and righteous with the temporal, metaphysical and the divine.

Subsequent writers, leery of human nature, scoffed at the idea that human beings could attain such perfection and would ridicule this vision. Early dystopian works like *Gulliver's Travels* by Jonathan Swift, *Erehwon* ("nowhere" spelled backwards) by Samuel Butler, and *Looking Backward* by Edward Bellamy, ridicule humankind and reveal that human virtues are too complex to align themselves with perfection. Fritz

Lang's silent film masterpiece *Metropolis* (1927) predicts the human slave culture that would emerge in subservience to machines. Francois Truffaut's *Fahrenheit 451* was the visual realization of Ray Bradbury's broad swipe at anti-intellectual fascist cultures that censor and burn books, hinting that the power of the written word would eventually disappear only to be replaced by the manufactured image—easy to consume, highly manipulative, but immediately forgettable. These dystopian works are polite visions compared to the real corrosion of utopian values waiting to be explored.

During the colonialization of indigenous peoples by European powers and after the Industrial Revolution, *realpolitik*, totalitarianism and genocide gripped the imagination of writers, who churned out works ridiculing any hope for civilizing humankind. Books like Evgent Zamyatin's *We*, Aldous Huxley *Brave New World*, and George Orwell's *1984*, present chilling visions of a social state in which society has lost its ability to bring people together in any hopeful way.

Dystopian literature is critical; therefore, it is an argument. Almost all dystopian literature and film embrace the following codes in order to pursue their respective arguments:

- Authority is corrupt
- The masses are oppressed
- There must be blind obedience to authority
- A faceless, well-equipped police state enforces laws
- Minorities are persecuted
- The use of terror and torture are instruments of order
- There are no governmental checks and balances
- Civil and human rights are eliminated
- Free movement is suspended
- Books are banned or burned, or both
- Language is corrupted, convoluted, misused, reduced
- Propaganda and brainwashing techniques are used
- The consumption of alcohol, drugs and pornography is encouraged or tolerated
- The presence of an enemy is necessary, whether real or fictional
- The concentration of power is in the hands of a few
- Society is divided into a caste system
- There is a calculated dissemination of money
- Religion is either eliminated or amplified to extremes
- The establishment of authority borders on the semi-divine
- There is a constant conflict between the inner world and outer world
- People never had it so good, though things have never been worse

In addition to Lang's *Metropolis*, there are many films that adhere to the codes above and explore in detail how the superstate corrodes human values and brings about the state of dystopia. Here are just a few of the better ones: *The Trial* (962), *V of Vendetta* (2006), *Soylent Green* (1973), *Silent Running* (1972), *Never Let Me Go* (2010), *Moon*

(2010), *Minority Report* (2002), *Logan's Run* (1976), *La jetee* (1962), *The Handmaid's Tale* (1990), *Brazil* (1985), *Blade Runner* (1982), *A Scanner Darkly* (2006), and *Children of Men* (2006). For the purposes of this paper, our focus will be on three films that represent distinct illustrations of dystopian films, marked by time, style, and the consistency and subversion of dystopian codes: Francois Truffaut's adaptation of Ray Bradbury's *Fahrenheit 451* (1966), George Lucas's expansion of his student film, *THX-1138* (1971), and Michael Radford's adaptation of George Orwell's *1984* (1984)

The demands of creating a visual world based on a dystopian book are considerable. A book can express ideas and the reader's mind can create images of the bleak landscape of dystopia. A film, however, has to do what the mind does: It has to create something familiar out of something unfamiliar—in this case, something that reveals a **world out of balance**. Unless one has lived in a dystopian society, it is hard to know what one looks like. Because this idea is often presented as an idea of the future, the dystopian film is often lumped in with pure science fiction. This is a mistake. Where science fiction often creates a shiny, technological view of the future, dystopian fiction presents a future in retreat, in decay, despite its technology, whether it is advancing or declining.

Film has shown a remarkable ability to present dystopian literature in convincing ways, creating worlds that are as frightening and psychologically disturbing as any monster movie—the difference being that dystopian monsters are almost always human authority figures. In fact, the whole genre of dystopian cinema is framed around the corruption of authority, particularly in the way authority demands absolute fealty and loyalty for the security and comfort it provides its otherwise debased, starving, and brutalized citizens—the very citizens who represent the failure of this authority but are powerless to do anything about it. Looking at the films of Truffaut, Lucas and Radford, we can see how these filmmakers from three different decades use authority to tell compelling stories about how power corrupts, especially in the name of security and keeping people maximally complacent and as docile as well-bred pets. Each film addresses the codes of dystopia and presents a recipe for a world out of balance and a reason why paradise and utopia elude us.

Francois Truffaut's *Fahrenheit 451* is a sobering account of Ray Bradbury's novel, more so because it <u>is</u> a film in totality, as the viewer is separated from words right from the start. There are no printed credits and no evidence of the existence of printed words available anywhere in the film except those books about to be consumed by flames. This is a vision about a future that outlaws the reading of books, terrorizing and punishing those who break the law, and ritualizing the burning of books as a public entertainment spectacle. This is not far fetched, as it is based on historical episodes of "literary cleansing" in Mussolini's Italy, Hitler's Germany, Stalin's Russia, and in odd episodes of the American South burning banned school books. [In our time we have seen this with the burning of Islamic texts and Beatle and Dixie Chicks records.]

Truffaut and cinematographer Nicholas Roeg create an anti-septic world where everything is in order, where people are little more than automatons who spend most of their time working, watching TV, and taking drugs to stay awake and fall asleep. Truffaut accomplishes this with an exceedingly simple film design and character definitions: the sets are modern, but with no shine or ornamentation; his characters are meek, busy, prone to taking and following orders, fearful of some mysterious, powerful force around them; and the dialogue is flat, absent of ideas and passion, and is only concerned with the junk culture of TV and an obsession with every kind of sport imaginable.

When the main characters, Clarisse (Julie Christie) and Montag (Oscar Werner), try to break out of this ceaseless sameness, they have to come to terms with the force behind this book-hating authority, represented by The Commander (Cyril Cusack). Cusack delivers Bradbury's dystopian ideas in perfect code in a kind, grandfatherly manner, assuring his underlings and others that books are evil because they distract people from life. He clearly wants a world where no one thinks, no one is different, no one uses his imagination to empower dreams, and no one develops the intellect to challenge The Commander's twisted authority and the security that authority provides. In the end The Commander loses, as he is no match for human memory, for he simply cannot wipeout the remembrance of books. In the film's final scene, Truffaut guides us to a forest to where Montag flees, where people live and have dedicated their lives to memorizing whole books, keeping the oral tradition of storytelling and thinking alive and using that tradition to keep hope alive, knowing that life is dynamic, messy, diverse, and built on natural conflict and not blind obedience.

This pattern repeats itself in George Lucas's *THX 1138*, except that instead of books being the victim, love and individuality are outlawed by an authority represented by computer technology. Robert Duval plays THX-1138 (he has no name, just a number) and lives in an underground world called "White limbo," which Lucas drenches in antiseptic, artificial white light and white sets. Duval moves about as a mindless droid, dressed in white coveralls, is hairless, fully drugged and clueless. The philosophy behind this computer culture, represented by OMM (Donald Pleasance), is "Work hard, increase production, prevent accidents, and be happy" (Lucas). Almost every scene is cranked out with the glare of technological overkill, consuming any remnant of human joy or fraternal interaction. The film reaches a turning point when THX meets LUH 03147 (Maggie MaComie) and falls in love with her.

Their love begins a rebellion against the vast computer culture that swallows everyone and wants to outlaw emotion because emotion, like books, individualizes thought and fills the imagination with hope and questions. Love connects us with other people and makes us stronger and helps us answer questions we cannot answer by ourselves. Both Duval and Macomie's characters wean themselves off drugs and realize the security OMM propagandizes is fiction and soulless. There is one scene in particular where they make love, praying that nobody is watching them, but it seems everyone is watching them; yet, what they are watching is a grotesque distortion of what love is, as the image is warped and out of focus.

LUH is caught and re-drugged, while THX become a fugitive from "justice." Lucas ends the film with THX running from the robocops and escaping "White Limbo," heading to the upper world and emerging into a blast of sunlight. We are left to decide if this is a new beginning or an ironic end. "White Limbo" may be a retreat from this sunlit world, which may be a nuclear fried Earth. Lucas can be forgiven for his ambiguity, as this was his first major effort out of film school. However, with great instinct, he realizes that a true dystopian film depicts **a world out of balance**, where authority, pretending to bring tranquillity, draws people away from each other and forces them into a ceaseless, institutional security-driven monotony that makes life seem hopeless.

This hopelessness is perhaps best represented by Michael Radford's powerful rendering of Orwell's *1984*. Whereas Truffaut and Lucas end their respective films with a sense of hope, Radford is true to Orwell's vision and to the political ends of dystopia: There is no hope. Orwell's thesis: If an omniscient state authority can find the psychological path to our darkest fears, it will use them against us in such a way that we will betray the ones we love; we will willingly live in squalor and accept permanent poverty as normalcy; we will work endless hours for the worst of all human purposes—war. We will also denounce family, friends, marriage, mother, father, sister, brother, lover and everything else except our unbending loyalty to the authority of Big Brother. And we will do all of this to remain secure within the boundaries of a superstate threatened by other superstates, whether they exist or not, because all knowledge of them is either outlawed or revised on a daily basis.

Radford's film design is a virtual "rubblescape": a society in "planned" decay—rubbish and ruins everywhere—a permanent ghetto where everyone is under suspicion for violating laws that do not exist. Ninety-eight percent of the population (The Proles) is impoverished, drunk, and pornographically blissed out; one percent (The Outer Party) works continuously and miserably on behalf of the other one percent (The Inner Party) who hides behind immense wealth and absolute power. The presence of telescreens is everywhere, privacy is abolished, nonsense statistics bilge from speakers bragging about how wonderful everything is, but everything is on the decline. It is like living in a permanent war zone as war is permanent—an encoded security trap of the security apparatus of dystopian society.

Big Brother, represented by O'Brien (Richard Burton), lures Orwell's two heroes, Winston Smith (John Hurt) and Julia (Suzanna Hamilton), into the arms of the Thought Police, represented by the Prole antique dealer, Mr. Charrington (again, played with sinister menace by the "grandfatherly" Cyril Cusack). In the Ministry of Truth, Winston and Julia are taught to believe lies (2+2=5), are physically tortured, then psychologically tortured until they betray each other and themselves. In the end they are faceless, mindless and hopeless.

Radford uses the same tools as Truffaut and Lucas, but with different results. One gets a sense that the former directors' characters are going to survive. With Radford, every bit of space and time surrounding Winston and Julia make the viewer fear for them because it is inevitable that this massively corrupt authority cannot be broken. Big Brother breaks their spirit because it robs Winston and Julia of their innate ability to think and reason. Big Brother eliminates words, thoughts, love—even God. Everything is gone.

In one particular gruesome scene, after O'Brien has tortured Winston on the rack, he stands Winston up before a mirror, and pulls out one of his rotting teeth. Winston reacts: "You did this to me. You reduced me to this." O'Brien simply states, "No Winston. You did this to yourself" (Orwell 273). Earlier O'Brien says, "You are rotting away. You are a bag of filth…. You are the last man" (272), assuring Winston that the whole and wellness of humanity is an afterthought to the concentrated power of the few. Winston sees O'Brien's visual prophecy of the future of humankind in the mirror before him: He looks like the result of " a boot stomping on a human face—forever (267)."

This is such a hard, bitter, nearly impossible truth to consider, especially in light of the grace we hope for in life. The tone of the entire film is depressing, monotonous, yet reflective of the dead spirit that awaits any society that allows itself to be regimented and crushed by authority's malignant neglect of it. People together create utopia; people disconnected from each other create dystopia. It is in the best interest of a corrupt power to keep people apart, to keep them unnaturally busy and overworked, to keep them drunk and drugged, to keep them distracted by dumb mass media, to make them distrust each other, to make them fear others without sufficient reason except for unfounded prejudices, to promise them just enough to get by (and to seal that promise by threatening to take everything away if they don't obey the laws). There is much to believe that people are willing to be deceived and to suffer the above for the sake of the smallest sense of security hosted by others, even if it is a brutal police state. History has proven that. Dystopian film or literature is a warning in the form of the above political recipe. All three of these films use aspects of this recipe to represent their version of dystopia and they have one thing in common: it is not security, but unity that give people power over absolute authority.

Bibliography

Honig, Doug.www.aclu.org
Lucas, George. *THX-1138*. Los Angeles: American Zoetrope/ Warner Bros. Inc., 1971.
Orwell, George. *1984*. New York: New American Library, 1949.
Rockwell, Craig. www.lewisandclarktrail.org
Thomas, Linda. www. mynorthwest.com

38. *1984* Projects

1. **PROPAGANDA POSTER**: Most authoritarian organizations use the medium of the poster to convey certain messages. Usually for the kinds of appeal corrupt authorities seek, exaggeration is the method they use to convince the masses of some basic lie they are selling as truth. Research propaganda posters and you'll find a large sampling of the kinds of nonsense foul authoritarians and totalitarians in history have created to propagandize their points of view. Create your own powerful propaganda poster message about something you believe that with the right assemblage of words and images could convey a "truth" or an action for your audience to take.

2. **COLLAGE or POWERPOINT or SCRAPBOOK**: In the world today there is a small but persistent population of totalitarian/ fascist leaders who are subjecting their citizens to the same kinds of suffering the Party subjected its citizens to in *1984*. Using any of the three mediums mentioned above, create an inventory of these political tyrants, with images, maps of their respective countries, a description of their fascist policies, and an explanation comparing their policies to the Party's in *1984*.

3. **UNPERSON SCRAPBOOK**: Assemble a two-part photo scrapbook of at least TEN pictures of a person who matters in your life. Each photo must be accompanied with an anecdotal story (when and why the photo was taken, its significance, etc.). Then make that person an UNPERSON, filling the second half of your scrapbook with blank spaces where the original photo would be, now covering it with some abstraction (Winston used brown packing tape) to obliterate the image. Write about the effect of the absence of this person in your life at the stage the original photo was taken. Each entry is like your final memory of that time with that person, now preserved in writing, as there is no longer any proof this person existed other than what is in your memory. (Consider how Winston catalogues his memories: a mental photo of his mother & sister; another one of St. Clemens' Church; one of Katherine; another of 'that place with no darkness; one of Aaronson, etc. Bundle them together and that's his mental memory reference to the past, which O'Brien says does not exist).

4. **DRAMATIZATION PROJECTS**: (5-7 minutes maximum)

   A. **Take a Scene** from *1984* and dramatize it. It can be a monologue, soliloquy, or duologue. You can cherry pick scenes and compress them together. For example, Winston has many private thoughts regarding O'Brien, but they are spread out in Book III. Locate them, join them together and create an internal soliloquy (that you speak aloud). You can use a props, stare out of a window—use any subtle action you want to convey the spilling out of your thoughts across your tongue into the world. If you do a duologue, the scenes between Julia and Winston are very powerful in their evocation and discovery of love and other things important to them. Contract their conversations and create one whole conversational scene between them to reveal the essence of their growing understanding of each other.

B. You can also make a **VIDEO** of your dramatization and choose a piece of **INSTRUMENTAL** music/ soundscape to provide an atmosphere for your soliloquy/duologue. Make sure your camera work is interesting and the AUDIO IS GOOD.

C. You can also do this dramatization **OFF-CAMERA**, as a **VOICEOVER** narration, using the camera to capture images that suggest something parallel to what you are saying. Find some dingy, dank, dreadful part of the school that looks like it could be the door to Room 101, or some other location, that suggests the tone of your dramatization.

5. DISPLAY CASE/ SHOPPING BAG: Create a shopping bag / display case full of VICTORY items, with each item showing *1984*-like ingredients and language. There must be a minimum of five items for a bag; ten fir a display case. For the DISPLAY CASE several students can champion this project. See me.

6. ARTIFACTS: At Charrington's Junk Shoppe, Winston buys a coral glass paperweight—not for its value, but for its uselessness. We surround ourselves with artifacts—things that have meaning only to us, but are junk to others. I have this amazingly stupid film advertisement for a movie called *Gorgo*—possibly the worst Godzilla-like movie ever made. Weirdly enough, it's one of the oldest things I own. I encased it in plastic so it would not rot away. Totally useless, but for some reason I won't junk it. It conjures up something in me that I can't quite describe—mostly a clear memory of my childhood at that specific time and all the people I knew, the places I frequented, and the feelings I had. Find an artifact in your life that resonates this way. Bring it in. Write about it and share it with the class.

7. ARTISTIC RENDERING: Choose a person, place or something in *1984* and using any art medium, crate an original work rendering your choice. It could be an image of Julia & Winston exchanging their first note; O'Brien's fatherly face bestowing fascist wisdom on Winston; the interior of Charrington's Junk Shoppe—anything that conveys what art must convey: personal meaning.

8. ROOM 101: What is in your ROOM 101? Choose any EXPRESSIVE medium at all and either reveal this irrational fear, or try to make us guess what it is.

9. FILM & MUSIC: The themes of *1984* have been explored in other movies and in music. Bring in a reel of film clips or a song cycle of different performers who have tried to emulate Orwell's ideas and present them to the class. Do not merely present them: Be prepared to ask and be asked questions regarding your project,

10. YOUR IDEA_____

39. Why Orwell Still Matters

The Guardian's Stuart Jeffries wrote in 2013:

> *Try this passage from* **Nineteen Eighty-Four** *where Orwell writes about the 20th century as the period in which "human equality became technically possible" and in which, simultaneously 'practices which had long been abandoned, in some cases for hundreds of years – imprisonment without trial, the use of war prisoners as slaves, public executions, torture to extract confessions, the use of hostages, and the deportation of whole populations – not only become common again, but were tolerated by people who considered themselves enlightened and progressive.'*

If one has been following world history for the past thirty years —Western history in particular—Jeffries' reference makes a compelling case for George Orwell's prescience and aggregate warnings. It seems in the 'first world' we have partially descended into the abyss of social injustice and dystopian ruination described by Orwell in *1984*'s 'illegal book', *The Theory and Practice of Oligarchical Collectivism' by Emmanuel Goldstein*. As *1984* is a satire of the future, not even Orwell could have imagined that his masterwork would appear as the very blueprint for our ruination. For that theoretical architecture, Orwell has been ridiculed and misunderstood by many. Thankfully, there are many more who consider him an avatar of political wisdom and defend him for the courage it takes to give truth to experience, which is the ultimate form of relevance. His 'experiences' cobble together a political tapestry of ideas to be avoided, not followed.

The late essayist Christopher Hitchens makes a compelling case for George Orwell's continued relevance in his book, *Why Orwell Matters*. With surgical detail and wit, he deconstructs many of the criticisms leveled at Orwell during his time by contemporary thinkers who believed Orwell a hypocrite, elitist, and ideological troublemaker. Thankfully, Hitchens' defense is not fawning, as he reveals Orwell to be flawed, but a person capable of change and insight, possessing a revolutionary intellect informed by experience far out the range of his critics, and forged by fighting against, and living under, totalitarian and fascist rule. *1984* is Orwell's crowning achievement—not because it is so compelling a tale and satire; rather, because it is a profound reflection of his own experiences and passions.

Hitchens explores a number of motifs in Orwell's life that reflects the ideological, intellectual, and political underpinnings of *1984*. Students of Orwell and of *1984*, in particular, can see how a man and his work are hinged to his experiences, his times, and the impositions put upon any man through, at best, the serial misunderstandings of his detractors, and at worse, the outright fabrications of those who want the 'doors' of Orwell's inventions to swing their way. Lauded, vilified, used and abused, Orwell emerges not so much as a "saint" (using writer Philip Larkin's word), but as a true revolutionary. Hitchens mines and refines a variety of observations that should instruct the reader of *1984* of specific contexts in how the novel developed as a work and survived as one of the most important books of the last 100 years:

Introduction: The Figure

- "He [Orwell] would appear never to have diluted his opinions in the hope of seeing his byline disseminated to the paying customers; this alone is a clue to why he still matters" (5).

- Orwell's insights into what Nietzsche called the 'master-slave relationship' were shaped by his experiences in post-colonial England and his 'visceral' and 'intellectual' repulsion to the modernist empires of Nazism and Stalinism. "[His] fiction manifests a continued awareness of the awful pleasures and temptations of servility, and many of its most vivid scenes would have been inconceivable without it" (6-7).

- His contemporary relevance is still evident in "his views on the importance of language, which have anticipated much of what we now debate under the rubric of psychobabble, bureaucratic speech, and political correctness" […] and "his fascination with objective and verifiable truth—a central problem in the discourse now offered us by post-modern theorists…" (11).

- Orwell is valued for his intellectual honesty and, as American writer Lionel Trilling observed, a modesty which informed his ability to "communicate to us the sense that what he has done, anyone of us could do" (12). As an affront to those who despised him, Trilling goes on to celebrate Orwell's virtues of "sportsmanship and gentlemanliness and dutifulness and physical courage…" and, as Orwell testifies, possessing the "power of facing unpleasant facts" (13)—all of these things practiced in his life and in his writings.

1. Orwell and Empire

- As a sub-divisional police officer in the Burmese town of Moulmein, Orwell grew to hate imperialism and participating in "the dirty work of an Empire" (17). Though he professed a 'private animosity' towards the suffering natives who made his life unbearable, he was of another, more virtuous mind to realize that he was living in a world of lies and self-deception where censorship abounds and free speech is impermissible. It is here where Hitchens sees Orwell himself emerge as the conflicted model for Winston Smith. Smith grouses about the indifference of the Proles, but believes they will rise up and defeat Big Brother.

- His escalating dislike of "colonial mentality" and "the class system at home" is heightened by an incident in Colombo during his first day in Asia when he witnessed a "white policeman [delivering] a savage blow to a local coolie…" (20). In *1984* the memory of this incident is mirrored in O'Brien's vision of a "boot stomping on a human face forever" (Orwell 266-267). He continued to refine his thoughts on "racialism [as] something totally different. It is the invention not of conquered nations but of *conquering nations* [Italics—mine]. It is a way of pushing exploitation beyond the point that is normally possible, by pretending that the exploited *are not human beings*" (20-21), [Italics—Orwell]. In the novel, O'Brien degrades Winston to a point where his body is rotting away and is no more viable than rubbish, erasing any visage of humanity.

- "His rooted opposition to imperialism is a strong and consistent theme throughout his writings. […] [In] general he insisted that the whole colonial 'racket' was corrupting to the British and degrading to the colonized. […] Orwell upheld the view that the war should involve *decolonization*" (22), [Italics—mine]. In *1984* Winston's evolving empathy for the Proles reflects Orwell's sympathy for the downtrodden and colonialized, and he worked tirelessly for all who were marginalized by imperial ideologies. 'Goldstein's book' is a work of revelatory deconstruction of Orwell's insights into the extremes of imperialism, so much so that the patient reader can see where the roots of fascism and totalitarianism first form.

- Orwell's grasp of propaganda grew from his experiences at the BBC, as evidenced by his observations regarding BBC censorship and its penchant for sanitizing history (25).

- His concept of Big Brother, specifically the "bombastic…ventriloquized [voice] for the masses" (25) grew from his resistance to Winston Churchill's "Finest Hour rhetoric" (25).

- Orwell actually modeled 'Room 101' in *1984*'s 'Ministry of Truth' from Room 101 in Portland Place at the BBC (25).

- Even the singing Prole woman, who Orwell so admires before he and Julia are arrested, has her incarnation in the 'charwomen'—the army of women who swept the floors of the BBC while singing in the early hours of the morning before business commenced (26).

- Hitchens goes some way in defending Orwell's Leftist leanings, which often confused his detractors as implicit support for Communism. To be sure, Orwell was unconditionally opposed to colonization. Though he despised Stalinism and totalitarianism, he equally condemned the imperialism of Great Britain and feared a lurching ambition in the United States to pick up the imperial baton after World War II (28-29).

- In *1984* the motif of narrowing the English language to the point of meaninglessness (e.g. 'Newspeak': *doubleplusungood*) may have been drawn from Orwell's realization that the "end of imperial rule would mean the withering of the English faculty in India" (32). Orwell wrote, "The best bridge between Europe and Asia, better than trade or battleships or aeroplanes, is the English language" (32). In the novel, when Ministry of Truth colleague Symes says, "The destruction of words is a beautiful thing," Orwell implies that when language is bleached of meaning, power can usurp the weak, and critical thought and revolution are futile. Furthermore, without meaningful language, the dream of a world where multicultural sympathies and universal understandings are explored will collapse into confusion, propaganda, and war.

2. Orwell and the Left

- During his career as a political writer, both the Right and Left vilified Orwell, partly, according to Hitchens, because of his 'immense potency' and 'effect' (39). Among critics of Orwell: Isaac Deutscher accused Orwell of 'moving millions to despair and apathy'; Raymond Williams suggested that Orwell '[spoiled] the morale of a whole generation'; Edward Thompson claimed, 'in authoring a work of fiction that was in fact, in rather cunning disguise, the work of an entire *culture*' (46) [Single quotes—Hitchens].

- Most representative of Orwell's detractors on the Left was Williams, a Communist during 1930-40: "[The] total effect of [Orwell's] work is an effect of paradox. He was a humane man who communicated an extreme inhuman terror; a man committed to decency who actualized a distinctive squalor" (48). Hitchens rightfully deconstructs the hypocrisy of both phrases and Williams' overall penchant for creating his own paradox in regard to Orwell (51). Accusing Orwell of being a literary and intellectual "vagrant" (52), Williams conveniently forgets that Orwell "was very moved" by his experiences in Catalonia and was a part of a "community of revolutionary sympathizers who had felt the shared experience of betrayal at the hands of Stalin" (53). Williams controverts his claim that Orwell despised the underclass by quoting a part of *1984* that actually demonstrates the opposite—Winston's conclusion that the hope and salvation of humankind lie with the Proles.

- Williams also implies a kind of global parochialism practiced by Orwell, suggesting that Orwell's imagination (possibly best expressed in his *Animal Farm*) cannot possibly mirror the realities he criticizes, especially in regard to the physical and intellectual squalor of totalitarianism. However, Hitchens refutes this by quoting the Polish poet and essayist, Czeslaw Milosz: *Orwell fascinates…through his insight into details they know well…[.] Such a form of writing is forbidden by the New Faith because allegory, by nature manifold in meaning, would trespass beyond the prescriptions of socialist realism and the demands of sensors.* **Even those who knew Orwell only by hearsay are amazed that a writer who never lived in Russia should have so keen a perception into its life (54-55)** [Italics, brackets, boldface—mine].

- Long before the publications of *Animal Farm* and *1984*, Orwell's 'premonitions' about the cruelties of totalitarian socialism were born in his time in Catalonia (Spain): "This is where Orwell suffered the premonitory pangs of a man living under a police regime: a police regime ruling in the name of socialism and the people" (55). Unlike Williams and other detractors who saw Stalinism as an elixir to Nazism, Orwell did not 'repress' his misgivings and chose instead to 'face the truth' of Stalin's social tyranny. This insight was misunderstood by other intellectuals as a "hint of superiority" on Orwell's part and "aroused an "intense dislike" for him (55) [Single quotations—Hitchens].

- Just as *Goldstein's book* was "a secret book circulated only within the Inner Party, [*1984*] was itself a secret book circulated only within the Inner Party" of the Soviet state (55).

- Orwell's concept of the 'novel writing machines' (*1984*), which provided pornography for the Proles, came about through some guess work and detective work on Orwell's part regarding the 'writings' of 'Frank Richards', which "[were] too vast and too homogenized to be the work of one man" (58). In America, 'pulp fiction' paperbacks, magazines, and post-Code comic books used formulas that rarely deviated from the same plots and characterizations until the graphic novel came into being. Furthermore—other things to infuriate his detractors—Orwell had a keen eye for 'popular' culture: "[He] monitored the rise and fall of the ethnic joke [...]" and "the increasing influence of American [cinema] marketing techniques" [...] on the cultural manners and stereotypes of British culture (58).

- The satirical roots of his dystopian novels were present early in his writing career. Using parody in his review of Eugene Lyon's *Assignment in Utopia*, he reveals his own premonitions and certainties about the fraudulence of Stalinist socialism by translating the Trotsky trials into English terms and conditions, by swapping Right with Left and Left with Right, and by using Winston Churchill as the ambitious despot of Britain. Aided and abetted by a cast of sheep stealers, uber-Capitalists, graffiti propagandists, and a cartel of factory managers, Bishops, and Postal workers engaged in acts of universal sabotage, Churchill brings fanaticism, paranoia, censorship, and a political chicanery to Mother England (60-61).

- For Winston, *Goldstein's book* represents a treatise on revolution and hope. His own suspicions and convictions become articulated through Goldstein. Imagine how crushed he was when O'Brien tells him that *Goldstein's book* was authored by members of the Inner Party, adding that any single individual no longer authors books. Though in *1984* the figure of Goldstein is used to both inspire a rebellion against Big Brother and to arouse anger and hate among Outer Party members towards a perceived enemy, Goldstein may or may not exist and is therefore a virtual character in Orwell's virtual world. Goldstein, in fact, is based on Leon Trotsky, who found 'war and revolution inseparable.' Hitchens casts Goldstein not so much as social revolutionist but as a figure opposed to the war. And as the war Oceania is waging against Eastasia one moment and then Eurasia the next, like the virtual existence of Goldstein, the war is a virtual war. Though Orwell was not a follower of Trotsky, his Trotsky—Goldstein—is the witness to what Hitchens refers to as " 'the midnight of the century'—the clasping of hands between Hitler and Stalin" (63).

- Winston argues with O'Brien that the Proles will eventually rise up, defeat, and "tear [the Party] into pieces." O'Brien quickly dismisses the Proles as nothing but animals. In his own experiences in the Prole district, Winston encounters nothing from the Proles except filth, drunken degradation, stupefying indifference, and little historical memory of anything worthwhile for Winston to use in his own understanding of why things are the way they are. So why does he champion them as an instrument of salvation? Even when he is being tortured, Winston is a believer in the 'spirit' of the Proles? Hitchens suggests that the Proles may be modeled after the Polish during WWII:

"[The] Polish army fought as long as the French, against far heavier odds, nor did the Polish change sides in the middle of the war. It seems, in fact, that this nation of thirty million souls, with its long tradition of struggle against the Emperor and the Tsar, deserves its independence in any world where national sovereignty is possible. Like the Czechs, the Poles will rise again, though the old feudal life, with the private chapel in the cattle grounds and gamekeeper who is the baron's foster-brother, is vanished forever" (65).

The reference to the 'chapel', 'cattle grounds', 'gamekeeper' and the 'baron's foster brother' are the kinds of parallel sentiments Orwell loads into *1984* and reflect Winston's obsession with the past that has vanished under Big Brother.

- The frequent show trials of 'traitors' of Big Brother, broadcast on the ubiquitous Telescreens throughout Oceania, are modeled after the show trials of Spanish Catalan revolutionary leaders and the Soviet 'frame ups' (67). In the novel and in Michael Radford's excellent film adaptation, Winston and all of Oceania are surrounded by Telescreens broadcasting the 'confessions' of beaten-down Party 'traitors' Aaronson and his accomplices. According to Hitchens, Orwell and his wife were targeted for possible imprisonment and trial, as they were both accused of being 'Trotskyites' (67). The seed of *thoughtcrime* was planted in this potential, as Orwell points out that "I am not guilty of any definite act…but I was guilty of Trotskyism" (68). At he end of the novel, Winston has been 'cleansed ' of his sins against Big Brother, wanders about Oceania and sees his own 'confessions' broadcast for everyone to see.

- The interrogation process and torture of Winston Smith has its progenitor in George Kopp, a brigade commander of Orwell's in Barcelona. For his efforts against fascist Spain, Kopp was imprisoned, tortured, and was forced into close confinement with rats (68).

- The public manner in which the conflict in Spain was characterized and propagandized washed away the fascist tenets of Spanish authority and inspired Orwell to explore the nature of subjective and objective truth, which is at the heart of *doublethink*:

"The implied objective of this line of thought is a nightmare world in which the Leader, or some ruling clique, controls not only the future but the *past*. If the leader says of such and such an event, 'It never happened'…well it never happened. If he says that two and two are five, well then two and two are five" (69-70).

- In the novel when Winston not only accepts the possibility that 'two and two are five' after being tortured nearly beyond endurance, Orwell takes it a step further, as O'Brien reminds Winston that two and two can be anything the Party wants it to be, utterly annihilating both objective and subjective states of language: The truth becomes a subjective lie; the lie is spread as an objective truth, throwing out truth altogether (The Latin root 'ject' means to 'throw').

- Another of Orwell's detractors, Raymond Williams—a teacher at Cambridge University— accuses him of hyperbole and 'blueprinting' the terror Orwell creates in

1984. Williams all but accuses Orwell of inventing 'the Proles' as a way to debilitate 'the masses' (71). Hitchens frets about Williams inability to understand satire, but bristles against Williams' use of 'bureaucratese' to characterize his objections to Orwell, which Hitches funds 'drab' and vague. Orwell's own "Politics and the English Language" condemns the language of obfuscation: "Political language—and with variations this is true of all political parties, from Conservatives to Anarchists—*is designed to make lies sound truthful and murder respectable, and to give an appearance of solidity to pure wind*" (71), [Italics mine].

- Hitchens is infuriated when England's *New Left Review*, inspired by Williams, claims that *1984* will never amount to more than a 'curio'—a relic of imagination only and that Orwell's brand of totalitarianism is impossible. Hitchens goes on to detail three examples of Orwell's greatest fears realized—all post fascist Spain, post Nazi Germany, post Stalin-era totalitarianism:

    1) North Korea, with its cult of personality ('Dear Leader' = 'Big Brother'); its ceaseless broadcasting of propaganda, such as bulletins apprising North Koreans of their "radiant future"; a "society endlessly mobilized for war" (NK possesses the world's third largest military); its geographical, media, and political isolation from the rest of the world; "a pervasive atmosphere of scarcity and hunger"—in sum, the nearly identical twin to Orwell's Oceania (73-75).

    2) According to Hitchens, the transformation of Rhodesia into Zimbabwe by dictator Robert Mugabe in 1980 best resembles Orwell's *Animal Farm,* where, like 'Napoleon', once winning power, Mugabe anoints himself with absolute authority, practices widespread corruption, organizes fascist youth brigades, practices the tenets of a personality cult and megalomania, and instructs his henchmen to destroy his enemies through state-sponsored terrorism and death squads (76-77).

    3) In 1998, Barcelona conferred upon Orwell and the revolutionary leader, Andreas Nin, a recognition through atonement for the fascist atrocities that occurred in Catalonia during Franco's brutal reign: "Catalonia has freed itself from the fascism against which Orwell fought, and to which it never submitted. It has done so by means of a long and dignified struggle […] and has rescued its history and its records from years of falsification and denial" (77). To Hitchens this is the acknowledgement that fascism is not fiction and that its remedy is for good men and women to recognize the past and the sins of an authority unchecked, and, most importantly, to pursue the path of democracy [Brackets—mine].

3. Orwell and the Right

- In *1984*, one gets the impression from Winston's interaction with characters like Symes and Parsons, both of whom have a fanatical obsession with Big Brother orthodoxy, that Winston despised this kind of purity and allegiance (Symes' destruction of words and Parsons unthinking loyalty to everything Big Brother, which culminates in his thankfulness that his own children betrayed him to the *Thought Police*). In accepting

Julia's promiscuity he rails against the sexual repression that pervades Oceania. Yet, early on in his life, Orwell's intolerance of homosexuals and abortion points to the traditional values that informed this contradiction possibly rooted in a poor, parochial upbringing. Eventually, his experiences somewhat disposed him of his prejudices, made him mistrust authority and bureaucracy, and fed his own obsession with liberty and equality. Hitchens goes on to remark about Orwell's hatred of despotism and collectivism—respective boilerplate tenets of fascism and communism. If Orwell prefers any political philosophy, it is socialism, because, as Hitchens paraphrases one of Orwell's heroes, politician Aneurin Bevan: "[The] Socialism movement is the only movement in human history that sought to attain power only to give it away" (81-82).

• The paradox of *1984* is that Orwell framed his terrorist state around English Socialism (*Ingsoc*). Hitchens, however, infers that Orwell's use of *Ingsoc* as a political framing device is one that reminds readers that even an altruistic movement may suffer from authoritarianism and bureaucracy. Indeed, *The Inner Party* suffocates the masses with its regimentation, unwritten laws and regulations, the absence of *habeas corpus*, and the perversion of language, which cannot verify thought and reality (82).

• Villified by some in the popular press for 'attacking' the Labour Party, Orwell defends himself by writing that *1984* is meant to reveal "the perversions to which a centralized economy is liable and which have already been partly realized in Communism and fascism, [and that] totalitarianism, *if not fought against*, could triumph anywhere" (85), [Italics—Orwell; single quotes—mine].

• The concept of perpetual war is explored in *1984*, specifically in *Goldstein's book*. This has been realized through 'the Troubles' in Ireland, the various conflicts in the Mideast and Africa, and the 'war on terror' itself, to name a few. As economies and national securities are partially built on arms manufacturing and distribution, perpetual war is proliferate in carnage, in profit, and in the manipulation of the masses through fear. Add to this the question of what to do with unemployed, poor, politically malleable men, as well as the arguable natural aggression of the male species, and we have a casserole of causes nurturing the reality of perpetual wars.

• Orwell's insight grew from his thoughts on the Cold War (a term which he coined) and, before that, his distrust of the Soviet Union when it was an ally with the West against Nazi Germany. Specifically, theorizing that perpetual war must feed off the concept of the *unconquerable*, Orwell's 'wars' in *1984* have no beginning and no end. At any given time Oceania can be at war with Eurasia and then Eastasia, and no one is wise to the deception or dare question the whims of war of the Party, as civic dissent is a *thoughtcrime*. The great irony is that while territories are unconquerable, individuals can be defeated. O'Brien's dismantling of Winston puts to rest Winston's belief that somehow the human spirit will rise and defeat Big Brother. In order for war to proliferate, the will and conscience of individuals must not.

- Hitchens reflects on James Burnham's influence on Orwell (93), who proffers this ugly truth: Regarding nuclear threat, "[The] kind of world-view, the kind of beliefs, and the social structure that would probably prevail in a State which was once *unconquerable* and in a permanent state of 'cold war' with its neighbors" are the ideological ingredients of perpetual war (86). On the brink of nuclear annihilation during The Cuban Missile Crisis, the West and the Soviet Union recognized the concept of the 'unconquerable' through *mutually assured destruction* (M.A.D.), [Italics—Orwell].

- The US and Soviet Union fashioned military doctrines recognizing M.A.D. as an international policy, therefore perpetuating a preference for 'cold war' over outright war (Italics—mine). When the Cold War ended, the theatre of perpetual war shifted peripherally to Africa, the Balkans and the Mideast.

- Hitchens asserts that the threat of nuclear annihilation by either one of the two superpowers was "used to petrify and immobilize dissent" (87).

- With perpetual war comes a perpetual war economy. *1984* presents a rubblescape of horrendous living conditions as a result of the Oceania's war economy. This is a singular vindication for Orwell, as it alludes to the dissolution of the Soviet Bloc nations, whose withering poverty made necessary the end of the Cold War. The Soviet Union could not survive a perpetual cold war, which was brought about by a ceaseless arms race with the United States. It was just a matter of which country would wither first. The Soviets blinked, the United States prevailed, the map of Europe was redrawn, the conditions of East Germany, in particular, demonstrated the bankruptcy of a centralized bureaucracy and the paranoid police state apparatus, wars broke out in the Balkans, and the United States brokered an economic détente with China so it could turn its attention to solidifying its position as the world's only military and economic superpower. Yet, this was no 'victory'; no nation was conquered. It could be argued that both were destabilized and remain so. Corruption prevails in Russia, and a return to hard line Communism is on the rise. The United States has a crumbling infrastructure, bankrupted cities, a declining middle class, and an obsession with fear and security in its war on terror, which is the new 'perpetual war' (87-88).

- For Orwell (and Hitchens), the Cold War also meant the distortion of history through the perpetuation of lies, a theme explored through Winston's obsession with Jones, Rutherford and Aaronson—alleged traitors to Big Brother. When Winston confronts O'Brien with the truth, O'Brien shows Winston a picture of these Brotherhood conspirators, tosses it in the 'memory hole' (fire), and assures Winston that they are just a hallucination. According to Hitchens, Orwell crusaded against the lie that German soldiers murdered 10,000 men of the Polish officer corps in Latyn during World War II. The Soviet lawyers at Nuremburg assured a war-exhausted world that Germany was to blame. The objections of Orwell and others were met with indifference. Hitchens believes this indifference was fueled by the West's unwillingness to 'heat up' the Cold War. In 1990, the Russian Federation admitted culpability to this war crime (88).

- Another incrimination against those who were reluctant to 'offend' a former war ally, the West's attitude towards Orwell's *Animal Farm* fueled its censorship and confiscation of the Ukrainian edition, for which Orwell wrote the foreword. Ukraine had suffered much under the Nazis and Stalin's political purges and agricultural policies, the latter bringing about a nation-wide famine. The survivors of this famine "were able to decipher the meaning of the pigs (and of the name Napoleon) without any undue difficulty, a task of interpretation that had defeated conservatism's most deft and subtle literary critic" (92). However, most of the copies were seized by the American military authorities in Germany and eventually turned over to the Red Army for destruction (92). In this way, *Animal Farm* becomes part of the inspiration and ideological blueprint for *Goldstein's book*.

- A major inspiration for the monolithic themes in *Goldstein book*, and perhaps for the intellectual cynicism of O'Brien, was James Burnham, an American intellectual, reformed anti-Communist, and a "chief theorist of the idea of America as an empire" (93). In analyzing Burnham's rhetorical style, Hitchens deduces Burnham to be a cheerleader, or at the very least, a reluctant admirer of Stalin and the dark ethos of similar 'great men' [Single quotes—Burnham].

    As a columnist for William Buckley's *National Review*, Burnham cautioned the West of a 'Third World War' based on its struggle against Communism. In his book, *The Managerial Revolution*, Burnham infers that justice and civil manner are subjective and that a "rising class and new order of society have got to break through old moral codes just as they must break through old economic and political institutions" (96). Winston's vague remembrances of a better world inform his hatred of 'the new social order' of Big Brother—an order of monstrous decay, despair, and suffering. Hitchens takes Burnham to task for his early admiration of Nazism and his "overestimation" of Stalin. Even before Stalin was assailed as a mass murderer, Orwell had predilections to future terror: "The Russian regime will either democratize itself, or it will perish. The huge, invincible, everlasting slave empire of which Burnham appears to dream will not be established, or, if established, will not endure because slavery is no longer a stable basis for human society"(96). A careful reading of those chapters where O'Brien tortures and 'interviews' Winston reveals O'Brien's doctrinaire mindset, which reflects Burnham's devotion to *realpolitik* in the name of empire and survival. All moral codes and allusions to justice are reduced to quaint notions, outright delusions, or the harsh, implacable truth of the Darwinian polemic—in this case, only the powerful survive.

- In the year 1984, when the novel *1984* had its 'commemorative' touchstone moment, conservative critics of the novel recalibrated their objections by comparing the novel's 'outing' of totalitarianism by Orwell to their own dismissal of Franklin D. Roosevelt's National Recovery Act and The Tennessee Valley Authority as nothing more than governmental enabling of a Depression Era mentality to persist, ultimately leading to a permanent nanny state (100). Hitchens takes Norman Podheratz—then editor of *The Commentary*—to task for attacking Orwell personally by raising his early views on homosexuality, and misrepresenting Orwell as a nuclear hawk by taking his words out of context. While Podheratz misquotes Orwell by asserting that he believes in the wisdom of a centralized 'Great Power', Hitchens clarifies Orwell's actual opinion, which was that this 'Great Power' construct can occur only "if we fail to bring a Western Union into being" (100). He adds "that a socialist United States of Europe seems to me the only worthwhile political objective today"(100). Indeed, an elementary reading of *1984* would reveal Orwell's disdain of centralized and bureaucratized authority. Hitchens calls the attempt by conservatives to bring him into their corner a form of "body snatching" and concludes that Orwell may have had some socially conservative leanings, which he often worked out of his system through reasoning; however, in terms of politics, he was a socialist, making his 'body of work' one that cannot be snatched by critical revisionists (102).

4. Orwell and America

• Even though Orwell never visited America, it was not far from his criticisms, some of which surprised Hitchens. Hitchens believes that the American Revolution "is the only model revolution humanity has left to it" (104); whereas, Orwell finds America to be vulgar, crass, violent and obsessed with empire. He did believe the English language in America had more life to it than its stodgy British counterpart. Orwell contrasted the abject cruelty of American popular literature with the proper British way of classic male confrontations: In England, when a man knocks another man down, he will wait or even help his opponent to his feet; in America the victor will jump on his face (106-107). This is not very far from the image O'Brien gives to Winston of what the future of humanity looks like: a boot forever stomping on a human face.

• Like so many things about Orwell, there are apparent contradictions to his sympathies. His appreciation or denigration of America was built around collisions of untested perceptions. In describing the path of the typical hero of a British novel, the hero would account for what it is like to be English with all of the social pressures, family ties, history, and job responsibilities bearing down on character. In contrast, the American hero was free from these considerations and distraction, free to charge down the path of the hero with barely an obstruction in the way of a wild destiny that defined America itself as a land boundlessness and heroes with no strings attached (106). In *1984* Winston is hardly the America-type hero. He is beaten down, annoyed by the smallest detail of his squalid life, mistrustful of everyone, and is physically inert, ill, and in pain most of the time. Whatever action exists it is in his imagination and in his intellectual effort to come to terms with his despair. He is bound by his surroundings and is a kind of a marionette with steel cables restricting him from action...until he meets Julia. This is the encounter that brings him out of himself and closest to anything that represents an American novelist's motif for change and action. But Orwell shared with America a "revulsion from Stalin" and communism and had an admiration for "the immense technological superiority of the Americans, their understanding for what is and what is not impressive, [and] their intolerance of what is amateurish generally" (107).

• Hitchens locates Orwell's own literary antipathy toward America after World War II. This is where he may have refined his feelings about living in a democratic society occupied by an Allied force. Except for African American soldiers, he and others found American troops ill mannered. He was at the same time ashamed that the British soldier made far less than his American counterpart, putting into focus the idea that it was not just the poor American who fought the Nazis but the middle class (107). This dichotomy may have inspired the idea behind *Big Brother's* uber-loyal, professional army that did the nasty work of the *Party* and the *Thoughtpolice*. A loyalty paid for is more devoted and productive that soldiers conscripted from the lower ranks of society.

• In contrast, Orwell admired American writers like Mark Twain, Jack London, F. Scott Fitzgerald, Herman Melville, Henry James an others who defined and refined the American story—from social and class realism (Fitzgerald, James) to wild naturalism (London); whether through myth and invention (Twain) or hard reality and suffering (Steinbeck). In one critical occasion he even criticized the beloved Charles Dickens for disparaging America (110-111).

• To Hitchens, Orwell's lack of desire to visit America was a lost opportunity. Through the prodding of his friends, Orwell considered a visit to the American South, to write about life in Dixie (111). This climate would have been better for him, as there was also medicine in America not yet available in Europe that would treat his tuberculosis. By then, however, he was in his last days and was unable to come to the states. Hitchens lamented what Orwell would have seen in Mississippi and what he would have written (113). One of the great visions Winston Smith has prior to and during the recess from his torture was the vision of *The Golden Country*. Prompted by O'Brien, Winston is led to believe that there is a better place than this dilapidated land and time. As *1984* is a book of the search for murdered memories, Orwell's love of England's green spaces and country and America's vast boundless beauty may have played into this vision, making the denial of it as a possibility all the more crushing to Winston and the reader.

5. Orwell and "Englishness": *The Antinomies of St. George*

• Hitchens locates in Orwell something that citizens of free and progressive nations fear: the erosion and devolution of that nation's spirit and momentum. In *1984* Winston is searching for the past glories of England, hoping these were not just imagined but actually existed. This would give some form to his protest regarding *Big Brother*. Badgering drunks in Prole pubs to remember the past, and begging O'Brien to give credence to some form of revolt that has historical precedent, Winston cannot frame his own reality around any hope and must face the future without a past to validate it. Hitchens finds the blur of retrospection in Orwell's own contemplation of British history. His indifference to the Crown and the waning British Empire, his dismissal of Wales, and his prescience regarding the resurgence of Scottish nationalism, all deflate the "Englishness" of Orwell's Britain (116-118).

• As for the natural beauty and tranquility of England, Orwell wrote about the vanishing idyll in his *Homage to Catalonia*, evoking and lamenting an England asleep in the bosom of its own nostalgia, its natural grandeur, and the small details of its quaint countenance: "The railway cuttings smothered in wild flowers, the deep meadows where great shining horses browse and meditate, the slow moving streams […], the larkspurs in the cottage gardens, […]—all sleeping the deep, deep sleep of England, from which I sometimes fear that we shall never wake unless jerked out of it by the roar of bombs" (120). He evokes this fear throughout *1984* by painting with the ugliest and grayest tones possible an England reduced to rubble, its citizens in constant fear of daily bombings *(steamers),* perpetual war, economic destitution, and the elevation of permanent social paranoia. Winston's search for the artifacts of a better world is confined to Charrington's junk shop and the apartment he unknowingly leases from the head of the *Thoughtpolice.* Even Charrington plays into Winston's lamentations, knowing the further Winston falls into the rabbit hole of hope that a better world will triumph over *Big Brother*, the more devastating Winston's defeat will be. Yet, Orwell equips Charrington with a touch of the sentimental when he instructs one of his mindless *Thoughtpolice* to pick up the pieces of Winston's smashed paperweight, suggesting that power has its own share of regret. In Michael Radford's faithful adaptation of *1984*, Charrington, played with icy stoicism by Cyril Cusack, often betrays this stoicism with the sentimental expressions of a regretful patriarch. He knows and feels sympathy for Winston's lamentations, but is too doctrinaire to deviate from the eventual consequences of Winston's *thoughtcrime* he must prosecute. The look on Cyril Cusack's 'Charrington' betrays the disappointment he has with Winston for being so stupid and careless to be duped into hope. As a result, Winston's "Englishness" becomes fully degraded and turned into a delusion to be avoided.

• This dichotomy of "Englishness" carries over into Orwell's thoughts on religion, specifically the Anglicanism of the English church. While Orwell has an appreciation for its enduring history and a studied familiarity with its literature and architecture, he dismisses the supernatural authority of Christianity as propaganda, especially the "Roman Catholic form" (122), going so far as to satirize the Bible as rejected by a 'book-wallah' (itinerant peddler) in his *Burmese Days*—"What can it be that is in this black book? Some evil undoubtedly" (123).

• It was given to Anthony Powell, Orwell's friend, to make funeral arrangements for him, which consisted of odd references to scripture and peculiar secular ritual artifacts. "George Orwell's funeral service was one of the most harrowing I have ever attended," remarked Powell (124). This carries over into *1984* and Winston's bitter remembrances of his wife, Katherine, who was inclined toward blind religious belief and for whom Winston's memory remains mystifyingly purgatorial and unresolved. [The dark memory of Katherine reveals a harrowing conceit towards woman in general that betrays Orwell's elegant mind, I believe.]

• There were specific idiosyncrasies to Orwell's "Englishness": [He] defended the coloured subjects of the Empire at home and abroad. […]; Orwell wanted the whole colonial racket wound up. […]; Orwell thought the English were too scared to breed enough, and keenly wished to become a father himself […]; Orwell thought the English were too passive and placid, and reserved a particular dislike for policemen"(125). Hitchens reminds us that Orwell was ambivalent towards his own "Englishness," particularly in regard to his "kith and kin" (126). This dislike for police and uncertainty towards family bleed into *1984*. The cruelty of the *thoughtpolice* and the entire martial superstructure of *Oceania* unnerve Winston, while the themes of anti-family, anti-sex, and his own memories of a frigid, brainwashed wife vex his memories of an "Englishness" when love, family and fealty were whole and possible.

• *1984* is about many things having to do with Orwell's thoughts and his hatred of fascism and totalitarianism. In turn, these feelings and his experiences reveal much about patriotism itself, which is often confused with nationalism—the very parent of fascism. Orwell once compared fascism and democracy to "Tweedle Dum and Tweedle Dee, the latter being polluted by the "stupidity of Conservatives," consequently making Britain nationalistic and not "worth fighting for" (127). His wartime experience made Orwell regret his comparison and he subsequently confessed in an apology to readers in an essay in *The Partisan Review*: "I don't share the average English intellectual's hatred of his own country and am not dismayed by a British victory. *I hate to see England either humiliated or humiliating anybody else.* […] I want to think that the class distinctions and imperialist exploitation of which I am ashamed would not return" (127-128), [Italics—Hitchens].

• In *1984*, Orwell draws fresh images of England for Winston, alluding to the mythic *Golden Country* that beckons Winston's deliverance from the horrors of *Big Brother*. The closest he comes to this idyll is the forest area where he and Julia make love, not knowing that the *Thoughtpolice* are snapping photos of them having sex, these photos eventually to be distributed by the Party's *Pornosec Division* for the titillation of the *Proles*. The class distinctions eradicating any semblance of "Englishness" are further pulled apart by class *realpolitik*: The *Thoughtpolice* (Inner Party class), *Pornosec* (Outer Party labor class), and the *Proles* ('animals' according to O'Brien). All work against each other to restore, redeem, or even remember what was once a glorious, fertile, and quaint England.

• According to Hitchens, "Orwell as a writer was forever taking his own temperature. If the thermometer registered too high or too low, he took measures to correct matters" (128).

• Just as Orwell could be critical of something as fundamental as the metric system—he found that it lacked a visual representation of the objects being measured: a 'quart' is more visual than a 'litre', for example—so, too, "was his attention to the smallest inflections of words and language…" (130). His essay, "Politics and the English Language," is a plea for clarity and a polemic against "windy prose" and propaganda. Orwell believed that English would eventually become the international language and longed to keep it "unpolluted" by "blather and falsification" (131). This internationalism Orwell dreamed about is located in his politics of revolt, possibly believing that English can simultaneously be used and abused for political intent. Proof of this lies in *1984*, with the motif of language distortion and destruction a primary force in Oceania. The language of *Newspeak* is a linguistic contraption that reduces languages generally in order to eliminate the language of rebellion specifically. The goal of *Big Brother* is to advance *IngSoc*—English Socialism—through language as the reductive expression of all of its citizens to essentially 'unthink'.

• As the bucolic England of Orwell's time holds a place in is heart, especially his love of animals, he exploits the animal idyll in no small measure as a way to explain Stalinism in *Animal Farm*. One must recognize as a result of his totalitarian allegory that he is not a dreamy romantic when it comes to a simple love of nature. He knows that his own "Englishness" in this regard is a realization that those who work in nature—mostly rustics and agriculturalists—put up with nature as a way to make ends meet. "The fact is that those who really have to deal with nature have no cause to be in love with it" (132). Orwell hated pigs but loved dogs, and to push his allegory to its extremes, the 'conditioning' of Napoleon's dogs into SS-type bloodthirsty enforcers means jettisoning his affections for the sake of the narrative. The death of Boxer—the large but gentle horse of Manor Farm—nearly brings tragic force to the allegory, banishing any romantic affectations Orwell may possess in his "Englishness" (136). Except for the allusions to the *Golden Country*, the near absence of nature in *1984*, affirms that Oceania is little more than a nation-state gulag.

- At the center of Orwell's rebellion that is informed by some kind of "Englishness" is his respect for various English writers, like Rudyard Kipling, Thomas Rainsborough, Tom Paine, and Milton. Hitchens: "His favourite text of justification was Milton's line—'by the known rules of ancient liberty'—the English tradition that has had to be asserted against British authorities time and again" (138). In *1984* Winston has an encounter with Ampleforth who has been tasked to help 're-write' British literature so it conforms to unwritten Party doctrine (Single quotes—mine). Working on a "definitive collection of Kipling poems" (138), Ampleforth despairs that he cannot use 'God' to rhyme with 'rod' (as there is no concept of God in *Oceania**). Ampleforth complains that the failure of the English language is that it doesn't have enough rhymes—as if that is the real reason why *The Party* is accelerating its decrepitude. Winston's recurring dream of *The Golden Country* ends with him waking up with "the word 'Shakespeare' on his lips" (139). In that one stunning remembrance, Orwell recognizes the most vital part of "Englishness."

*There is great irony here, as Winston realizes in the end that the fourth maxim of the Party is *God Is Power*—the final reference to the language of *doublethink*.

6. Orwell and the Feminists: The Difficulty with Girls

- Hitchens writes of Orwell's difficulty with women—another chink in Orwell's armor that informs a peculiar misogyny. This may have stemmed from being raised by hard parents, his humiliating experiences at prep school, and his own self-image as "unappetizing" to the opposite sex. "The small Eric Blair was compelled to confront the idea of obscenity and indecency long before he has any concept of love or sex, let alone the relationship between the two" (143). Hitchens theorizes that he resigned from his post in Burma partly because of his discomfort with 'native women' and not just his "revulsion against imperialism" (143). He loathed the cultural repression of the Burmese people in general, and Burmese women in particular, therefore creating a dichotomy for his own views on feminism. In terms of physical beauty, Orwell gravitated toward appreciating male beauty, suggesting a certain level of homoeroticism, or making Orwell a practitioner of the "mass narcissism" of many men, who, if not homosexual, considered women "subordinate" (147). In *1984*, Winston's antipathy towards Katherine, his initial impressions of Julia ("I hate her"), and the elevation of the elegance of a woman's servitude and ignorance esteemed in his view of the singing Prole woman ("She is beautiful"), suggests a fixed attitude towards women. "Women are by no means invisible in Orwell's travelogue, but they occur as wives or daughters or young people caught in domestic drudgery" (147).

- Feminist Deidre Beddoe: "Orwell's awareness of class divisions in society went along with his lack of understanding of gender divisions" (47). Beddoe claims that Orwell's female characters rarely exhibit any intellectual qualities. Hitchens peruses Orwell's literary account of women without much to say in defense of Orwell, and reminds us that in *1984*, Julia dozes off during Winston's reading of the "dangerous" *Goldstein book*. However, in defense of Orwell, Hitchens reminds us that the women in his adult life were "tough-minded" and intelligent, and that Orwell regretted the way he treated his first wife, Eileen O'Shaughnessy, and was "wordless upon her death" (149).

- Let me remind the student that Julia is much more than what she seems, even to critics of Orwell and *1984*. She is the one character who the *Thought Police* cannot break psychologically by appealing to her deepest irrational fear, unless the fear of having a partial lobotomy is on the menu of irrational fears. While Winston gives Julia up in *Room 101*, we do not know what happened to Julia in that room, if anything. When they meet in the *Chestnut Tree Café*, Julia admits to betraying him immediately, but Orwell's one reference to the scar on her forehead, behind which is the frontal lobe, suggests she would not be able to remember anything of the sort. In short, in this reader's opinion, they couldn't get to Julia. Orwell also gives Julia a conviction Winston readily abandons when, at the Ministry of Truth, O'Brien asks him if he is willing to give up everything and everyone (including Julia) for *The Brotherhood*. Julia immediately says no to this, fearlessly, right in front of O'Brien, which jars Winston into recanting his willingness to do absolutely anything for *The Brotherhood*. Whatever this motif is, intentional or not, Orwell redeems his misogyny for the sake of a love that transcends the horror these two characters experience. I would like to think that this is at least one redeeming feature of *1984*.

- Or is it love? Hitchens seems to think that Orwell's conflicted opinion of women resides in his attitude towards women and sex. Orwell's objection is against women who have "lost [their] sex, become shriveled and/or mannish" (150). Hitchens believes this attitude is wrapped up in some kind of virtue having to do more with his attitude against abortion, or that sexlessness is an affront to nature. This attitude informs *1984*. Through Winston's bitter remembrance of Katherine, Orwell emphasizes the sexlessness and wifely drudgery that reduces women to "invisible" characters in his narratives. Yet, even in this point, Orwell seems to have a more refined sensitivity towards women than the class lout. In his reference to Orwell's Gordon Comstock in *Keep the Aspidistra Flying*, his realization that the women he has impregnated is someone more than a one night stand after he considers what is growing in her womb. Comstock comes to terms with something more human than he is (he is a lout), realizing his connection to another life and not an inconvenience. As a result, Hitchens suggests that Orwell's stand on abortion has more to do with the natural beauty of a new human life than abortion as birth control (151-153).

In a strange way, the birthing process itself is embedded in the interrogation scene in *1984* with O'Brien 'delivering' Winston through a difficult 'labor' (torture), bringing Winston into the 'new world' of *Big Brother*. After being tortured on the rack, O'Brien cleans—'baptizes'—Winston, nourishes him back to health, and prepares him for the puberty of patriarchal reflection and adoration before sending him out to the cruel world, represented by *Room 101*, to an inconsequential life. As awful as Winston's experience is, Orwell will not 'abort' him (Single quotes—mine).

• Hitchens struggles with Orwell's notion of a gentle patriarchy built around a firm but loving father figure. On one hand, he defends Orwell for abhorring the gender "divisions of labor" and "the tyranny of domestic relations"; on the other hand, Hitchens believes Orwell's understanding of the war between the sexes is part of a natural order, justifying his "minimal" hypocrisy (154). This is evident throughout *1984* in many subtexts: *Big Brother's* policy of *ArtSem* in regard to sex and family, the *Anti-Sex League's* prohibition against sex and marriage, Winston's hatred for his wife Katherine, his deep regret for abandoning his mother and sister when he was much younger, his willingness to bed a Prole woman who repulsed him, his hate/love for Julia, his affections for the matriarchal singing Prole laundry woman, his 'demonstrated affections' for O'Brien—his patriarchal 'father' figure—after he is tortured beyond endurance, and finally, his love for *Big Brother* after he is totally broken and reassembled (Single quotes—mine).

7. 'The List'

• Hitchens refutes the accusations of some that Orwell secretly compiled a 'blacklist' of leftist subversives, contradicting the very mind that was "essentially 'right' about the three great issues of fascism, Stalinism and Empire"—a mind "enabled to be 'right' by a certain insistence on intellectual integrity and independence" (155). Noting the abnormalities in the accusations, Hitchens clarifies that it was Orwell's guess that the 'defeatist' intellectuals of England had no real loyalty to political factions and would sell out in the event of a dictatorship (157), noting in Orwell's essay in a 1942 issue of *The Partisan Review* how willingly intellectuals of the Vichy government in France were ready to collaborate with the Nazis (157). For this, some contemporary critics condemned Orwell for being no better than the *Thought Police* weaning Winston to be a willing subversive against himself. On the contrary, Orwell railed against the British Communist Party for condemning a British naval blockade of Germany and "the sorts of intellectual [—] who could transfer their allegiance from one despotic regime to another" (158).

• In *1984*, the children of Winston's neighbor, Parsons, denounce their father as a *Thought Criminal* and he is arrested. In a bleak holding cell of the *Ministry of Truth*, Parsons confesses to Winston how proud he is of this denunciation and admits that he was unaware of his own betrayal of *Big Brother*, calling *Thoughtcrime* "insidious." This is perhaps conjured from Orwell's experiences in Spain where denunciation, informing and betrayal were a Soviet strategy to weed out subversives, or 'thought criminals.' One model—Pavlik Morozov, a 14-year-old 'Pioneer' (i.e. Soviet 'boy scout')—had turned in his family to the Soviet police for the offense of hoarding grain (158). Though his neighbors killed him, he remained a martyr to the name of fealty to the Party (Single quote—mine).

• Orwell's objection to the radical left sprung from his revulsion to the doctrinaire, even when it masqueraded as progress against conservatism. "He showed a lifelong hatred for all forms of censorship, proscription and blacklisting," even defending the right of habeas corpus for one with whom he was in total disagreement (159). According to Hitchens it was Orwell's task to convince the radical left and the democratic left that

"Stalinism was a negation of socialism and not a version of it," and that communist sympathizers, some like the writers of *The Daily Worker*, needed to work this out (159). Peppered throughout *1984* are character epithets of *Outer Party* members, like Parsons, Symes and Ampleforth, 'sympathizing' with the goals of *Big Brother* (Single quotes—mine). O'Brien's repudiation of every probing question Winston asks is the prime example of the unequivocal subjugation of the individual mind to the collective will. The icy elegance and lack of rhetorical flourish in Goldstein's book reflects the mechanisms of those who wrote it, namely *The Inner Party*. The super irony is that while *the Book* reveals the truth, the truth matters not.

- To Orwell, Stalinism was a personal threat to his expression as a writer. Communist sympathizers who worked in British publishing and politics threatened to ban and blacklist his books, and nearly saw the suppression of *Animal Farm* at the hands of one member of the British **Ministry of Information** (Boldface mine). Not merely reacting to this personal calamity, Orwell authored a set of safeguards to protect others, specifically British civil servants, regardless of their political views (160). Orwell was one of the first to protest the Soviet occupation of Czechoslovakia and the ethnic cleansing of its German inhabitants. Those intellectuals who denounced Orwell as a traitor to socialism, never mentioned his efforts on their behalf (161).

- In this section, Hitchens goes to great lengths to defend Orwell's alleged trespasses against those he thought were counterproductive to socialist causes, at times pausing to validate some of Orwell's inconsistencies (e.g. his views on homosexuality). On balance, however, Hitchens puts into political and historical context the hypocrisies of his critics, while revealing his passions about human rights and his loathing of anything tyrannical. Hitchens sums up the gist of Orwell's detractors as somewhat trivial and feels history has vindicated Orwell: "[Nobody] suffered or could have suffered from Orwell's private opinion; he said nothing in 'private' that he did not consistently say in public" (167). What this has to do with *1984* requires one to understand the difficulty human nature has in accommodating true revolutionary freedom. Winston wanders the bleak rubblescape of Oceania suspecting that once upon a time humankind had a greater dream than the oppression he and others must endure, only realizing in the end that humans will do terrible things to each other to proffer their own forms of freedom apart from those who they believe are unworthy of those forms.

- One case in particular stands as an affront to Orwell and history itself. Konni Zillacus, a figure of England's Labour Left, described the Soviet zones of East Germany and Poland as "revolutionary democracy, democracy in the primitive and original sense of Abraham Lincoln's great definition of 'government of the people, by the people, and for the people'" (167), [Single quotes Hitchens]. One critic inferred that *1984* was Orwell's wish for the world to end. Criticisms *in extremis* are self- serving. Orwell often maintained that *1984* was not a prophecy, but a warning. Hitchens: "[The Cold War] involved a confrontation with the poisonous illusion that the Soviet system had a claim on the democratic Left. In this essential confrontation, Orwell kept his little corner of the Cold War fairly clean" (169).

8. Generosity and Anger: *The Novels*

- Orwell was uncomfortable with his writing and lamented the fact that he lived in a world where fascism, horror, and the suffering of human beings provoked "an awareness of the enormous injustice and misery in the world, and a guilt-stricken feeling that one ought to be doing something about it" (172). He felt that this urgency prevented him from writing literature that could explore virtues and aesthetics. Perhaps Orwell believed that his works functioned more as historical memoirs and essay narratives than pure literature. Hitchens implies that Orwell's attitude towards his own work is "adolescent," and goes on to say that his early novels, with all their faults, were just "precursors" to *Animal Farm* and *1984*—novels that "are evidence themselves of Orwell's determination to take the risk of fiction at almost any cost" (174). Hitchens suggest that Orwell's two masterpieces may have moved literature itself from 'bourgeois' narratives to a new place of importance and prominence, as they ushered in decades of works by others that were angry **and** literary, as well as absurd and existential. Ideas like the 'master-slave' relationship and the agony of betrayal introduced earlier in *Burmese Days*, become graphic and psychologically institutionalized in *1984*. Yet, despite its status today, Orwell thought his *1984* "a ghastly mess, a good idea ruined"—a confession he made to his friend Anthony Powell (177). However, recognizing Orwell's lapses to racism, homophobia, and misogyny, Hitchens comes to Orwell's defense repeatedly, advocating that present in almost all of his novels is a passion for life, a hatred for injustice, and a deep suspicions of empire.

- In one subtle observation among many, Hitchens points out that "Orwell [often] allowed himself a moment of identification with the overseer as opposed to the underdog" (183). His deference to authority informed his deconstruction of it. In *1984*, as readers, we are trapped in Winston's fixation with the possibilities that O'Brien (overseer) is part of the *Brotherhood* working in concert to topple *Big Brother*. Even when this notion is betrayed, and after Winston is brutally tortured, he defers to O'Brien and embraces the patriarchal tone of O'Brien's assurance that he—Winston—is powerless. Subsequently, Winston is resolved to behave this way. Through this 'identification' we can see the insidiousness of the overseer and contemplate what maladaptive psych-techics construct such authority. In O'Brien's case it is his unyielding will to *Big Brother*, built largely upon the philosophy of defeat, which, except for some motifs regarding Julia, permeates this novel.

- During the period of his book *Coming Up for Air*, "Orwell was fatally divided in his mind over the question of whether war or Nazism presented the greater danger…" (185). In 'civilized' Europe, immediately after The Middle Ages and during the Age of Reformation, war was announced through seasoned diplomats, and the warring sides had time to prepare for what warriors and kings considered the 'noble battle.' Fascism and Nazi Germany ended this and added a dimension to war that no longer alluded to 'honor and sacred homage', replacing it with all-out murder, carnage and genocide that are not easily understood by historians. In *1984*, when Winston reads *Goldstein's book*, he comes to a passage that suggests Hitler lost the war because his persecution of Jews was too irrational for war and therefore distracted him from the war's effort. O'Brien implies that the new centurions of perpetual war will not make that mistake of using war as a personal crusade, as the goal of war is not victory, but power—the more implacable the better. Orwell may be suggesting that in order for the 'righteousness' of the German race to persist, the 'righteousness' that informed their 'master race' ethos, resulting in ethnic cleansing and genocide, had to be eradicated: *Doublethink* at its most frightening. (Single quote—mine):

- Hitchens claims Orwell's first four novels were an "amateur throat clearing" (186). Orwell admitted that "*Animal Farm* was the first book in which I tried, with full consciousness of what I was doing, to fuse political purpose and artistic purpose into one whole" (186). Hitchens celebrates the fable's success on many historic and narrative levels, but faults Orwell for his allegorical blunder in *Animal Farm* by collapsing Lenin and Trotsky into Snowball's character, just as he faults Orwell in *1984* for creating the one dimensional dichotomy of *Big Brother* and *Emmanuel Goldstein*. If *Animal Farm* mirrors the 'great Soviet experiment', Hitchens seems to suggest that Lenin and Trotsky contributed individually to the rise of Stalinism. More importantly is Orwell's prescience regarding how Stalinism gave way to corruption and eventually resulted in post-Cold War cronyism and crime that invoked the capitalist ways of the West (187). One must remember that at the end of *Animal Farm*, the pigs and the humans look alike—both walking erect—and farmer Jones has returned to co-manage the farm, even changing its name back to 'Manor Farm.'

- To Hitchens, and to many others, Orwell delivers everything he and his life experiences are about in *1984*. Even his publisher, Frederic Warburg, could barely recover from shock after reading it: "[Here] is a study in pessimism unrelieved, except by the thought that if a man can conceive *1984*, he can also will to avoid it" (188). A close reading of *1984* will bear this out, as well as a new appraisal of Julia's character, in my opinion. However, Hitchens says that "*1984* is more like rage than anger, rage against the dying of the light" (188). A book about "tearing human minds into pieces then putting them back together again in new shapes of your own choosing (O'Brien), (189), borrows this motif and others from Russian novelist, Evgeny Zamyatin (*We*), Fydor Dostoyevsky (*Notes from the Underground*), and the ' great Soviet experiment' itself (*The Five Year Plan, 2+2=5*) (189). Hitchens believes *1984* is the first time an Orwell novel rose to the level of his essays, which have undeniable insight into the growth of totalitarianism in the 20th Century. As mentioned before, when Parsons willingly accepts his guilt, pisses himself in rank fear and humiliation, and is thankful that he was discovered to be a *thoughtcriminal*, he represents the will to be dominated, which Hitchens believes is how much ordinary "humans relish cruelty and war and absolute capricious authority and are bored by humane and civilized pursuits" (191). In terms of Hitchens finding anyone heroic in *1984,* he maintains that, "There will always be Trotskys, Goldsteins and even Winston Smiths, but it must be understood that the odds are overwhelming against them" (191). I believe that it is up to the reader to summon publisher Warburg's belief that if we can conjure this nightmare, we can wake up from it.

9. Deconstructing the Post-modernists: Orwell and Transparency

- Hitchens deconstructs Orwell's insistence on 'plain language' as a way to expose the hypocrisy of intellectuals who covet vagueness and mistake it for profundity. Orwell was particularly keen on making sure that when confronting the abstract and the difficult, he did not fall back on existing dialects, such as jargon and slogans, to delineate the profound. In *1984*, the language of *Newspeak* retards meaning by scaling down its subtleties, abstractions, and its poetry. Symes applauds the 'destruction of words' as a beautiful thing, not because its 'beauty' celebrates simplicity, but because it obliterates the effort it takes to give words meaning and resonance. Hitchens cannot prove, but suspects that for Orwell, "a common language with accepted and mutually understood rules was an indispensible condition for an open democracy" (196).

- *Newspeak* represents a uniformity Orwell fears will infect the future of language. His opening salvo in *1984* foreshadows this fear when Winston writes in his illegal journal, "From the age of uniformity, from the age of solitude, from the age of Big Brother, from the age of doublethink—greetings!" (198).

- The degradation of literature to pornography in *1984* speaks to Orwell's (and Winston's) conjuring of *Oldspeak*, outlawed by Big Brother. This "old speech is organically connected to the ancient truths preserved and transmitted by literature"(198). *Newspeak* is not a search of truth nor is it literature. Orwell's *1984* is his belief in literature itself and its potential, when honestly and clearly realized, to root out the truth through new abstractions that do not conform to worn out dialects but, instead, summon the imagination, even if what is summoned is brutal.

- Skepticism is a healthy tool to measure the universe. Verifiable fact is an affront to skepticism, and as far as fictional literature goes, Hitchens confers upon Orwell a unique viability to his imagination. Hitchens consigns Orwell's detractors to the sarcastic, to those who merely guess at Orwell's intentions, and to those who inveigh against his 'authenticity.' Hitchens believes Orwell transcends his critics' 'vulgar assumptions': "Perhaps Orwell stumbles on the near impossible: the synthesis of the empiricist dialectic" (203)—the collusion of the sensory and the logical. In *1984* Winston rhapsodizes about something gone wrong, something he remembers, something lost, something he is looking for, something that has more value than what the world of *Big Brother* offers, even while his imagination fails to fully assemble truth. However, even under torture, Winston advocates for some sense of truth, a feeling or suspicion of meaning and vindication for the old, more human ways, while O'Brien provides him an icy logic for human annihilation.

- Always for Orwell was the purity of language that cannot tolerate the 'intellectual rot' that distorts a verifiable truth, as language helps us to "penetrate the supposed secrets of authority" (204), even in the form of fiction. Orwell's intellectual honesty makes good on the esteem he has for literature, as most of what happens in *1984* has sobering presence in today's politics and history.

10. In Conclusion

- "Orwell's views have been vindicated by time [...]; [What] he illustrates by his commitment to language as the partner of truth, is that 'views' do not really count; that it matters not what you think, but *how* you think; and that politics are relatively unimportant, while principles have a way of enduring, as do the few irreducible individuals who maintain allegiance to them" (211).

Note: I want to remind teachers and students that I have attempted to use Christopher Hitchens' *Why Orwell Matters* largely in reference to *1984*. Hitchens explores in great detail many of Orwell's major writings, the early novels, and Orwell's life as it is reflected in his works. His book is a loving evocation of Orwell's continuing influence as a political writer and a defense against those who have misunderstood, maligned, or exploited Orwell for questionable purposes.

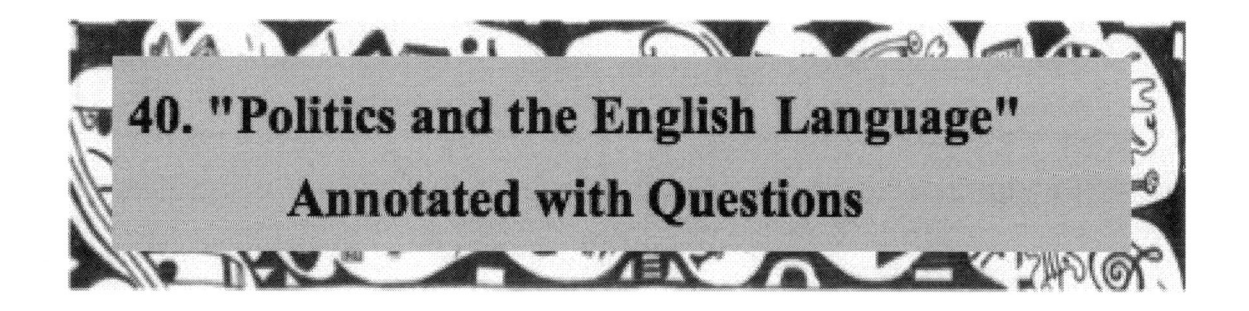

40. "Politics and the English Language" Annotated with Questions

In this landmark essay written in 1946—three years before the publication of *1984*, George Orwell assesses the state of the English language in regard to political misuse and the loss of vibrancy in the language itself. *1984* reflects the extremes of this degeneration through the elimination of language and the subsequent effects of its impact on thinking. His invention, *the Thought Police*, is the ultimate expression of a society made helpless through the perversion and loss of language. With meaningful language purged, the logical affront to authority is *thought*. The novel is a reminder that critical thinking is in direct proportion to the knowledge and use of words: No words, no thoughts; no thoughts, no action; no action, no dissent against that which suppresses thought; and that which suppresses thought may be largely attributed to the deliberate and habitual misuse of language.

In *1984*, where language is muted and rendered inconsequential (*Duckspeak*), the *Thought Police* are now free to arrest citizens for 'actionable' crimes, like *Facecrime* or *Crimespeak*. Orwell warns us that the state of language has a corollary to mass communications and political rhetoric—the former stripped of meaning; the latter bloated with lies, distortions, half-truths and the deceptive spectacle of the abuser composing fear and comforting meaninglessness.

Annotating, raising questions, and providing exercises about Orwell's essay should serve to alert the student and teacher of current abuses of language. One does not have to go far to find examples of the 'politics of language,' nor the infantilizing of language in popular mass media and personal media. Both exploit words for effect rather than meaning, and process a one-way dialogue that seeks no conversation and provides no relevance.

Politics and the English Language
by George Orwell

Most people who bother with the matter at all would admit that the English language is in a bad way, but it is generally assumed that we cannot by conscious action do anything about it. Our civilization is decadent and our language — so the argument runs — must inevitably share in the general collapse. It follows that any struggle against the abuse of language is a sentimental archaism, like preferring candles to electric light or hansom cabs to aeroplanes. Underneath this lies the half-conscious belief that language is a natural growth and not an instrument which we shape for our own purposes.

> **1. What is the nature of our indifference to language? Is there inevitability to language suffering because of other forms of communication, such as images, icons, and the clipped expressions of social media?**
>
> **2. Have our purposes for language changed? Be specific.**

Now, it is clear that the decline of a language must ultimately have political and economic causes: it is not due simply to the bad influence of this or that individual writer. But an effect can become a cause, reinforcing the original cause and producing the same effect in an intensified form, and so on indefinitely. A man may take to drink because he feels himself to be a failure, and then fail all the more completely because he drinks. It is rather the same thing that is happening to the English language. It becomes ugly and inaccurate because our thoughts are foolish, but the slovenliness of our language makes it easier for us to have foolish thoughts. The point is that the process is reversible. Modern English, especially written English, is full of bad habits which spread by imitation and which can be avoided if one is willing to take the necessary trouble. If one gets rid of these habits one can think more clearly, and to think clearly is a necessary first step toward political regeneration: so that the fight against bad English is not frivolous and is not the exclusive concern of professional writers. I will come back to this presently, and I hope that by that time the meaning of what I have said here will have become clearer. Meanwhile, here are five specimens of the English language as it is now habitually written.

> **3. Are our thoughts 'foolish' and 'frivolous' because our lives are foolish and frivolous?**
>
> **4. The habits of 'imitation' are important in early learning. Orwell suggests that imitation leads to bad habits in language. What are these bad habits?**
>
> **5. Why is it as important for all of us, and not just professional writers, to get out of the habit of 'imitation'?**

These five passages have not been picked out because they are especially bad — I could have quoted far worse if I had chosen — but because they illustrate various of the mental vices from which we now suffer. They are a little below the average, but are fairly representative examples. I number them so that I can refer back to them when necessary:

1. I am not, indeed, sure whether it is not true to say that the Milton who once seemed not unlike a seventeenth-century Shelley had not become, out of an experience ever more bitter in each year, more alien *[sic]* to the founder of that Jesuit sect which nothing could induce him to tolerate.

Professor Harold Laski (Essay in Freedom of
Expression)

2. Above all, we cannot play ducks and drakes with a native battery of idioms which prescribes egregious collocations of vocables as the Basic *put up with* for *tolerate*, or *put at a loss* for *bewilder*.

Professor Lancelot Hogben (Interglossia)

3. On the one side we have the free personality: by definition it is not neurotic, for it has neither conflict nor dream. Its desires, such as they are, are transparent, for they are just what institutional approval keeps in the forefront of consciousness; another institutional pattern would alter their number and intensity; there is little in them that is natural, irreducible, or culturally dangerous. But *on the other side*, the social bond itself is nothing but the mutual reflection of these self-secure integrities. Recall the definition of love. Is not this the very picture of a small academic? Where is there a place in this hall of mirrors for either personality or fraternity?

Essay on psychology in Politics (New York)

4. All the 'best people' from the gentlemen's clubs, and all the frantic fascist captains, united in common hatred of Socialism and bestial horror at the rising tide of the mass revolutionary movement, have turned to acts of provocation, to foul incendiarism, to medieval legends of poisoned wells, to legalize their own destruction of proletarian organizations, and rouse the agitated petty-bourgeoise to chauvinistic fervor on behalf of the fight against the revolutionary way out of the crisis.

Communist pamphlet

5. If a new spirit is to be infused into this old country, there is one thorny and contentious reform which must be tackled, and that is the humanization and galvanization of the B.B.C. Timidity here will bespeak canker and atrophy of the soul. The heart of Britain may be sound and of strong beat, for instance, but the British lion's roar at present is like that of Bottom in Shakespeare's *A Midsummer Night's Dream* — as gentle as any sucking dove. A virile new Britain cannot continue indefinitely to be traduced in the eyes or rather ears, of the world by the effete languors of Langham Place, brazenly masquerading as 'standard English'. When the Voice of Britain is heard at nine o'clock, better far and infinitely less ludicrous to hear aitches honestly dropped than the present priggish, inflated, inhibited, school-ma'amish arch braying of blameless bashful mewing maidens!

Letter in Tribune

> ***Before you read on…***
>
> **6. List all the issues of expression in these passages (e.g., double negatives, etc.).**
>
> **7. It would be interesting for students to divide up these examples and re-write them according to what they think the passages mean.**

Each of these passages has faults of its own, but, quite apart from avoidable ugliness, two qualities are common to all of them. The first is staleness of imagery; the other is lack of precision. The writer either has a meaning and cannot express it, or he inadvertently says something else, or he is almost indifferent as to whether his words mean anything or not. This mixture of vagueness and sheer incompetence is the most marked characteristic of modern English prose, and especially of any kind of political writing. As soon as certain topics are raised, the concrete melts into the abstract and no one seems able to think of turns of speech that are not hackneyed: prose consists less and less of *words* chosen for the sake of their meaning, and more and more of *phrases* tacked together like the sections of a prefabricated hen-house. I list below, with notes and examples, various of the tricks by means of which the work of prose-construction is habitually dodged.

> **8. Orwell states that "prose consists less and less of *words* chosen for the sake of their meaning, and more and more of *phrases* tacked together like the sections of a prefabricated henhouse." What does he mean?**

DYING METAPHORS. A newly invented metaphor assists thought by evoking a visual image, while on the other hand a metaphor which is technically 'dead' (e. g. iron resolution) has in effect reverted to being an ordinary word and can generally be used without loss of vividness. But in between these two classes there is a huge dump of worn-out metaphors which have lost all evocative power and are merely used because they save people the trouble of inventing phrases for themselves. Examples are: *Ring the changes on, take up the cudgel for, toe the line, ride roughshod over, stand shoulder to shoulder with, play into the hands of, no axe to grind, grist to the mill, fishing in troubled waters, on the order of the day, Achilles' heel, swan song, hotbed.* Many of these are used without knowledge of their meaning (what is a 'rift', for instance?), and incompatible metaphors are frequently mixed, a sure sign that the writer is not interested in what he is saying. Some metaphors now current have been twisted out of their original meaning without those who use them even being aware of the fact. For example, *toe the line* is sometimes written as *tow the line*. Another example is *the hammer and the anvil*, now always used with the implication that the anvil gets the worst of it. In real life it is always the anvil that breaks the hammer, never the other way about: a writer who stopped to think what he was saying would avoid perverting the original phrase.

> **9. What is the power of metaphor? Why do we complicate the clarity of meaning by utilizing metaphor? When Orwell uses 'prefabricated henhouses' as a metaphor for stale expressions, would he have achieved more clarity by saying, *Prose consists less and less of words chosen for the sake of their meaning, and more and more of phrases that suggest meaning but are too general and overused to mean anything*? If no, why not? Is he suggesting more than that with his metaphor?**

OPERATORS OR VERBAL FALSE LIMBS. These save the trouble of picking out appropriate verbs and nouns, and at the same time pad each sentence with extra syllables which give it an appearance of symmetry. Characteristic phrases are *render inoperative, militate against, make contact with, be subjected to, give rise to, give grounds for, have the effect of, play a leading part (role) in, make itself felt, take effect, exhibit a tendency to, serve the purpose of,* etc., etc. The keynote is the elimination of simple verbs. Instead of being a single word, such as *break, stop, spoil, mend, kill*, a verb becomes a *phrase*, made up of a noun or adjective tacked on to some general-purpose verb such as *prove, serve, form, play, render*. In addition, the passive voice is wherever possible used in preference to the active, and noun constructions are used instead of gerunds (*by examination of* instead of *by examining*). The range of verbs is further cut down by means of the *-ize* and *de-* formations, and the banal statements are given an appearance of profundity by means of the *not un-* formation. Simple conjunctions and prepositions are replaced by such phrases as *with respect to, having regard to, the fact that, by dint of, in view of, in the interests of, on the hypothesis that*; and the ends of sentences are saved by anticlimax by such resounding commonplaces as *greatly to be desired, cannot be left out of account, a development to be expected in the near future, deserving of serious consideration, brought to a satisfactory conclusion,* and so on and so forth.

---

10. Simplify or clarify the following: *render inoperative, militate against, make contact with, be subjected to, give rise to, give grounds for, have the effect of, play a leading part (role) in, make itself felt, take effect, exhibit a tendency to, serve the purpose of, with respect to, having regard to, the fact that, by dint of, in view of, in the interests of, on the hypothesis that, greatly to be desired, cannot be left out of account, a development to be expected in the near future, deserving of serious consideration, brought to a satisfactory conclusion.*

PRETENTIOUS DICTION. Words like *phenomenon, element, individual (as noun), objective, categorical, effective, virtual, basic, primary, promote, constitute, exhibit, exploit, utilize, eliminate, liquidate,* are used to dress up a simple statement and give an air of scientific impartiality to biased judgments. Adjectives like *epoch-making, epic, historic, unforgettable, triumphant, age-old, inevitable, inexorable, veritable,* are used to dignify the sordid process of international politics, while writing that aims at glorifying war usually takes on an archaic colour, its characteristic words being: *realm, throne, chariot, mailed fist, trident, sword, shield, buckler, banner, jackboot, clarion.* Foreign words and expressions such as *cul de sac, ancien regime, deus ex machina, mutatis mutandis, status quo, gleichschaltung, weltanschauung,* are used to give an air of culture and elegance. Except for the useful abbreviations *i. e., e. g.* and *etc.,* there is no real need for any of the hundreds of foreign phrases now current in the English language. Bad writers, and especially scientific, political, and sociological writers, are nearly always haunted by the notion that Latin or Greek words are grander than Saxon ones, and unnecessary words like *expedite, ameliorate, predict, extraneous, deracinated, clandestine, subaqueous,* and hundreds of others constantly gain ground from their Anglo-Saxon numbers[1]. The jargon peculiar to Marxist writing (*hyena, hangman, cannibal, petty bourgeois, these gentry, lackey, flunkey, mad dog, White Guard,* etc.) consists largely of words translated from Russian, German, or French; but the normal way of coining a new word is to use Latin or Greek root with the appropriate affix and, where necessary, the size formation. It is often easier to make up words of this kind (*deregionalize, impermissible, extramarital, non-fragmentary* and so forth) than to think up the English words that will cover one's meaning. The result, in general, is an increase in slovenliness and vagueness.

> **11. Why are the following words 'pretentious':** *Phenomenon, element, individual* **(as noun),** *objective, categorical, effective, virtual, basic, primary, promote, constitute, exhibit, exploit, utilize, eliminate, liquidate*?
>
> **12. Explain Orwell's 'categorical' objections to the following groups of words:**
>
> A. *realm, throne, chariot, mailed fist, trident, sword, shield, buckler, banner, jackboot, clarion.*
>
> B. *epoch-making, epic, historic, unforgettable, triumphant, age-old, inevitable, inexorable, veritable*
>
> C. **What are Orwell's objections to the use of 'foreign' expressions? Could this be a personal bias shaped by his experiences?**

MEANINGLESS WORDS. In certain kinds of writing, particularly in art criticism and literary criticism, it is normal to come across long passages which are almost completely lacking in meaning(2). Words like *romantic, plastic, values, human, dead, sentimental, natural, vitality,* as used in art criticism, are strictly meaningless, in the sense that they not only do not point to any discoverable object, but are hardly ever expected to do so by the reader. When one critic writes, 'The outstanding feature of Mr. X's work is its living quality', while another writes, 'The immediately striking thing about Mr. X's work is its peculiar deadness', the reader accepts this as a simple difference opinion. If words like *black* and *white* were involved, instead of the jargon words *dead* and *living*, he would see at once that language was being used in an improper way. Many political words are similarly abused. The word *Fascism* has now no meaning except in so far as it signifies 'something not desirable'. The words *democracy, socialism, freedom, patriotic, realistic, justice* have each of them several different meanings which cannot be reconciled with one another. In the case of a word like *democracy*, not only is there no agreed definition, but the attempt to make one is resisted from all sides. It is almost universally felt that when we call a country democratic we are praising it: consequently the defenders of every kind of regime claim that it is a democracy, and fear that they might have to stop using that word if it were tied down to any one meaning. Words of this kind are often used in a consciously dishonest way. That is, the person who uses them has his own private definition, but allows his hearer to think he means something quite different. Statements like *Marshal Petain was a true patriot, The Soviet press is the freest in the world, The Catholic Church is opposed to persecution,* are almost always made with intent to deceive. Other words used in variable meanings, in most cases more or less dishonestly, are: *class, totalitarian, science, progressive, reactionary, bourgeois, equality.*

> **13. Find examples of art, film, music or literary criticism and point out those words or expressions that are vague or meaningless. Try to determine what the critic is attempting to say, and provide clearer expressions on his or her behalf.**
>
> **14. Orwell writes that** *"democracy, socialism, freedom, patriotic, realistic, justice; class, totalitarian, science, progressive, reactionary, bourgeois, equality"* **are words that have lost their meaning because they have no distinction or they are used in a dishonest way. Consider each of these words and explain Orwell's criticisms.**

Now that I have made this catalogue of swindles and perversions, let me give another example of the kind of writing that they lead to. This time it must of its nature be an imaginary one. I am going to translate a passage of good English into modern English of the worst sort. Here is a well-known verse from *Ecclesiastes*:

I returned and saw under the sun, that the race is not to the swift, nor the battle to the strong, neither yet bread to the wise, nor yet riches to men of understanding, nor yet favour to men of skill; but time and chance happeneth to them all.

Here it is in modern English:

Objective considerations of contemporary phenomena compel the conclusion that success or failure in competitive activities exhibits no tendency to be commensurate with innate capacity, but that a considerable element of the unpredictable must invariably be taken into account.

This is a parody, but not a very gross one. Exhibit (3) above, for instance, contains several patches of the same kind of English. It will be seen that I have not made a full translation. The beginning and ending of the sentence follow the original meaning fairly closely, but in the middle the concrete illustrations — race, battle, bread — dissolve into the vague phrases 'success or failure in competitive activities'. This had to be so, because no modern writer of the kind I am discussing — no one capable of using phrases like 'objective considerations of contemporary phenomena' — would ever tabulate his thoughts in that precise and detailed way. The whole tendency of modern prose is away from concreteness. Now analyze these two sentences a little more closely. The first contains forty-nine words but only sixty syllables, and all its words are those of everyday life. The second contains thirty-eight words of ninety syllables: eighteen of those words are from Latin roots, and one from Greek. The first sentence contains six vivid images, and only one phrase ('time and chance') that could be called vague. The second contains not a single fresh, arresting phrase, and in spite of its ninety syllables it gives only a shortened version of the meaning contained in the first. Yet without a doubt it is the second kind of sentence that is gaining ground in modern English. I do not want to exaggerate. This kind of writing is not yet universal, and outcrops of simplicity will occur here and there in the worst-written page. Still, if you or I were told to write a few lines on the uncertainty of human fortunes, we should probably come much nearer to my imaginary sentence than to the one from *Ecclesiastes*.

> **15. Orwell's parody of the passage from *Ecclesiastes* is obvious, and the clutter of words in his modern 'translation' is nonsense. He considers the Biblical passage fresh and clear, and his concoction stale and vague. Why does he assert that his parody is more likely the course of action for most modern writers? Can you find examples of what he means?**

As I have tried to show, modern writing at its worst does not consist in picking out words for the sake of their meaning and inventing images in order to make the meaning clearer. It consists in gumming together long strips of words which have already been set in order by someone else, and making the results presentable by sheer humbug. The attraction of this way of writing is that it is easy. It is easier — even quicker, once you have the habit — to say *In my opinion it is not an unjustifiable assumption that* than to say *I think*. If you use ready-made phrases, you not only don't have to hunt about for the words; you also don't have to bother with the rhythms of your sentences since these phrases are generally so arranged as to be more or less euphonious. When you are composing in a hurry — when you are dictating to a stenographer, for instance, or making a public speech — it is natural to fall into a pretentious, Latinized style. Tags like *a consideration which we should do well to bear in mind* or *a conclusion to which all of us would readily assent* will save many a sentence from coming down with a bump. By using stale metaphors, similes, and idioms, you save much mental effort, at the cost of leaving your meaning vague, not only for your reader but for yourself. This is the significance of mixed metaphors. The sole aim of a metaphor is to call up a visual image. When these images clash — as in *The Fascist octopus has sung its swan song, the jackboot is thrown into the melting pot* — it can be taken as certain that the writer is not seeing a mental image of the objects he is naming; in other words he is not really thinking. Look again at the examples I gave at the beginning of this essay. Professor Laski (1) uses five negatives in fifty three words. One of these is superfluous, making nonsense of the whole passage, and in addition there is the slip — *alien* for akin — making further nonsense, and several avoidable pieces of clumsiness which increase the general vagueness. Professor Hogben (2) plays ducks and drakes with a battery which is able to write prescriptions, and, while disapproving of the everyday phrase *put up with*, is unwilling to look *egregious* up in the dictionary and see what it means; (3), if one takes an uncharitable attitude towards it, is simply meaningless: probably one could work out its intended meaning by reading the whole of the article in which it occurs. In (4), the writer knows more or less what he wants to say, but an accumulation of stale phrases chokes him like tea leaves blocking a sink. In (5), words and meaning have almost parted company. People who write in this manner usually have a general emotional meaning — they dislike one thing and want to express solidarity with another — but they are not interested in the detail of what they are saying. A scrupulous writer, in every sentence that he writes, will ask himself at least four questions, thus: What am I trying to say? What words will express it? What image or idiom will make it clearer? Is this image fresh enough to have an effect? And he will probably ask himself two more: Could I put it more shortly? Have I said anything that is avoidably ugly? But you are not obliged to go to all this trouble. You can shirk it by simply throwing your mind open and letting the ready-made phrases come crowding in. The will construct your sentences for you — even think your thoughts for you, to a certain extent — and at need they will perform the important service of partially concealing your meaning even from yourself. It is at this point that the special connection between politics and the debasement of language becomes clear.

> **16.** From above: "People who write in this manner usually have a general emotional meaning — they dislike one thing and want to express solidarity with another — but they are not interested in the detail of what they are saying." The manner to which Orwell refers is 'vague' writing; the 'emotional meaning' clouds expression. Why do emotions cloud reasoning? How do we resist getting emotional about things for which we have passion?

> **Orwell's recommendations for the 'scrupulous' writer:**
> 1. What am I trying to say?
> 2. What words will express it?
> 3. What image or idiom will make it clearer?
> 4. Is this image fresh enough to have an effect?
> 5. Could I put it more shortly?
> 6. Have I said anything that is avoidably ugly?

In our time it is broadly true that political writing is bad writing. Where it is not true, it will generally be found that the writer is some kind of rebel, expressing his private opinions and not a 'party line'. Orthodoxy, of whatever colour, seems to demand a lifeless, imitative style. The political dialects to be found in pamphlets, leading articles, manifestos, White papers and the speeches of undersecretaries do, of course, vary from party to party, but they are all alike in that one almost never finds in them a fresh, vivid, homemade turn of speech. When one watches some tired hack on the platform mechanically repeating the familiar phrases — *bestial, atrocities, iron heel, bloodstained tyranny, free peoples of the world, stand shoulder to shoulder* — one often has a curious feeling that one is not watching a live human being but some kind of dummy: a feeling which suddenly becomes stronger at moments when the light catches the speaker's spectacles and turns them into blank discs which seem to have no eyes behind them. And this is not altogether fanciful. A speaker who uses that kind of phraseology has gone some distance toward turning himself into a machine. The appropriate noises are coming out of his larynx, but his brain is not involved, as it would be if he were choosing his words for himself. If the speech he is making is one that he is accustomed to make over and over again, he may be almost unconscious of what he is saying, as one is when one utters the responses in church. And this reduced state of consciousness, if not indispensable, is at any rate favourable to political conformity.

> **17.** What is 'orthodoxy'? Why does orthodoxy depend on bad writing—'a lifeless, imitative style'?
>
> **18.** Some of the familiar phrases to which Orwell refers—*bestial, atrocities, iron heel, bloodstained tyranny, free peoples of the world, stand shoulder to shoulder* —

> are of his time and country. What are some of the stale phrases used today in political writing and speaking?
>
> **19. In his own writing here, how does Orwell present an image of lifeless political speech? What does Orwell mean when he claims that "this state of reduced consciousness...is favourable to political conformity"?**

In our time, political speech and writing are largely the defense of the indefensible. Things like the continuance of British rule in India, the Russian purges and deportations, the dropping of the atom bombs on Japan, can indeed be defended, but only by arguments which are too brutal for most people to face, and which do not square with the professed aims of the political parties. Thus political language has to consist largely of euphemism, question-begging and sheer cloudy vagueness. Defenseless villages are bombarded from the air, the inhabitants driven out into the countryside, the cattle machine-gunned, the huts set on fire with incendiary bullets: this is called *pacification*. Millions of peasants are robbed of their farms and sent trudging along the roads with no more than they can carry: this is called *transfer of population* or *rectification of frontiers*. People are imprisoned for years without trial, or shot in the back of the neck or sent to die of scurvy in Arctic lumber camps: this is called *elimination of unreliable elements*. Such phraseology is needed if one wants to name things without calling up mental pictures of them. Consider for instance some comfortable English professor defending Russian totalitarianism. He cannot say outright, 'I believe in killing off your opponents when you can get good results by doing so'. Probably, therefore, he will say something like this:

'While freely conceding that the Soviet regime exhibits certain features which the humanitarian may be inclined to deplore, we must, I think, agree that a certain curtailment of the right to political opposition is an unavoidable concomitant of transitional periods, and that the rigors which the Russian people have been called upon to undergo have been amply justified in the sphere of concrete achievement.'

The inflated style itself is a kind of euphemism. A mass of Latin words falls upon the facts like soft snow, blurring the outline and covering up all the details. The great enemy of clear language is insincerity. When there is a gap between one's real and one's declared aims, one turns as it were instinctively to long words and exhausted idioms, like a cuttlefish spurting out ink. In our age there is no such thing as 'keeping out of politics'. All issues are political issues, and politics itself is a mass of lies, evasions, folly, hatred, and schizophrenia. When the general atmosphere is bad, language must suffer. I should expect to find — this is a guess which I have not sufficient knowledge to verify — that the German, Russian and Italian languages have all deteriorated in the last ten or fifteen years, as a result of dictatorship.

> **20. "In our time, political speech and writing are largely the defense of the indefensible" is an oft-quoted phrase from this essay. "Euphemism, question-begging and sheer cloudy vagueness" constitute what Orwell feels is indefensible, and he goes to give examples of how political speech softens, or makes vague, brutal realities. What are some contemporary examples of political speech? Here are a few examples to start you off:**

> a. *Sorties*: a combat mission of a number of aircraft, usually to drop bombs on targets.
>
> b. *Outsourcing*: this once meant obtaining products from another source; now it means shipping jobs overseas.
>
> c. *ethnic cleansing*: genocide
>
> 21. What does Orwell mean when he writes: "All issues are political issues, and politics itself is a mass of lies, evasions, folly, hatred, and schizophrenia"? How does this translate into other aspects of society that contribute to the deterioration of language, like media, the arts, education, entertainment?

But if thought corrupts language, language can also corrupt thought. A bad usage can spread by tradition and imitation even among people who should and do know better. The debased language that I have been discussing is in some ways very convenient. Phrases like *a not unjustifiable assumption, leaves much to be desired, would serve no good purpose, a consideration which we should do well to bear in mind,* are a continuous temptation, a packet of aspirins always at one's elbow. Look back through this essay, and for certain you will find that I have again and again committed the very faults I am protesting against. By this morning's post I have received a pamphlet dealing with conditions in Germany. The author tells me that he 'felt impelled' to write it. I open it at random, and here is almost the first sentence I see: '[The Allies] have an opportunity not only of achieving a radical transformation of Germany's social and political structure in such a way as to avoid a nationalistic reaction in Germany itself, but at the same time of laying the foundations of a co-operative and unified Europe.' You see, he 'feels impelled' to write — feels, presumably, that he has something new to say — and yet his words, like cavalry horses answering the bugle, group themselves automatically into the familiar dreary pattern. This invasion of one's mind by ready-made phrases (*lay the foundations, achieve a radical transformation*) can only be prevented if one is constantly on guard against them, and every such phrase anaesthetizes a portion of one's brain.

> 22. "Look back through this essay, and for certain you will find that I have again and again committed the very faults I am protesting against." Orwell's honesty is refreshing, recognizing that good writing is difficult and "very convenient," and that the effort should be made to keep writing simple and fresh.
>
> 23. Take a chance: Rewrite the post Orwell receives and to which he objects, using clarity and brevity to make the observation fresh.
>
> 24. Throughout this study guide, I know I have committed errors in clarity and figurative imagery. When you find them, please tell me how I erred and contact me at: emorneau@gmail.com. Thanks.

I said earlier that the decadence of our language is probably curable. Those who deny this would argue, if they produced an argument at all, that language merely reflects existing social conditions, and that we cannot influence its development by any direct tinkering with words and constructions. So far as the general tone or spirit of a language goes, this may be true, but it is not true in detail. Silly words and expressions have often disappeared, not through any evolutionary process but owing to the conscious action of a minority. Two recent examples were *explore every avenue* and *leave no stone unturned*, which were killed by the jeers of a few journalists. There is a long list of flyblown metaphors which could similarly be got rid of if enough people would interest themselves in the job; and it should also be possible to laugh the *not un-* formation out of existence (3), to reduce the amount of Latin and Greek in the average sentence, to drive out foreign phrases and strayed scientific words, and, in general, to make pretentiousness unfashionable. But all these are minor points. [...]

> **25. What "silly words and expressions" used today should be dropped from the English language? For example, does *awesome* mean anything anymore?**
>
> **26. Why does Orwell object to formations preceded by *not* and *un*? What would our language look like if we did this? Give examples.**

[...] The defense of the English language implies more than this, and perhaps it is best to start by saying what it *does not* imply.

To begin with it has nothing to do with archaism, with the salvaging of obsolete words and turns of speech, or with the setting up of a 'standard English' which must never be departed from. On the contrary, it is especially concerned with the scrapping of every word or idiom which has outworn its usefulness. It has nothing to do with correct grammar and syntax, which are of no importance so long as one makes one's meaning clear, or with the avoidance of Americanisms, or with having what is called a 'good prose style'. On the other hand, it is not concerned with fake simplicity and the attempt to make written English colloquial. Nor does it even imply in every case preferring the Saxon word to the Latin one, though it does imply using the fewest and shortest words that will cover one's meaning. What is above all needed is to let the meaning choose the word, and not the other way around. [...]

> **27. What does Orwell mean by this last sentence?**

[...] In prose, the worst thing one can do with words is surrender to them. When you think of a concrete object, you think wordlessly, and then, if you want to describe the thing you have been visualising you probably hunt about until you find the exact words that seem to fit it. When you think of something abstract you are more inclined to use words from the start, and unless you make a conscious effort to prevent it, the existing dialect will come rushing in and do the job for you, at the expense of blurring or even changing your meaning. [...]

> **28. Why is it dangerous for writers to invent the meaning of abstractions? For example, if *love* is an abstraction, how can a writer make it concrete and meaningful?**

[...] Probably it is better to put off using words as long as possible and get one's meaning as clear as one can through pictures and sensations. Afterward one can choose — not simply *accept* — the phrases that will best cover the meaning, and then switch round and decide what impressions one's words are likely to make on another person. This last effort of the mind cuts out all stale or mixed images, all prefabricated phrases, needless repetitions, and humbug and vagueness generally. But one can often be in doubt about the effect of a word or a phrase, and one needs rules that one can rely on when instinct fails. I think the following rules will cover most cases:

> i. **Never use a metaphor, simile, or other figure of speech which you are used to seeing in print.**
>
> ii. **Never use a long word where a short one will do.**
>
> iii. **If it is possible to cut a word out, always cut it out.**
>
> iv. **Never use the passive where you can use the active.**
>
> v. **Never use a foreign phrase, a scientific word, or a jargon word if you can think of an everyday English equivalent.**
>
> vi. **Break any of these rules sooner than say anything outright barbarous.**
>
> **[Table and Boldface—mine]**

These rules sound elementary, and so they are, but they demand a deep change of attitude in anyone who has grown used to writing in the style now fashionable. One could keep all of them and still write bad English, but one could not write the kind of stuff that I quoted in those five specimens at the beginning of this article.

I have not here been considering the literary use of language, but merely language as an instrument for expressing and not for concealing or preventing thought. Stuart Chase and others have come near to claiming that all abstract words are meaningless, and have used this as a pretext for advocating a kind of political quietism. Since you don't know what Fascism is, how can you struggle against Fascism? One need not swallow such absurdities as this, but one ought to recognise that the present political chaos is connected with the decay of language, and that one can probably bring about some improvement by starting at the verbal end. If you simplify your English, you are freed from the worst follies of orthodoxy. You cannot speak any of the necessary dialects, and when you make a stupid remark its stupidity will be obvious, even to yourself. Political language — and with variations this is true of all political parties, from Conservatives to Anarchists — is designed to make lies sound truthful and murder respectable, and to give an appearance of solidity to pure wind. One cannot change this all in a moment, but one can at least change one's own habits, and from time to time one can even, if one jeers loudly enough, send some worn-out and useless phrase — some *jackboot, Achilles' heel, hotbed, melting pot, acid test, veritable inferno*, or other lump of verbal refuse — into the dustbin where it belongs.

> **29. "Political language — and with variations this is true of all political parties, from Conservatives to Anarchists — is designed to make lies sound truthful and murder respectable, and to give an appearance of solidity to pure wind." This is another oft-quoted maxim from this essay. Can you give examples of political language today that corresponds to this maxim?**

---

1) An interesting illustration of this is the way in which the English flower names which were in use till very recently are being ousted by Greek ones, *snapdragon* becoming *antirrhinum, forget-me not* becoming *myosotis*, etc. It is hard to see any practical reason for this change of fashion: it is probably due to an instinctive turning-away from the more homely word and a vague feeling that the Greek word is scientific.

2) Example: 'Comfort's catholicity of perception and image, strangely Whitmanesque in range, almost the exact opposite in aesthetic compulsion, continues to evoke that trembling atmospheric accumulative hinting at a cruel, an inexorably serene timelessness... Wrey Gardiner scores by aiming at simple bull's-eyes with precision. Only they are not so simple, and through this contented sadness runs more than the surface bitter-sweet of resignation'. (*Poetry Quarterly*.)

3) One can cure oneself of the *not un-* formation by memorizing this sentence: *A not unblack dog was chasing a not unsmall rabbit across a not ungreen field.*

THE END

___BD___
George Orwell: 'Politics and the English Language'
First published: *Horizon*. — GB, London. — April 1946.

Something to Consider

Orwell's criticisms of the abuse of the English language may seem rigid or dated to some. English is a vibrant language, difficult to learn, let alone master, and the fluidity of change brought about by science and culture inevitably shape our expressions. Add to this the visual component of modern learning and communication, and the written language is positioned for abuse and indifference. In fact, the impact of media on the written word probably has more to do with its decline than the willing misuse of language. Just as the written word can be made vague or meaningless, the array of images that convey a story, a political theme, or almost any subject, has a greater chance of being manipulated for effect and not substance. Media education therefore is essential to understanding the subtleties of media manipulation. Perhaps a media literate society will make the effort to treat words with more respect and bring word literacy to a position of authority over what composes truth and relevance.

41. George Orwell: Notes on Nationalism, Complete

http://orwell.ru/library/essays/nationalism/english/e_nat#fnm_1

Somewhere or other Byron makes use of the French word *longeur*, and remarks in passing that though in England we happen not to have the word, we have the thing in considerable profusion. In the same way, there is a habit of mind which is now so widespread that it affects our thinking on nearly every subject, but which has not yet been given a name. As the nearest existing equivalent I have chosen the word 'nationalism', but it will be seen in a moment that I am not using it in quite the ordinary sense, if only because the emotion I am speaking about does not always attach itself to what is called a nation — that is, a single race or a geographical area. It can attach itself to a church or a class, or it may work in a merely negative sense, against something or other and without the need for any positive object of loyalty.

By 'nationalism' I mean first of all the habit of assuming that human beings can be classified like insects and that whole blocks of millions or tens of millions of people can be confidently labelled 'good' or 'bad'. But secondly — and this is much more important — I mean the habit of identifying oneself with a single nation or other unit, placing it beyond good and evil and recognising no other duty than that of advancing its interests. *Nationalism is not to be confused with patriotism.* Both words are normally used in so vague a way that any definition is liable to be challenged, but one must draw a distinction between them, since two different and even opposing ideas are involved. By 'patriotism' I mean devotion to a particular place and a particular way of life, which one believes to be the best in the world but has no wish to force on other people. Patriotism is of its nature defensive, both militarily and culturally. Nationalism, on the other hand, is inseparable from the desire for power. The abiding purpose of every nationalist is to secure more power and more prestige, *not* for himself but for the nation or other unit in which he has chosen to sink his own individuality.

So long as it is applied merely to the more notorious and identifiable nationalist movements in Germany, Japan, and other countries, all this is obvious enough. Confronted with a phenomenon like Nazism, which we can observe from the outside, nearly all of us would say much the same things about it. But here I must repeat what I said above, that I am only using the word 'nationalism' for lack of a better. Nationalism, in the extended sense in which I am using the word, includes such movements and tendencies as Communism, political Catholicism, Zionism, Anti-Semitism, Trotskyism and Pacifism. It does not necessarily mean loyalty to a government or a country, still less to one's own country, and it is not even strictly necessary that the units in which it deals should actually exist. To name a few obvious examples, Jewry, Islam, Christendom, the Proletariat and the White Race are all of them objects of passionate nationalistic feeling:

but their existence can be seriously questioned, and there is no definition of any one of them that would be universally accepted.

It is also worth emphasizing once again that nationalist feeling can be purely negative. There are, for example, Trotskyists who have become simply enemies of the U.S.S.R. without developing a corresponding loyalty to any other unit. When one grasps the implications of this, the nature of what I mean by nationalism becomes a good deal clearer. A nationalist is one who thinks solely, or mainly, in terms of competitive prestige. He may be a positive or a negative nationalist — that is, he may use his mental energy either in boosting or in denigrating — but at any rate his thoughts always turn on victories, defeats, triumphs and humiliations. He sees history, especially contemporary history, as the endless rise and decline of great power units, and every event that happens seems to him a demonstration that his own side is on the upgrade and some hated rival is on the downgrade. But finally, it is important not to confuse nationalism with mere worship of success. The nationalist does not go on the principle of simply ganging up with the strongest side. On the contrary, having picked his side, he persuades himself that it is the strongest, and is able to stick to his belief even when the facts are overwhelmingly against him. Nationalism is power-hunger tempered by self-deception. Every nationalist is capable of the most flagrant dishonesty, but he is also — since he is conscious of serving something bigger than himself — unshakably certain of being in the right.

Now that I have given this lengthy definition, I think it will be admitted that the habit of mind I am talking about is widespread among the English intelligentsia, and more widespread there than among the mass of the people. For those who feel deeply about contemporary politics, certain topics have become so infected by considerations of prestige that a genuinely rational approach to them is almost impossible. Out of the hundreds of examples that one might choose, take this question: Which of the three great allies, the U.S.S.R., Britain and the USA, has contributed most to the defeat of Germany? In theory, it should be possible to give a reasoned and perhaps even a conclusive answer to this question. In practice, however, the necessary calculations cannot be made, because anyone likely to bother his head about such a question would inevitably see it in terms of competitive prestige. He would therefore *start* by deciding in favour of Russia, Britain or America as the case might be, and only *after* this would begin searching for arguments that seemed to support his case. And there are whole strings of kindred questions to which you can only get an honest answer from someone who is indifferent to the whole subject involved, and whose opinion on it is probably worthless in any case. Hence, partly, the remarkable failure in our time of political and military prediction. It is curious to reflect that out of al the 'experts' of all the schools, there was not a single one who was able to foresee so likely an event as the Russo-German Pact of 1939 (2). And when news of the Pact broke, the most wildly divergent explanations were of it were given, and predictions were made which were falsified almost immediately, being based in nearly every case not on a study of probabilities but on a desire to make the U.S.S.R. seem good or bad, strong or weak. Political or military commentators, like astrologers, can survive almost any mistake, because their more devoted followers do not look to them for an appraisal of the facts but for the stimulation of nationalistic loyalties (3). And aesthetic judgments, especially literary judgments, are often corrupted in the same way as political ones. It would be difficult for an Indian Nationalist to enjoy reading Kipling or for a Conservative to see merit in Mayakovsky, and there is always a temptation to claim that any book whose tendency one disagrees with must be a bad book from a *literary* point of view. People of strongly nationalistic outlook often perform this sleight of hand without being conscious of dishonesty.

In England, if one simply considers the number of people involved, it is probable that the dominant form of nationalism is old-fashioned British jingoism. It is certain that this is still widespread, and much more so than most observers would have believed a dozen years ago. However, in this essay I am concerned chiefly with the reactions of the intelligentsia, among whom jingoism and even patriotism of the old kind are almost dead, though they now seem to be reviving among a minority. Among the intelligentsia, it hardly needs saying that the dominant form of nationalism is Communism — using this word in a very loose sense, to include not merely Communist Party members, but 'fellow travellers' and Russophiles generally. A Communist, for my purpose here, is one who looks upon the U.S.S.R. as his Fatherland and feels it his duty t justify Russian policy and advance Russian interests at all costs. Obviously such people abound in England today, and their direct and indirect influence is very great. But many other forms of nationalism also flourish, and it is by noticing the points of resemblance between different and even seemingly opposed currents of thought that one can best get the matter into perspective.

Ten or twenty years ago, the form of nationalism most closely corresponding to Communism today was political Catholicism. Its most outstanding exponent — though he was perhaps an extreme case rather than a typical one — was G. K. Chesterton. Chesterton was a writer of considerable talent who whose to suppress both his sensibilities and his intellectual honesty in the cause of Roman Catholic propaganda. During the last twenty years or so of his life, his entire output was in reality an endless repetition of the same thing, under its laboured cleverness as simple and boring as 'Great is Diana of the Ephesians.' Every book that he wrote, every scrap of dialogue, had to demonstrate beyond the possibility of mistake the superiority of the Catholic over the Protestant or the pagan. But Chesterton was not content to think of this superiority as merely intellectual or spiritual: it had to be translated into terms of national prestige and military power, which entailed an ignorant idealisation of the Latin countries, especially France. Chesterton had not lived long in France, and his picture of it — as a land of Catholic peasants incessantly singing the *Marseillaise* over glasses of red wine — had about as much relation to reality as *Chu Chin Chow* has to everyday life in Baghdad. And with this went not only an enormous overestimation of French military power (both before and after 1914-18 he maintained that France, by itself, was stronger than Germany), but a silly and vulgar glorification of the actual process of war. Chesterton's battle poems, such as *Lepanto* or *The Ballad of Saint Barbara*, make *The Charge of the Light Brigade* read like a pacifist tract: they are perhaps the most tawdry bits of bombast to be found in our language. The interesting thing is that had the romantic rubbish which he habitually wrote about France and the French army been written by somebody else about Britain and the British army, he would have been the first to jeer. In home politics he was a Little Englander, a true hater of jingoism and imperialism, and according to his lights a true friend of democracy. Yet when he looked outwards into the international field, he could forsake his principles without even noticing he was doing so. Thus, his almost mystical belief in the virtues of democracy did not prevent him from admiring Mussolini. Mussolini had destroyed the representative government and the freedom of the press for which Chesterton had struggled so hard at home, but Mussolini was an Italian and had made Italy strong, and that settled the matter. Nor did Chesterton ever find a word to say about imperialism and the conquest of coloured races when they were practiced by Italians or Frenchmen. His hold on reality, his literary taste, and even to some extent his moral sense, were dislocated as soon as his nationalistic loyalties were involved.

Obviously there are considerable resemblances between political Catholicism, as exemplified by Chesterton, and Communism. So there are between either of these and for instance Scottish nationalism, Zionism, Anti-Semitism or Trotskyism. It would be an oversimplification to say that all forms of nationalism are the same, even in their mental atmosphere, but there are certain rules that hold good in all cases. The following are the principal characteristics of nationalist thought:

OBSESSION. As nearly as possible, no nationalist ever thinks, talks, or writes about anything except the superiority of his own power unit. It is difficult if not impossible for any nationalist to conceal his allegiance. The smallest slur upon his own unit, or any implied praise of a rival organization, fills him with uneasiness which he can relieve only by making some sharp retort. If the chosen unit is an actual country, such as Ireland or India, he will generally claim superiority for it not only in military power and political virtue, but in art, literature, sport, structure of the language, the physical beauty of the inhabitants, and perhaps even in climate, scenery and cooking. He will show great sensitiveness about such things as the correct display of flags, relative size of headlines and the order in which different countries are named (4). Nomenclature plays a very important part in nationalist thought. Countries which have won their independence or gone through a nationalist revolution usually change their names, and any country or other unit round which strong feelings revolve is likely to have several names, each of them carrying a different implication. The two sides of the Spanish Civil War had between them nine or ten names expressing different degrees of love and hatred. Some of these names (e. g. 'Patriots' for Franco-supporters, or 'Loyalists' for Government-supporters) were frankly question-begging, and there was no single one of the which the two rival factions could have agreed to use. All nationalists consider it a duty to spread their own language to the detriment of rival languages, and among English-speakers this struggle reappears in subtler forms as a struggle between dialects. Anglophobe-Americans will refuse to use a slang phrase if they know it to be of British origin, and the conflict between Latinizers and Germanizers often has nationalist motives behind it. Scottish nationalists insist on the superiority of Lowland Scots, and socialists whose nationalism takes the form of class hatred tirade against the B.B.C. accent and even the often gives the impression of being tinged by belief in sympathetic magic — a belief which probably comes out in the widespread custom of burning political enemies in effigy, or using pictures of them as targets in shooting galleries.

INSTABILITY. The intensity with which they are held does not prevent nationalist loyalties from being transferable. To begin with, as I have pointed out already, they can be and often are fastened up on some foreign country. One quite commonly finds that great national leaders, or the founders of nationalist movements, do not even belong to the country they have glorified. Sometimes they are outright foreigners, or more often they come from peripheral areas where nationality is doubtful. Examples are Stalin, Hitler, Napoleon, de Valera, Disraeli, Poincare, Beaverbrook. The Pan-German movement was in part the creation of an Englishman, Houston Chamberlain. For the past fifty or a hundred years, transferred nationalism has been a common phenomenon among literary intellectuals. With Lafcadio Hearne the transference was to Japan, with Carlyle and many others of his time to Germany, and in our own age it is usually to Russia. But the peculiarly interesting fact is that re-transference is also possible. A country or other unit which has been worshipped for years may suddenly become detestable, and some other object of affection may take its place with almost no interval. In the first version of H. G. Wells' Outline of History, and others of his writings about that time, one finds the United States praised almost as extravagantly as Russia is praised by Communists today: yet within a few years this uncritical admiration had turned into hostility. The bigoted Communist who changes in a space of weeks, or even days, into an equally bigoted Trotskyist is a common spectacle. In continental Europe Fascist movements were largely recruited from among Communists, and the opposite process may well happen within the next few years. What remains constant in the nationalist is his state of mind: the object of his feelings is changeable, and may be imaginary.

But for an intellectual, transference has an important function, which I have already mentioned shortly in connection with Chesterton. It makes it possible for him to be much *more* nationalistic — more vulgar, more silly, more malignant, more dishonest — that he could ever be on behalf of his native country, or any unit of which he had real knowledge. When one sees the slavish or boastful rubbish that is written about Stalin, the Red Army, etc. by fairly intelligent and sensitive people, one realises that this is only possible because some kind of dislocation has taken place. In societies such as ours, it is unusual for anyone describable as an intellectual to feel a very deep attachment to his own country. Public opinion — that is, the section of public opinion of which he as an intellectual is aware — will not allow him to do so. Most of the people surrounding him are sceptical and disaffected, and he may adopt the same attitude from imitativeness or sheer cowardice: in that case he will have abandoned the form of nationalism that lies nearest to hand without getting any closer to a genuinely internationalist outlook. He still feels the need for a Fatherland, and it is natural to look for one somewhere abroad. Having found it, he can wallow unrestrainedly in exactly those emotions from which he believes that he has emancipated himself. God, the King, the Empire, the Union Jack — all the overthrown idols can reappear under different names, and because they are not recognised for what they are they can be worshipped with a good conscience. Transferred nationalism, like the use of scapegoats, is a way of attaining salvation without altering one's conduct.

INDIFFERENCE TO REALITY. All nationalists have the power of not seeing resemblances between similar sets of facts. A British Tory will defend self-determination in Europe and oppose it in India with no feeling of inconsistency. Actions are held to be good or bad, not on their own merits, but according to who does them, and there is almost no kind of outrage — torture, the use of hostages, forced labour, mass deportations, imprisonment without trial, forgery, assassination, the bombing of civilians — which does not change its moral colour when it is committed by 'our' side. The *Liberal News Chronicle* published, as an example of shocking barbarity, photographs of Russians hanged by the Germans, and then a year or two later published with warm approval almost exactly similar photographs of Germans hanged by the Russians (5). It is the same with historical events. History is thought of largely in nationalist terms, and such things as the Inquisition, the tortures of the Star Chamber, the exploits of the English buccaneers (Sir Francis Drake, for instance, who was given to sinking Spanish prisoners alive), the Reign of Terror, the heroes of the Mutiny blowing hundreds of Indians from the guns, or Cromwell's soldiers slashing Irishwomen's faces with razors, become morally neutral or even meritorious when it is felt that they were done in the 'right' cause. If one looks back over the past quarter of a century, one finds that there was hardly a single year when atrocity stories were not being reported from some part of the world; and yet in not one single case were these atrocities — in Spain, Russia, China, Hungary, Mexico, Amritsar, Smyrna — believed in and disapproved of by the English intelligentsia as a whole. Whether such deeds were reprehensible, or even whether they happened, was always decided according to political predilection.

The nationalist not only does not disapprove of atrocities committed by his own side, but he has a remarkable capacity for not even hearing about them. For quite six years the English admirers of Hitler contrived not to learn of the existence of Dachau and Buchenwald. And those who are loudest in denouncing the German concentration camps are often quite unaware, or only very dimly aware, that there are also concentration camps in Russia. Huge events like the Ukraine famine of 1933, involving the deaths of millions of people, have actually escaped the attention of the majority of English Russophiles. Many English people have heard almost nothing about the extermination of German and Polish Jews during the present war. Their own anti-Semitism has caused this vast crime to bounce off their consciousness. In nationalist thought there are facts which are both true and untrue, known and unknown. A known fact may be so unbearable that it is habitually pushed aside and not allowed to enter into logical processes, or on the other hand it may enter into every calculation and yet never be admitted as a fact, even in one's own mind.

Every nationalist is haunted by the belief that the past can be altered. He spends part of his time in a fantasy world in which things happen as they should — in which, for example, the Spanish Armada was a success or the Russian Revolution was crushed in 1918 — and he will transfer fragments of this world to the history books whenever possible. Much of the propagandist writing of our time amounts to plain forgery. Material facts are suppressed, dates altered, quotations removed from their context and doctored so as to change their meaning. Events which it is felt ought not to have happened are left unmentioned and ultimately denied (6). In 1927 Chiang Kai Shek boiled hundreds of Communists alive, and yet within ten years he had become one of the heroes of the Left. The re-alignment of world politics had brought him into the anti-Fascist camp, and so it was felt that the boiling of the Communists 'didn't count', or perhaps had not happened. The primary aim of propaganda is, of course, to influence contemporary opinion, but those who rewrite history do probably believe with part of their minds that they are actually thrusting facts into the past. When one considers the elaborate forgeries that have been committed in order to show that Trotsky did not play a valuable part in the Russian civil war, it is difficult to feel that the people responsible are merely lying. More probably they feel that their own version *was* what happened in the sight of God, and that one is justified in rearranging the records accordingly.

Indifference to objective truth is encouraged by the sealing-off of one part of the world from another, which makes it harder and harder to discover what is actually happening. There can often be a genuine doubt about the most enormous events. For example, it is impossible to calculate within millions, perhaps even tens of millions, the number of deaths caused by the present war. The calamities that are constantly being reported — battles, massacres, famines, revolutions — tend to inspire in the average person a feeling of unreality. One has no way of verifying the facts, one is not even fully certain that they have happened, and one is always presented with totally different interpretations from different sources. What were the rights and wrongs of the Warsaw rising of August 1944? Is it true about the German gas ovens in Poland? Who was really to blame for the Bengal famine? Probably the truth is discoverable, but the facts will be so dishonestly set forth in almost any newspaper that the ordinary reader can be forgiven either for swallowing lies or failing to form an opinion. The general uncertainty as to what is really happening makes it easier to cling to lunatic beliefs. Since nothing is ever quite proved or disproved, the most unmistakable fact can be impudently denied. Moreover, although endlessly brooding on power, victory, defeat, revenge, the nationalist is often somewhat uninterested in what happens in the real world. What he wants is to feel that his own unit is getting the better of some other unit, and he can more easily do this by scoring off an adversary than by examining the facts to see whether they support him. All nationalist controversy is at the debating-society level. It is always entirely inconclusive, since each contestant invariably believes himself to have won the victory. Some nationalists are not far from schizophrenia, living quite happily amid dreams of power and conquest which have no connection with the physical world.

I have examined as best as I can the mental habits which are common to all forms of nationalism. The next thing is to classify those forms, but obviously this cannot be done comprehensively. Nationalism is an enormous subject. The world is tormented by innumerable delusions and hatreds which cut across one another in an extremely complex way, and some of the most sinister of them have not yet impinged on the European consciousness. In this essay I am concerned with nationalism as it occurs among the English intelligentsia. In them, much more than in ordinary English people, it is unmixed with patriotism and therefore can be studied pure. Below are listed the varieties of nationalism now flourishing among English intellectuals, with such comments as seem to be needed. It is convenient to use three headings, Positive, Transferred, and Negative, though some varieties will fit into more than one category:

Positive Nationalism

(I) NEO-TORYISM. Exemplified by such people as Lord Elton, A. P. Herbert, G. M. Young, Professor Pickthorn, by the literature of the Tory Reform Committee, and by such magazines as the *New English Review* and the *Nineteenth Century and After*. The real motive force of neo-Toryism, giving it its nationalistic character and differentiating it from ordinary Conservatism, is the desire not to recognise that British power and influence have declined. Even those who are realistic enough to see that Britain's military position is not what it was, tend to claim that 'English ideas' (usually left undefined) must dominate the world. All neo-Tories are anti-Russian, but sometimes the main emphasis is anti-American. The significant thing is that this school of thought seems to be gaining ground among youngish intellectuals, sometimes ex-Communists, who have passed through the usual process of disillusionment and become disillusioned with that. The anglophobe who suddenly becomes violently pro-British is a fairly common figure. Writers who illustrate this tendency are F. A. Voigt, Malcolm Muggeridge, Evelyn Waugh, Hugh Kingsmill, and a psychologically similar development can be observed in T. S. Eliot, Wyndham Lewis, and various of their followers.

(II) CELTIC NATIONALISM. Welsh, Irish and Scottish nationalism have points of difference but are alike in their anti-English orientation. Members of all three movements have opposed the war while continuing to describe themselves as pro-Russian, and the lunatic fringe has even contrived to be simultaneously pro-Russian and pro-Nazi. But Celtic nationalism is not the same thing as anglophobia. Its motive force is a belief in the past and future greatness of the Celtic peoples, and it has a strong tinge of racialism. The Celt is supposed to be spiritually superior to the Saxon — simpler, more creative, less vulgar, less snobbish, etc. — but the usual power hunger is there under the surface. One symptom of it is the delusion that Eire, Scotland or even Wales could preserve its independence unaided and owes nothing to British protection. Among writers, good examples of this school of thought are Hugh McDiarmid and Sean O'Casey. No modern Irish writer, even of the stature of Yeats or Joyce, is completely free from traces of nationalism.

(III) ZIONISM. This the unusual characteristics of a nationalist movement, but the American variant of it seems to be more violent and malignant than the British. I classify it under Direct and not Transferred nationalism because it flourishes almost exclusively among the Jews themselves. In England, for several rather incongruous reasons, the intelligentsia are mostly pro-Jew on the Palestine issue, but they do not feel strongly about it. All English people of goodwill are also pro-Jew in the sense of disapproving of Nazi persecution. But any actual nationalistic loyalty, or belief in the innate superiority of Jews, is hardly to be found among Gentiles.

Transferred Nationalism

(I) COMMUNISM.

(II) POLITICAL CATHOLICISM.

(III) COLOUR FEELING. The old-style contemptuous attitude towards 'natives' has been much weakened in England, and various pseudo-scientific theories emphasising the superiority of the white race have been abandoned **(7)**. Among the intelligentsia, colour feeling only occurs in the transposed form, that is, as a belief in the innate superiority of the coloured races. This is now increasingly common among English intellectuals, probably resulting more often from masochism and sexual frustration than from contact with the Oriental and Negro nationalist movements. Even among those who do not feel strongly on the colour question, snobbery and imitation have a powerful influence. Almost any English intellectual would be scandalised by the claim that the white races are superior to the coloured, whereas the opposite claim would seem to him unexceptionable even if he disagreed with it. Nationalistic attachment to the coloured races is usually mixed up with the belief that their sex lives are superior, and there is a large underground mythology about the sexual prowess of Negroes.

(IV) CLASS FEELING. Among upper-class and middle-class intellectuals, only in the transposed form — i. e. as a belief in the superiority of the proletariat. Here again, inside the intelligentsia, the pressure of public opinion is overwhelming. Nationalistic loyalty towards the proletariat, and most vicious theoretical hatred of the bourgeoisie, can and often do co-exist with ordinary snobbishness in everyday life.

(V) PACIFISM. The majority of pacifists either belong to obscure religious sects or are simply humanitarians who object to the taking of life and prefer not to follow their thoughts beyond that point. But there is a minority of intellectual pacifists whose real though unadmitted motive appears to be hatred of western democracy and admiration of totalitarianism. Pacifist propaganda usually boils down to saying that one side is as bad as the other, but if one looks closely at the writings of younger intellectual pacifists, one finds that they do not by any means express impartial disapproval but are directed almost entirely against Britain and the United States. Moreover they do not as a rule condemn violence as such, but only violence used in defence of western countries. The Russians, unlike the British, are not blamed for defending themselves by warlike means, and indeed all pacifist propaganda of this type avoids mention of Russia or China. It is not claimed, again, that the Indians should abjure violence in their struggle against the British. Pacifist literature abounds with equivocal remarks which, if they mean anything, appear to mean that statesmen of the type of Hitler are preferable to those of the type of Churchill, and that violence is perhaps excusable if it is violent enough. After the fall of France, the French pacifists, faced by a real choice which their English colleagues have not had to make, mostly went over to the Nazis, and in England there appears to have been some small overlap of membership between the Peace Pledge Union and the Blackshirts. Pacifist writers have written in praise of Carlyle, one of the intellectual fathers of Fascism. All in all it is difficult not to feel that pacifism, as it appears among a section of the intelligentsia, is secretly inspired by an admiration for power and successful cruelty. The mistake was made of pinning this emotion to Hitler, but it could easily be retransferred.

Negative Nationalism

(I) ANGLOPHOBIA. Within the intelligentsia, a derisive and mildly hostile attitude towards Britain is more or less compulsory, but it is an unfaked emotion in many cases. During the war it was manifested in the defeatism of the intelligentsia, which persisted long after it had become clear that the Axis powers could not win. Many people were undisguisedly pleased when Singapore fell or when the British were driven out of Greece, and there was a remarkable unwillingness to believe in good news, e.g. el Alamein, or the number of German planes shot down in the Battle of Britain. English left-wing intellectuals did not, of course, actually want the Germans or Japanese to win the war, but many of them could not help getting a certain kick out of seeing their own country humiliated, and wanted to feel that the final victory would be due to Russia, or perhaps America, and not to Britain. In foreign politics many intellectuals follow the principle that any faction backed by Britain must be in the wrong. As a result, 'enlightened' opinion is quite largely a mirror-image of Conservative policy. Anglophobia is always liable to reversal, hence that fairly common spectacle, the pacifist of one war who is a bellicose in the next.

(II) ANTI-SEMITISM. There is little evidence about this at present, because the Nazi persecutions have made it necessary for any thinking person to side with the Jews against their oppressors. Anyone educated enough to have heard the word 'anti-Semitism' claims as a matter of course to be free of it, and anti-Jewish remarks are carefully eliminated from all classes of literature. Actually anti-Semitism appears to be widespread, even among intellectuals, and the general conspiracy of silence probably helps exacerbate it. People of Left opinions are not immune to it, and their attitude is sometimes affected by the fact that Trotskyists and Anarchists tend to be Jews. But anti-Semitism comes more naturally to people of Conservative tendency, who suspect Jews of weakening national morale and diluting the national culture. Neo-Tories and political Catholics are always liable to succumb to anti-Semitism, at least intermittently.

(III) TROTSKYISM. This word is used so loosely as to include Anarchists, democratic Socialists and even Liberals. I use it here to mean a doctrinaire Marxist whose main motive is hostility to the Stalin regime. Trotskyism can be better studied in obscure pamphlets or in papers like the *Socialist Appeal* than in the works of Trotsky himself, who was by no means a man of one idea. Although in some places, for instance in the United States, Trotskyism is able to attract a fairly large number of adherents and develop into an organised movement with a petty fuhrer of its own, its inspiration is essentially negative. The Trotskyist is *against* Stalin just as the Communist is *for* him, and, like the majority of Communists, he wants not so much to alter the external world as to feel that the battle for prestige is going in his own favour. In each case there is the same obsessive fixation on a single subject, the same inability to form a genuinely rational opinion based on probabilities. The fact that Trotskyists are everywhere a persecuted minority, and that the accusation usually made against them, i. e. of collaborating with the Fascists, is obviously false, creates an impression that Trotskyism is intellectually and morally superior to Communism; but it is doubtful whether there is much difference. The most typical Trotskyists, in any case, are ex-Communists, and no one arrives at Trotskyism except via one of the left-wing movements. No Communist, unless tethered to his party by years of habit, is secure against a sudden lapse into Trotskyism. The opposite process does not seem to happen equally often, though there is no clear reason why it should not.

In the classification I have attempted above, it will seem that I have often exaggerated, oversimplified, made unwarranted assumptions and have left out of account the existence of ordinarily decent motives. This was inevitable, because in this essay I am trying to isolate and identify tendencies which exist in all our minds and pervert our thinking, without necessarily occurring in a pure state or operating continuously. It is important at this point to correct the over-simplified picture which I have been obliged to make. To begin with, one has no right to assume that everyone, or even every intellectual, is infected by nationalism. Secondly, nationalism can be intermittent and limited. An intelligent man may half-succumb to a belief which he knows to be absurd, and he may keep it out of his mind for long periods, only reverting to it in moments of anger or sentimentality, or when he is certain that no important issues are involved. Thirdly, a nationalistic creed may be adopted in good faith from non-nationalistic motives. Fourthly, several kinds of nationalism, even kinds that cancel out, can co-exist in the same person.

All the way through I have said, 'the nationalist does this' or 'the nationalist does that', using for purposes of illustration the extreme, barely sane type of nationalist who has no neutral areas in his mind and no interest in anything except the struggle for power. Actually such people are fairly common, but they are not worth the powder and shot. In real life Lord Elton, D. N. Pritt, Lady Houston, Ezra Pound, Lord Vanisttart, Father Coughlin and all the rest of their dreary tribe have to be fought against, but their intellectual deficiencies hardly need pointing out. Monomania is not interesting, and the fact that no nationalist of the more bigoted kind can write a book which still seems worth reading after a lapse of years has a certain deodorising effect. But when one has admitted that nationalism has not triumphed everywhere, that there are still peoples whose judgements are not at the mercy of their desires, the fact does remain that the pressing problems — India, Poland, Palestine, the Spanish civil war, the Moscow trials, the American Negroes, the Russo-German Pact or what have you — cannot be, or at least never are, discussed upon a reasonable level. The Eltons and Pritts and Coughlins, each of them simply an enormous mouth bellowing the same lie over and over again, are obviously extreme cases, but we deceive ourselves if we do not realise that we can all resemble them in unguarded moments. Let a certain note be struck, let this or that corn be trodden on — and it may be corn whose very existence has been unsuspected hitherto — and the most fair-minded and sweet-tempered person may suddenly be transformed into a vicious partisan, anxious only to 'score' over his adversary and indifferent as to how many lies he tells or how many logical errors he commits in doing so. When Lloyd George, who was an opponent of the Boer War, announced in the House of Commons that the British communiques, if one added them together, claimed the killing of more Boers than the whole Boer nation contained, it is recorded that Arthur Balfour rose to his feet and shouted 'Cad!' Very few people are proof against lapses of this type. The Negro snubbed by a white woman, the Englishman who hears England ignorantly criticised by an American, the Catholic apologist reminded of the Spanish Armada, will all react in much the same way. One prod to the nerve of nationalism, and the intellectual decencies can vanish, the past can be altered, and the plainest facts can be denied.

If one harbours anywhere in one's mind a nationalistic loyalty or hatred, certain facts, although in a sense known to be true, are inadmissible. Here are just a few examples. I list below five types of nationalist, and against each I append a fact which it is impossible for that type of nationalist to accept, even in his secret thoughts:

BRITISH TORY: Britain will come out of this war with reduced power and prestige.

COMMUNIST: If she had not been aided by Britain and America, Russia would have been defeated by Germany.

IRISH NATIONALIST: Eire can only remain independent because of British protection.

TROTSKYIST: The Stalin regime is accepted by the Russian masses.

PACIFIST: Those who 'abjure' violence can only do so because others are committing violence on their behalf.

All of these facts are grossly obvious if one's emotions do not happen to be involved: but to the kind of person named in each case they are also *intolerable*, and so they have to be denied, and false theories constructed upon their denial. I come back to the astonishing failure of military prediction in the present war. It is, I think, true to say that the intelligentsia have been more wrong about the progress of the war than the common people, and that they were more swayed by partisan feelings. The average intellectual of the Left believed, for instance, that the war was lost in 1940, that the Germans were bound to overrun Egypt in 1942, that the Japanese would never be driven out of the lands they had conquered, and that the Anglo-American bombing offensive was making no impression on Germany. He could believe these things because his hatred for the British ruling class forbade him to admit that British plans could succeed. There is no limit to the follies that can be swallowed if one is under the influence of feelings of this kind. I have heard it confidently stated, for instance, that the American troops had been brought to Europe not to fight the Germans but to crush an English revolution. One has to belong to the intelligentsia to believe things like that: no ordinary man could be such a fool. When Hitler invaded Russia, the officials of the MOI issued 'as background' a warning that Russia might be expected to collapse in six weeks. On the other hand the Communists regarded every phase of the war as a Russian victory, even when the Russians were driven back almost to the Caspian Sea and had lost several million prisoners. There is no need to multiply instances. The point is that as soon as fear, hatred, jealousy and power worship are involved, the sense of reality becomes unhinged. And, as I have pointed out already, the sense of right and wrong becomes unhinged also. There is no crime, absolutely none, that cannot be condoned when 'our' side commits it. Even if one does not deny that the crime has happened, even if one knows that it is exactly the same crime as one has condemned in some other case, even if one admits in an intellectual sense that it is unjustified — still one cannot *feel* that it is wrong. Loyalty is involved, and so pity ceases to function.

The reason for the rise and spread of nationalism is far too big a question to be raised here. It is enough to say that, in the forms in which it appears among English intellectuals, it is a distorted reflection of the frightful battles actually happening in the external world, and that its worst follies have been made possible by the breakdown of patriotism and religious belief. If one follows up this train of thought, one is in danger of being led into a species of Conservatism, or into political quietism. It can be plausibly argued, for instance — it is even possibly true — that patriotism is an inoculation against nationalism, that monarchy is a guard against dictatorship, and that organised religion is a guard against superstition. Or again, it can be argued that no unbiased outlook is possible, that all creeds and causes involve the same lies, follies, and barbarities; and this is often advanced as a reason for keeping out of politics altogether. I do not accept this argument, if only because in the modern world no one describable as an intellectual can keep out of politics in the sense of not caring about them. I think one must engage in politics — using the word in a wide sense — and that one must have preferences: that is, one must recognise that some causes are objectively better than others, even if they are advanced by equally bad means. As for the nationalistic loves and hatreds that I have spoken of, they are part of the make-up of most of us, whether we like it or not. Whether it is possible to get rid of them I do not know, but I do believe that it is possible to struggle against them, and that this is essentially a *moral* effort. It is a question first of all of discovering what one really is, what one's own feelings really are, and then of making allowance for the inevitable bias. If you hate and fear Russia, if you are jealous of the wealth and power of America, if you despise Jews, if you have a sentiment of inferiority towards the British ruling class, you cannot get rid of those feelings simply by taking thought. But you can at least recognise that you have them, and prevent them from contaminating your mental processes. The emotional urges which are inescapable, and are perhaps even necessary to political action, should be able to exist side by side with an acceptance of reality. But this, I repeat, needs a *moral* effort, and contemporary English literature, so far as it is alive at all to the major issues of our time, shows how few of us are prepared to make it.

1945

---

1) Nations, and even vaguer entities such as Catholic Church or the proletariat, are commonly thought of as individuals and often referred to as 'she'. Patently absurd remarks such as 'Germany is naturally treacherous' are to be found in any newspaper one opens and reckless generalization about national character ('The Spaniard is a natural aristocrat' or 'Every Englishman is a hypocrite') are uttered by almost everyone. Intermittently these generalizations are seen to be unfounded, but the habit of making them persists, and people of professedly international outlook, e.g., Tolstoy or Bernard Shaw, are often guilty of them.

2) A few writers of conservative tendency, such as Peter Drucker, foretold an agreement between Germany and Russia, but they expected an actual alliance or amalgamation which would be permanent. No Marxist or other left-wing writer, of whatever colour, came anywhere near foretelling the Pact.

3) The military commentators of the popular press can mostly be classified as pro-Russian or anti-Russian pro-blimp or anti-blimp. Such errors as believing the Maginot Line impregnable, or predicting that Russia would conquer Germany in three months, have failed to shake their reputation, because they were always saying what their own particular audience wanted to hear. The two military critics most favoured by the intelligentsia are Captain Liddell Hart and Major-General Fuller, the first of whom teaches that the defence is stronger that the attack, and the second that the attack is stronger that the defence. This contradiction has not prevented both of them from being

accepted as authorities by the sme public. The secret reason for their vogue in left-wing circles is that both of them are at odds with the War Office.

4) Certain Americans have expressed dissatisfaction because 'Anglo-American' is the form of combination for these two words. It has been proposed to submit 'Americo-British'.

5) The *News Chronicle* advised its readers to visit the news film at which the entire execution could be witnessed, with close-ups. The *Star* published with seeming approval photographs of nearly naked female collaborationists being baited by the Paris mob. These photographs had a marked resemblance to the Nazi photographs of Jews being baited by the Berlin mob.

6) An example is the Russo-German Pact, which is being effaced as quickly as possible from public memory. A Russian correspondent informs me that mention of the Pact is already being omitted from Russian year-books which table recent political events.

7) A good example is the sunstroke superstition. Until recently it was believed that the white races were much more liable to sunstroke that the coloured, and that a white man could not safely walk about in tropical sunshine without a pith helmet. There was no evidence whatever for this theory, but it served the purpose of accentuating the difference between 'natives' and Europeans. During the war the theory was quietly dropped and whole armies manoeuvred in the tropics without pith helmets. So long as the sunstroke superstition survived, English doctors in India appear to have believed in it as firmly as laymen.

THE END

42. Thoughts on *Newspeak*

We live in a world of clipped expressions, fueled by a culture that intentionally limits language. Icons, visuals, and signs replace words; blogs replace newspapers; Twitter limits characters; punctuation and spelling are abandoned for expediency and novelty; sound bytes and bumper stickers reduce complex ideas into slogans; mass media strives to be more immediate than contemplative, superficial and passive, rather than thorough and probing; and somewhere in all of this, this truth is over-simplified, exaggerated, distorted through emotion, or abandoned altogether. The goal of modern mass media is not expression, but compression. This compression either stirs up reaction or distraction. Seldom do media conversations mediate thoughtful pro-action.

George Orwell could never have predicted the devices and the stunning technological culture that would arise from post-war science, but he certainly pointed to the effect: the dumbing down of people in general, the dissemination of propaganda, and the consolidation of power through those corporations and governments that own the channels of mass media and exploit the benefits of limiting language to their own ends.

In *1984*, except for the *Telescreens*, the technology is familiar and crude, often primitive; however, Orwell reminds us that the technology of delivering communication is secondary to the language itself. The official language of *Oceania* is *Newspeak*. As a language it is intended to inseminate the citizens of *Oceania* with *IngSoc*— the ideological premises and principles of *Big Brother*.

The novel takes place during the time when the English language is still transitioning into *Newspeak*—the target date for completion is 2050. In fact, one character, Symes, is busy working on both eradicating words and reducing words and expressions to their dullest representations, all for the purpose of curbing any thoughts of rebellion. Symes even brags about the 'beauty' of destroying words.

This 'destruction' is accomplished by eliminating the duality of language. Instead of **good** or **bad**, **someone** or **no one**, for example, the new lexicon uses compounds, prefixes, or suffixes to eliminate traditional negatives: **bad** is now **ungood**; articulating extremes: **virtuous** is **doubleplusgood**; a **nobody** is an **unperson**, and so on to ridiculous lengths, rendering language cumbersome and foolish: Being **unplusdoubtful** of the **doubleplusunpurposefulness** of language establishes one's **doubleplusunappreciation** for words. By saddling language with such idiocy, language becomes meaningless.

Newspeak leaves no room for nuance. The **A Vocabulary** of *Newspeak* consists of everyday words and expressions—words that cannot give themselves to anything but literal interpretation (e.g. walking, eating, drinking). The **B Vocabulary** consists of words with political, ideological, or figurative significance. These words become neutered or targeted for elimination, such as the word **science**—which becomes so segmented that each separate field of science is unhinged from relevance as a unified concept. A word like **orthodoxy** loses its associative and connotative power by being reduced to **goodthink**. In the world of IngSoc, **The US Constitution** would be changed to **crimethink.**

The most alarming aspect the *Newspeak* is that in rendering language unviable or infantile, the task of completing a *Newspeak Dictionary* spells doom for the very dictionary itself. This accounts for the reluctance of the Inner Party to fulfill this mission entirely, keeping the citizens of *Oceania* in a constant state of befuddlement and at risk of committing *thoughtcrime*. As there is no such thing as crime in *Oceania*, as there are no laws, the lack of duality itself makes for invisible, powerless citizens.

Something to Consider

It is inferred by a close reading of *Goldstein's book* and the text of *1984* that Orwell believes the key to undermining corrupt authority is literacy and how literacy informs thought. A knowledge of words, and an interest in reading that adds to this knowledge, refines thought and is effective in detecting language that manipulates, lies, exaggerates, stupefies, advances blind conformity, and unthinking self-corruption. Cultures that do not form a habit of reading lag behind those cultures that encourage literacy. Literacy is the tool for debate, compromise, and diplomacy, which all hinge on the pursuit of logic and the rhetoric of argument. Arguments that cannot be reconciled with words are reconciled with action, which is often thoughtless and violent. However, action is often romanticized and mythologized and given urgency by those who want short-term solutions to long-term problems, propagandizing action as heroic. Solutions not quickly forthcoming give rise to impatience and emotion, which cloud the issues and intensify the conflict. The results are battles, wars, and carnage. Oceania does not advance forward as a culture because language is purposely taken away from its citizens, and with that, thought loses its ability to rationalize the very reality that allows for such an undoing.

If this book succeeds in helping you understand Orwell's masterpiece, you will know this by the skepticism you experience when authority manipulates language. You will know that language is a beautiful representation of humanity and a blunt instrument against totalitarianism. EM 2015

43. Bibliography of Dystopian Literature

18th Century

- *Gulliver's Travels* (**1726**) by **Jonathan Swift**

19th Century

- *A Sojourn in the City of Amalgamation, in the Year of Our Lord, 19--* (**1835**) by Oliver Bolokitten
- *The World As It Shall Be* (**1846**) by **Émile Souvestre**
- *Paris in the Twentieth Century* (**1863**) by **Jules Verne**.
- *Vril, the Power of the Coming Race* (1871) by **Edward Bulwer-Lytton**, originally printed as *The Coming Race*
  http://en.wikipedia.org/wiki/List_of_dystopian_literature - cite_note-4
- *Erewhon* (**1872**) by **Samuel Butler**
- *The Begum's Fortune* (**1879**) by **Jules Verne**
- *The Fixed Period* (**1882**) by **Anthony Trollope**
- *The Republic of the Future* (**1887**) by Anna Bowman Dodd
- *The Inner House* (**1888**) by **Walter Besant**
- *Caesar's Column* (**1890**) by **Ignatius L. Donnelly**
- *Pictures of the Socialistic Future* (1890) by **Eugen Richter**
- *The Time Machine* (**1895**) by **H. G. Wells**
- *When The Sleeper Wakes* (**1899**) by **H. G. Wells**

20th Century

1900's

- *The First Men in the Moon* (**1901**) by **H. G. Wells**
- *The Iron Heel* (**1908**) by **Jack London**
- *Lord of the World* (**1908**) by **Robert Hugh Benson**
- *The Machine Stops* (**1909**) by **E. M. Forster**
- *Trylogia Księżycowa* (1901-1911) by **Jerzy Żuławski**

1910's

- *The Air Trust* (**1915**) by **George Allan England**

- *City of Endless Night* (as "Children of Kultur") **(1919)** by **Milo Hastings**
- *The Heads of Cerberus* **(1919)** by "Francis Stevens" (**Gertrude Barrows Bennett**)
- *Philip Dru: Administrator* **(1912)** by (**Edward Mandell House**)

1920's

- *Useless Hands* **(1920)** by **Claude Farrère**
- *R.U.R.: Rossums's Universal Robots* **(1921)** by **Karel Capek**
- *We* **(1921)** by **Yevgeny Zamyatin**
- *The Trial* **(1925)** by **Franz Kafka**
- *Man's World* **(1926)** by **Charlotte Haldane**

1930's

- "The City of the Living Dead" **(1930)** by **Laurence Manning** and **Fletcher Pratt**
- *Brave New World* **(1932)** by **Aldous Huxley**
- *The New Gods Lead* **(1932)** by **S. Fowler Wright**
- *To Tell The Truth...* **(1933)** by Amabel Williams-Ellis
- *It Can't Happen Here* **(1935)** by **Sinclair Lewis**
- *Land Under England* **(1935)** by **Joseph O'Neill**
- *We Have Been Warned* **(1935)** by **Naomi Mitchison**
- *War with the Newts* **(1936)** by **Karel Čapek**
- *In the Second Year* **(1936)** by **Storm Jameson**
- *Swastika Night* **(1937)** by **Katharine Burdekin**
- *The Wild Goose Chase* **(1937)** by **Rex Warner**
- *Anthem* **(1938)** by **Ayn Rand**
- *Out of the Silent Planet* (1938) by **C.S. Lewis**
- *Invitation to a Beheading* by **(1938)** by **Vladimir Nabokov**
- *The Arrogant History of White Ben* **(1939)** by **Clemence Dane**
- *Impromptu in Moribundia* **(1939)** by **Patrick Hamilton**
- *Over the Mountain* **(1939)** by **Ruthven Todd**

1940's

- *Darkness at Noon* **(1940)** by **Arthur Koestler**
- *"If This Goes On—"* (1940) by **Robert A. Heinlein**
- *Kallocain* (1940) by **Karin Boye**
- *The Aerodrome* **(1941)** by **Rex Warner**
- *Perelandra* **(1943)** by **C.S. Lewis**
- *Cities of the Plain* **(1943)** by **Alex Comfort**
- *The Riddle of the Tower* **(1944)** by **J. D. Beresford** and **Esmé Wynne-Tyson**
- *That Hideous Strength* **(1945)** by **C.S. Lewis**
- *Animal Farm* **(1945)** by **George Orwell**

- *Bend Sinister* (**1947**) by **Vladimir Nabokov**
- *Doppelgangers* (**1947**) by **Gerald Heard**
- *Ape and Essence* (**1948**) by **Aldous Huxley**
- *Sometime Never: A Fable for Supermen* by **Roald Dahl**
- *Nineteen Eighty-Four* (**1949**) by **George Orwell**

1950's

- *The Day of the Triffids* (1951) by **John Wyndham**
- *Limbo*, (vt. *Limbo 90*) (**1952**) by **Bernard Wolfe**
- *Player Piano* (also known as *Utopia 14*) (1952) by **Kurt Vonnegut**
- *Fahrenheit 451* (**1953**) by **Ray Bradbury**
- *One* (also published as *Escape to Nowhere*) (**1953**) by **David Karp**
- *Love Among the Ruins* (1953) by **Evelyn Waugh**
- *The Foundation Pit* (1953) by **Andrey Platonov**
- *The Space Merchants* (**1953**) by **Frederik Pohl** and **C. M. Kornbluth**
- *Lord of the Flies* (1954) by **William Golding**
- *Tunnel in the Sky* (1955) by **Robert A. Heinlein**
- *The Chrysalids* (1955) by **John Wyndham**
- *The City and the Stars* (1956) by **Arthur C. Clarke**
- *The Golden Archer: A Satirical Novel of 1975* (**1956**) by Gregory Mason
- *Minority Report* (1956) by **Philip K. Dick**
- *Atlas Shrugged* (1957) by **Ayn Rand**
- *Alas, Babylon* (1959) by **Pat Frank**

1960's

- *Facial Justice* (**1960**) by **L. P. Hartley**
- *A Canticle for Leibowitz* (**1960**) by **Walter M. Miller**
- "Harrison Bergeron" (**1961**) by **Kurt Vonnegut**
- *The Joy Makers* (**1961**) by **James Gunn**
- *The Old Men at the Zoo* (**1961**) by **Angus Wilson**
- *A Clockwork Orange* (**1962**) by **Anthony Burgess**
- *The Wanting Seed* (**1962**) by **Anthony Burgess**
- *Planet of the Apes* (**1963**) by **Pierre Boulle**
- *Cloud On Silver* (US title *Sweeney's Island*) (**1964**) by **John Christopher**
- *Farnham's Freehold* (**1964**) by **Robert A. Heinlein**
- *Nova Express* (1964) by **William S. Burroughs**
- *The Penultimate Truth* (1964) by **Philip K. Dick**
- *Epp* (1965) by **Axel Jensen**
- *Logan's Run* (**1967**) by **William F. Nolan** and **George Clayton Johnson**
- *Make Room! Make Room!* (**1966**) by **Harry Harrison**
- *Do Androids Dream of Electric Sheep?* (**1968**) by **Philip K. Dick**
- *Stand on Zanzibar* (**1968**) by **John Brunner**

- *Camp Concentration* (1968) by **Thomas M. Disch**
- *The Jagged Orbit* (1969) by **John Brunner**
- *The White Mountains* (1967) by **John Christopher**
- *The City of Gold and Lead* (1968) by **John Christopher**
- *The Pool of Fire* (1968) by **John Christopher**

1970's

- *This Perfect Day* (1970) by **Ira Levin**
- *The Bodyguard* (1970) by **Adrian Mitchell**
- *The Lathe of Heaven* (1971) by **Ursula K. Le Guin**
- *The Sheep Look Up* (1972) by **John Brunner**
- *334* (1972) by **Thomas M. Disch**
- *Flow My Tears, the Policeman Said* (1974) by **Philip K. Dick**
- *Walk to the End of the World* (1974) by **Suzy McKee Charnas**
- *The Shockwave Rider* (1975) by **John Brunner**
- *High-Rise* (1975) by **JG Ballard**
- *Solution Three* (1975) by **Naomi Mitchison**
- *The Girl Who Owned a City* (1975) by O. T. Nelson
- *Woman on the Edge of Time* (1976) by **Marge Piercy**
- *The Dark Tower* (1977) - unfinished, attributed to **C.S. Lewis**, published as *The Dark Tower and Other Stories*
- *A Scanner Darkly* (1977) by **Philip K. Dick**
- *The Turner Diaries* (1978) by **William L. Pierce** (Andrew Macdonald)
- *Alongside Night* (1979) by **J. Neil Schulman**
- *The Long Walk* (1979) by **Stephen King** (Richard Bachman)

1980's

- *Riddley Walker* (1980) by **Russell Hoban**
- *Lanark: A Life in Four Books* (1981) by **Alasdair Gray**
- *The Running Man* (1982) by **Stephen King** (Richard Bachman)
- *Sprawl trilogy*: *Neuromancer* (1984), *Count Zero* (1986) and *Mona Lisa Overdrive* (1988) by **William Gibson**
- *The Handmaid's Tale* (1985) by **Margaret Atwood**
- *Ender's Game* (1985) by **Orson Scott Card**
- *Watchmen* (1986-1987) by **Alan Moore** (writer), and **David Gibbons** (artist)
- *In the Country of Last Things* (1987) by **Paul Auster**.
- *Obernewtyn Chronicles* (1987–2008) by **Isobelle Carmody**
- *The Domination* (1988) by **S. M. Stirling**
- *V for Vendetta* (1988-1989) by **Alan Moore** (writer), and **David Lloyd** (illustrator).
- *When the Tripods Came* (1988) by **John Christopher**

1990's

- *Fatherland* (1992) by **Robert Harris**
- *The Children of Men* (1992) by **P.D. James**
- *Parable of the Sower* (1993) by **Octavia E. Butler**
- *The Giver* (1993) by Lois Lowry
- *Virtual Light* (1993) by **William Gibson**
- *Gun, with Occasional Music* (1994) by **Jonathan Lethem**
- *The Diamond Age, or A Young Lady's Illustrated Primer* (1995) by **Neal Stephenson**
- *Infinite Jest* (1996) by **David Foster Wallace**
- *Underworld* (1997) by **Don DeLillo**
- *The Right to Read* (1997) by **Richard Stallman**
- *Among the Hidden* (1998, first in the Shadow Children series) by **Margaret Peterson Haddix**
- *Battle Royale* (1999) by **Koushun Takami**
- *The Ice People* (1999) by **Maggie Gee**
-

21st Century

2000's

- *Scorch* (2000) by A.D. Nauman
- *Noughts and Crosses* (2001) by **Malorie Blackman**
- *Ella Minnow Pea* (2001) by **Mark Dunn**
- *Mortal Engines* (2001, first in Hungry City Chronicles) by **Philip Reeve**
- *Among the Betrayed* (2002, third in the Shadow Children series) by **Margaret Peterson Haddix**
- *Feed* (2002) by **M. T. Anderson**
- *The House of the Scorpion* (2002) by **Nancy Farmer**
- *Jennifer Government* (2003) by **Max Barry**
- *The City of Ember* (2003) by **Jeanne DuPrau**
- *Oryx and Crake* (2003) by **Margaret Atwood**
- *Manna* (2003) by **Marshall Brain**
- *Among the Brave* (2004, fifth in the Shadow Children series) by Margaret Peterson Haddix
- *The People of Sparks* (2004) by **Jeanne DuPrau**
- *Knife Edge* (2004) by **Malorie Blackman**
- *The Bar Code Tattoo* (2004) by **Suzanne Weyn**
- *Cloud Atlas* (2004) by **David Mitchell**
- *The Plot Against America* (2004) by **Philip Roth**
- *Checkmate* (2005) by Malorie Blackman

- *Divided Kingdom* (2005) by **Rupert Thomson**
- *Never Let Me Go* (2005) by **Kazuo Ishiguro**
- *Among the Enemy* (2005, sixth in the Shadow Children series) by Margaret Peterson Haddix
- *Uglies* (2005) by **Scott Westerfeld**
- *Pretties* (2005) by Scott Westerfeld
- *Among the Free* (2006, seventh in the Shadow Children series) by Margaret Peterson Haddix
- *Specials* (2006) by Scott Westerfeld
- *Armageddon's Children* (2006) by Terry Brooks
- *Bar Code Rebellion* (2006) by Suzanne Weyn.
- *The Road* (2006) by Cormac McCarthy
- *The Book of Dave* (2006) by **Will Self**
- *Day of the Oprichnik (День Опричника)* (2006) by **Vladimir Sorokin**
- *Genesis* (2006) by **Bernard Beckett**
- *Incarceron* (2007) by Catherine Fisher
- **Unwind** (2007) by Neal Shusterman
- *The Pesthouse* (2007) by **Jim Crace**
- *Extras* (2007) by Scott Westerfeld
- *From the New World* (2008) by Yusuke Kishi
- *Blind Faith* (2007) by **Ben Elton**
- *Gone* (2008) by **Michael Grant**
- *World Made By Hand* (2008) by **James Howard Kunstler**
- *Sapphique* (2007) by Catherine Fisher
- *The Declaration* (2008) by Gemma Malley
- *The Host* (2008) by **Stephenie Meyer**
- *Double Cross* (2008) by **Malorie Blackman**
- *The Hunger Games* (2008) by **Suzanne Collins**
- *The Resistance* (2008) by Gemma Malley
- *The Forest of Hands and Teeth* (2009) by Carrie Ryan
- *The Maze Runner* (2009) by **James Dashner**
- *The Year of the Flood* (2009) by Margaret Atwood
- *Shades of Grey* (2009) by **Jasper Fforde**
- *Catching Fire* (2009) by Suzanne Collins
- *Z213: Exit* (2009) by **Dimitris Lyacos**
- *Last Light* (2007) by **Alex Scarrow**
- **The Windup Girl** (2009) by **Paolo Bacigalupi**

2010's

- *The Passage* (2010) by **Justin Cronin**
- *The Envy Chronicles* (2010) by Joss Ware
- *Matched* (2010) by **Ally Condie**
- *Monsters of Men* (2010) by **Patrick Ness**
- *Mockingjay* (2010) by **Suzanne Collins**
- *Rondo* (2010) by John Maher
- *Delirium* (2010) by **Lauren Oliver**

- *Super Sad True Love Story* (2010) by **Gary Shteyngart**
- *The Scorch Trials* (2010) by **James Dashner**
- *The Prophecies* (2011-2012) by Linda Hawley
- *Wither* (2011) by Lauren DeStefano
- *Wool* (2011-2012) by Hugh Howey
- *Across The Universe* (2011) by Beth Revis
- *Divergent* (2011) by Veronica Roth
- *Crossed* (2011) by **Ally Condie**
- *Legend* (2011) by **Marie Lu**
- *Shatter Me* (2011) by Tahereh Mafi
- *The Death Cure* (2011) by **James Dashner**
- *Insurgent* (2012) by **Veronica Roth**
- *Ready Player One* (2011) by **Ernest Cline**
- *Article 5* by **Kristen Simmons**
- *Crewel* (2012) by Gennifer Albin
- *Under the Never Sky* (2012) by Veronica Rossi
- *Revealing Eden* (2012) by **Victoria Foyt**
- *Reached* (2012) by **Ally Condie**
- *Agenda 21* (2012) by **Glenn Beck**
- *Blood Zero Sky* (2012) by **J. Gabriel Gates**
- *Dominion* (2012) by **C.J. Sansom**
- *Bleeding Edge* (2013) by **Thomas Pynchon**
- *MaddAddam* (2013) by **Margaret Atwood**
- *Prodigy* (2013) by **Marie Lu**
- *The 5th Wave* (2013) by Rick Yancey
- *Allegiant* (2013) by **Veronica Roth**
- *Champion (2013) by Marie Lu*
- *The Bone Season* (2013) by **Samantha Shannon**
- *The Circle* (2013) by **Dave Eggers**
- *The Last Human* (2014) by **Ink Pieper**
- *J* (2014) by **Howard Jacobson**

44. Dystopian Filmography

12 Monkeys (1995)
1984 (1956 & 1984)
2081 (2009)
A Scanner Darkly (2006)
Aachi &Sspak (2009)
Aeon Flux (2005)
Atlas Shrugged, Part 1 (2011)

Babylon AD (2008)
Battle Royale (2000)
Battle Royale II: Requiem   (2003)
Blade Runner (1982)
Blindness (2008)
Book of Eli (2010)
The Bothersome Man (2006)
Brave New World (1998)
Brazil (1985)
The Breed (2010)
Bunraku (2010)

Children of Men (2006)
Class of 1999 (1990)
Cloud Atlas (2012)
Code 46 (2003)

The Dark Knight Rises   (2012)
Dark Metropolis (2010)
Daybreakers (2010)
Death Race (200)8
Death Race 2000 (1975)
Demolition Man (1993)
District 9 (2009)
District 13 (2004)
District 13: Ultimatum   (2009)
Doomsday (2008)
Dredd (2012)
The End of Evangelion   (1997)
Escape from L.A. (1996)
Escape from New York   (1981)

Equilibrium (2002)

Fahrenheit 451 (1966)
FAQ: Frequently Asked Questions (2004)
Fortress (1993)
Fortress 2: Re-Entry (2000)
Gamer (2009)
Gattaca (1997)

The Handmaid's Tale (1990)
Harrison Bergeron (1995)
The Hunger Games (2012)

Idiocracy (2006)
The Island (2005)
In Time (2011)

Judge Dredd (1995)

Kin-dza-dza! (1986)

La jetée (1962)
Land of the Blind (2006)
Lockout (2012)
Logan's Run (1976)
Looper (2012)

The Manchurian Candidate   (2004)
The Matrix (1999)
The Matrix Reloaded (2003)
The Matrix Revolutions   (2003)
Maximum Shame (2010)
Megiddo: The Omega Code 2 (1999)
Metropolis (1927)
Minority Report (2002)
Moon (2009)

Never Let Me Go (201)0

Nineteen Eighty-Four (1984, 1958)

Oblivion (2013)
The Omega Man (1971)

Priest (2011)
Privilege (1967)
Punishment Park (1971)

Revengers Tragedy (2003)
The Running Man (1987)

Screamers (1995)
Serenity (2005)
Silent Running (1972)
Sleeper (1973)

Sleeping Dogs 1977)
Soldier (1998)
Southland Tales (2007)
Soylent Green (1973)
Strange Daysm (1995)

THX 1138 (1971)
The Trial (1962)
Total Recall (2012)
Turkey Shoot (1982)

Ultraviolet (2006)
V for Vendetta (2006)
Welt am Draht (1973)
Z.P.G. (1972)

45. Familiar Dystopian Graphic Novels

"Blame!"

"20th Century Boys"

"Batman: The Dark Knight Returns

"Akira"

"Appleseed"

"Battle Angel Alita"

"Eden: It's an Endless World"

"Fist of the North Star"

"Ghost in the Shell"

"Wanted

"The Incal"

"Judge Dredd

"Marshal Law

"Nikopol Trilogy"

"Ruins"

"Transmetropolitan"

"V for Vendetta"

"Watchmen"

"Y: The Last Man"

"X-Men"

Biography

Edward Morneau taught English, Media Studies, Film Studies, and Theatre Arts for thirty-five years in several school systems in the New Hampshire and Boston areas. He is the author of several books, including: *Willy Loman, Nosferatu*; *Billy Budd, WTF?*; and *Teacher on Rye*. He lives in Salem, MA and has dedicated a small part of his life to finding the perfect bowl of chowder.

Forthcoming Focus Study Guides

Lord of the Flies (William Golding)

Billy Budd (Coxe & Chapman's play adaptation of Herman Melville's novel, *Billy Budd, Sailor*)

Death of a Salesman (Arthur Miller)

Childhood's End (Arthur C. Clarke)

APPENDIX

19. Practice Essay Questions

1. Choose and write about two of the topics listed in the CONCEPT/MOTIF BANK in Section 14. Consider their relationship to each other in terms of commonalities, cause and effect, or contrasts. Choose these CONCEPTS carefully, as you will continue developing this topic in more formal essay assignments. This is a good chance to explore freewriting as a path structured composition.

2. In 1949, George Orwell used his experience writing about and witnessing *fascism* in Europe and *totalitarianism* in the Soviet Union and China, and consequently wrote *1984* as a warning to the future. The future has done a poor job of heeding Orwell's warning. Some of the above concepts and motifs are political, social and cultural realities in many parts of the world today, including the USA. Choose a concept and argue for or against its practice. Give examples to back up your assertions.

3. What is the nature of love between Winston and Julia. At what point do we learn that Julia is more committed to her relationship with Winston than he is with her? Who is witness to this remarkable expression of loyalty, and what are the probable consequences to Julia? In terms of Winston and Julia evolving into true revolutionaries against Big Brother, why is hers a complete revolution? In answering this, why does Winston's commitment to the revolution fall short, despite his willingness to do anything to destroy Big Brother?

4. One of he first things that female Holocaust prisoners did when they were liberated from the concentration camps was to wash their clothes and hair and apply rouge and lipstick. For some this was even more important than eating. Why? What is the significance of Julia getting made up and wearing a dress for Winston? When we compare the urgent preference for the Holocaust survivors to Julia's looking for a lost aspect of her, what is being suggested about the state of affairs in Oceania, especially for women?

4. It must have been shattering for Winston when O'Brien revealed that he took part of writing Goldstein's manifesto. The double irony of this sabotages Winston's last hope for any truth in the world of Big Brother. We, the reader, also feel betrayed because we go into literature and history with a hope that what we read has an unimpeachable quality of truth and speculation. Throughout the world, and even in the United States, the authorship of literature and history sometimes has fraudulent intentions. A few southern states in America downplay their role in resisting the abolition the slavery and adjust their textbooks accordingly. China heavily censors the Internet, while North Korea forbids it altogether, choosing many aspects of Orwell's blueprint to consolidate and maintain power through propaganda. North Koreans live in misery, but are told they live in

paradise. The dichotomy is achievable when authority is corrupt. It would be of interest to the student to explore these hypocrisies, as this dichotomy is not isolated to totalitarian regimes, but is practiced in otherwise altruistic democratic institutions, like schools, for instance. For example, 'school pride' is a rallying point for students, but on what achievements is this pride based? School sports are a source of pride, but is this pride located in victories at the expense of sportsmanship?

5. In *1984* privacy is impossible. Is privacy a core concern for Americans? Why do so many in *1984* find solace in Big Brother, despite its constant oppression? Do we as Americans choose security over privacy? Are we in danger of compromising basic rights so the larger desire to remain safe is guaranteed? How is this an illusion, according to those who argue against this arrangement?

6. How is *1984* an attack on institutions that we still regard as sacred and viable? Do these institutions deserve to be attacked, as they are part of a larger hypocrisy? For example, Big Brother forbids family because loyalty to family compromises loyalty to Big Brother. Let's change terms: Work forbids family because loyalty to family compromises loyalty to one's career.

7. When O'Brien calls Winston, "The last man," what does he mean? In thinking about this, for what reason does Orwell invent Winston's character? Why does O'Brien seem to take special interest in breaking him down?

8. How is Julia a counter weight to Winston? How does she represent a different set of values? What is her function in the story and her unique challenge to dystopia?

9. How does Oceania use technology to keep its citizens under compete control and to get then to enthusiastically support a dystopia that keeps them in misery and destitution?

10. How is Radford's film design a reflection of dystopian ideals?

11. The last maxim in the book, not mentioned in the film, is: *God Is Power*. How is this the most perfect representation of *doublethink?*

12. Using the articles on Nationalism and Patriotism, discuss the differences, giving modern examples of each and citing how one or the other, or both, reflect *1984*.

13. *1984* was a warning to the future about the dangers of fascism and totalitarianism to free forms of government. One student suggested that the kind of extreme dystopian ruination occurring in *1984* could never be visited upon our democracy. Is he right? Are there already critical dystopian parallels in America that mirror *1984*?

14. Why does O'Brien mean about Winston not existing. Why do the Inner Party and its minions want to warp reality for the citizens of Oceania? Give examples of how this warping effect gives the Party more power.

15. The term *rubblescape* was invented to describe the *mise en scene* (What is 'put upon stage') in Michael Radford's adaptation of *1984*. When we look around our own communities, is there a growing *rubblecape* to our surroundings? What causes this and

why is there such rural, suburban, and urban neglect? How does living in a *rubblescape* impact our own personal spaces?

16. How close do the performances of John Hurt as Winston, Suzanna Hamilton as Julia, and Richard Burton as O'Brien, represent Orwell's original vision? What scenes best deliver the oppression and terror of *1984*? How effective are the minor characters in delivering Orwell's subtexts?

17. Review the codes of nationalism and patriotism. Which aspects of *1984* are extreme examples of nationalism? Which ones could be mistaken for patriotism?

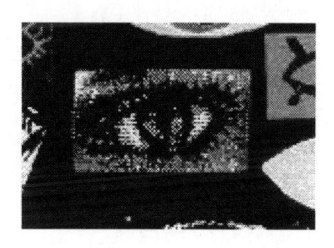

Beware the savage roar of
Nineteen Eighty-Four
—David Bowie

Printed in Great Britain
by Amazon